"If it were not for everyday performance, then we would live in a very gray world." Salomé

Artistic collector cups
Design no. 28; Ernst Fuchs
Rosenthal Archives, Selb

Dieter Struss

Dining Services, Figurines, Ornaments and Art Objects

Consultant: Petra Werner

4880 Lower Valley Rd. Atglen, PA 19310 USA

Library of Congress Catalog Card Number: 97-80094

Originally published in German as *Rosenthal, Service, Figuren, Zier- und Kunstobjekte* by Battenberg Verlag, Augsburg, 1995.
Translated by Dr. Edward Force, Central Connecticut State University.

Cover design by Zembsch' Studio, Munich, using a photo (Salomé) by Rudolf Majonica, Munich.
Layout by Konturwerk, Helga Schörnig

ISBN: 0-7643-0384-8
Printed in the United States of America

Published by Schiffer Publishing Ltd.
4880 Lower Valley Road
Atglen, PA 19310
Phone: (610) 593-1777; Fax: (610) 593-2002
E-mail: Schifferbk@aol.com
Please write for a free catalog.
This book may be purchased from the publisher.
Please include $3.95 for shipping.

Please try your bookstore first.

We are interested in hearing from authors with book ideas on related subjects.

Contents

Acknowledgements

Without the authors' research into the existing literature, and without the assistance of many Rosenthal admirers, this book could not have been written. I thank them all most heartily. In alphabetical order, I would particularly like to thank:

Dr. Cornelis Aldewereld and Ms. Helga Ratsch, of the Cultural Department of the Rosenthal AG in Selb; Ms. Monika Berg, Glass and Porcelain of the 20th Century, Munich; Mr. Nikolaus Debie, Rosenthal Studio-Haus, Munich; Dr. Berndt Fritz, Berlin, the former Rosenthal archivist; Ms. Elisabeth Hoffmann, Geschirrbörse Hoffmann, Vettelschöss; Director Wilhelm Siemen, Ms. Susanne Fraas and Mr. Wolfgang Schilling of the Museum der Deutschen Porzellanindustrie, Hohenberg/Eger.

I also owe particular thanks to Ms. Petra Werner, who is at home in the Rosenthal Archives in Selb as in the Museum der Deutschen Porzellanindustrie in Hohenberg/Eger, and who provided so much help to the author. Without her collaboration, this book could scarcely have been completed.

All the same, the author alone is responsible for any and all errors.

This book includes *only porcelain of the Rosenthal firm which also bears the Rosenthal trademark.* Thus, it does not include porcelain from the Rosenthal works of Haviland, Krister or Thomas.

Descriptions and pictures of all *Rosenthal hallmarks and trademarks* in this book are simplified. The author and publisher can accept *no responsibility* for the correctness of conclusions that are drawn from these reproductions.

For the *data* that are cited in this book, which are essentially based on information in the Rosenthal archives in Selb, the author and publisher can accept *no responsibility*, despite all efforts.

The Rosenthal Family and Firm

The Rosenthal firm stands out above others in four ways:

1. It is young as porcelain factories go. Founded in 1889 in Selb, Upper Franconia, east of Hof and close to the Czech border, it is "only" a little over a hundred years old.
2. The Rosenthal firm owes its ascendancy to only two generations of the family, namely Philipp Rosenthal (1855-1937) and his son Philip (English spelling), born in 1916.
3. The father and son always showed a keen interest in modern art and were constantly involved in uniting it with their production.
4. Both always showed a keen interest in advertising as well. Their method of linking the trade with their firm early and unusually closely played a major role in their success.

"White Gold"

Porcelain has been produced in Germany, more precisely in Europe, since 1709. At that time, Johann Friedrich Böttger discovered the "arcanum," the secret of the alchemists, for producing porcelain, the "white gold" of the Chinese, out of "soil," "dirt." This art spread quickly over Europe from Meissen, despite all efforts to protect the secret. Production began in Plauen, Prussia in 1713, in Vienna in 1717, in Venice in 1720, etc.

At first its production was limited to princely factories, for the capital needed for the highly complex technology was, and still is, enormous. Thus in Germany the business developed in Berlin, Höchst, Lud-wigsburg, Nymphenburg, etc., since every ruling prince wanted to produce his own porcelain. In the German Reich, there were ultimately seventeen princely factories.

As suggested by the Latin derivation of the word "manufacture," porcelain was originally produced and decorationated by hand. When the present-day successors speak of manufacturing, it is a matter of tradition, for there is scarcely one factory in existence where porcelain is produced or decorationated by hand today.

For at the same time as the discovery of the porcelain secrets, industrialization was taking place in Europe, and when the first small private factories were established in Thuringia, beginning in 1756, they called themselves "porcelain factories." This designation suits the huge application of technology, organization, capital, artistry and intelligence involved. In Germany, twenty-two new porcelain factories are said to have been espablished by the middle of the 19th century. Thus the "latecomer" Rosenthal was known as a porcelain factory from the start, even though it is famous today for its porcelain art.

The Rosenthal family

This Rosenthal family can be traced back to the end of the eighteenth century and members are found in 1811 in Werl, which is located on the Dortmund-Unna-Werl-Soest Autobahn. Philipp Abraham Rosenthal stated that he was born in Westönnen, a village east of Werl. He ran a successful cloth and dry-goods business, and was married to Sara Rosenberg of Geseke, near Paderborn. The fact that they were Jewish played a certain role at that time.

Philipp Rosenthal (1855-1937)

Philip Rosenthal (born 1916)

His son Abraham, born in 1821, inherited the store but, despite his father's success, converted it to another type. In 1856 he paid taxes on a business selling glass and porcelain. The business made a profit, the firm grew remarkably, and within ten years the yearly taxes increased elevenfold. Between 1877 and 1880, though, traces of the family and the business vanished from Werl.

A section of the production area of the Rosenthal Rotbühl Works in Selb.

Friedensreich Hundertwasser made the Rosenthal factory in Selb an "ecological art creation."

Shortly after his return, in 1880, he founded his own porcelain-painting business in Erkersreuth, near Selb in northeastern Upper Franconia, and exported his wares to the USA. A few years later, since he could not obtain enough porcelain to meet the demand for painted goods, he founded his own porcelain factory in Selb.

If the primary characteristic of the firm is its youth, then the second is that the firm has attained and expanded its international reputation in only two generations of the family. In 1934, because of his Jewish origins, the father [Philipp] had to give in to the Nazis and leave the firm. Yet the firm was able to retain its name of Rosenthal, since the brand name was well known outside Germany and brought in capital from its exports. In 1950, the son, Philip Rosenthal, born in 1916, entered the firm and took an important role in its further development. At first he was in charge of advertising; later he became the managing director.

Art and Advertising

The next characteristic that distinguishes the Rosenthal family from others is its extraordinary interest in modern art. Philipp Rosenthal was personally successful not only as an entrepreneur, but also as a designer, and his son was probably the first porcelain manufacturer who systematically invited large numbers of renowned modern artists, who originally had no close relationship to porcelain, to collaborate in the development of art and utility porcelain.

And finally, the father and son have both been characterized by their extraordinary talent for advertising. The father brought this particular interest with him from the USA. His booklet "Increasing Export Sales--an urgent problem" deals intensively with advertising. The title page also gives information about the versatility of his activity:

"Practical Suggestions from Geheimrat Dr.ing.h.c. Philipp Rosenthal, Presiding Member of the Reich Society of German Industry, Chairman of the Export Department of the Reich Society of German Industry, Chairman of the Central Office of Participants in the Leipzig Fair, Inc."

The steep ascent of the Rosenthal factories can be proved by some statistics:

porcelain painters

1881: 4

1884: 60

workers employed

1891: 225

1905: 1200

1913: 2500 (just before WWI)

1929: 7000 in a phase of stagnation that had begun in the porcelain industry in 1925, but had not yet affected Rosenthal.

1934: 4000

1939: 5500 (just before WWII)

1951: 6000 (just after WWII)

1979: 8400

1995: almost 3000 in the Federal Republic (after a phase of concentration). The Rosenthal firm now possesses two porcelain factories (Selb and Rotbühl in Selb), one ceramic factory (Kronach), one utensil factory (Neusorg), one furniture factory (Espelkamp), and two factories of the Thomas brand (Speichersdorf and Waldershof).

The Rosenthal Technology, with 4000 employees producing technological porcelain in large quantities, was sold to the Hoechst Dyeworks AG in 1979, and included factories in Britain and America. The Rosenthal AG is only 50% involved with the glass works in Amberg.

As early as 1897, after the conversion of the firm into a stock company, its growth took place by means of purchases or new ventures. Among the best-known porcelain brands owned by the Rosenthal AG are the Thomas firm in Marktredwitz (since 1908) that of Krister in Waldenburg, Silesia, and later in Landstuhl, in the Palatinate (since 1921, closed since 1992) and the Waldershof AG, formerly that of Johann Haviland (since 1937). In addition, the Rosenthal AG includes, among others, ceramic, glass, utensil and furniture firms in its empire, so that it is incorrect to speak only of a porcelain firm. One must rather speak of a business in the field of interior decoration.

After the firm had won a gold medal at the 1900 Paris World's Fair for its quality porcelain, it founded an art department at Selb in 1910; this moved into its own building in 1913 and into a new building in 1922-23. In 1920 a second art department was founded in the Bahnhof-Selb works at Selb-Plössberg which remained active until 1969-70.

A second beginning, of a very different kind, was made in 1964 with the encouragement of Arnold Bode of Kassel, founder of the "Documenta," with the first of three porcelain reliefs by modern artists, from which independent porcelain objects later developed from the relief. At the same time, Rosenthal became one of the founders of the international "Group 21" for modern design, with such firms as Arabia, Braun, Finntex and Rörstrand also participating.

But new avenues were being followed not only in production, but also "outside," for example, with the building of the new Roybühl factory in Selb in 1967, and the glassworks in Amberg, Upper Palatinate, by Walter Gropius, the founder of the "Bauhaus," and his TAC (The Architects' Collaborative), to cite only two examples. The factory in Amberg, thanks to its eye-catching form, won the nickname of "The Glass Cathedral." Older buildings were decorationated and accentuated in modern style by such artists as Friedensreich Hundertwasser, Otto Piene and the like.

But the decisive step in the market breakthrough of Rosenthal porcelain with artistic features was probably the founding of the special Rosenthal sales departments in foreign porcelain specialty shops after 1905, and again after 1912 by Rosenthal's own shops inside and outside Germany.

What was deliberate self-limitation on the one hand brought the quality of the brand to the foreground in an unusual way on the other. Philip Rosenthal took up his father's idea again and expanded it considerably after 1959. Today Rosenthal has fifteen "studio-houses" in the Federal Republic; they began to open in 1960, and in addition to Rosenthal products, they offer only products of similar prestige. There are also four "table-top shops," eight "Rosenthal studio houses" and five "Rosenthal Concession Shops" in Europe. Add to this more than 658 suitable "Rosenthal Studio Departments" in Germany and 685 in Europe--with a minimum of 25 square meters and interior decoration selected by Rosenthal.

On this solid foundation, Rosenthal introduced the "Studio Line" in 1961; it also included appropriate objects of the fifties. Since then, all the artistically outstanding new creations have appeared under this name, while the new offerings of estabilshed objects has continued under the name of "Rosenthal CLASSIC."

It must also be mentioned that this development has also been strongly dependent on the technical progress made in the Rosenthal factories, along with social measures for the employees.

The founder of the Bauhaus, Walter Gropius, who also designed the "TAC" dining service for Rosenthal along with his colleagues, created, as his last great industrial structure, a glass building that is nicknamed "The Glass Cathedral," for the Rosenberg firm in Amberg in 1968-70.

Rosenthal Porcelain between Art and Fashion

Dining Services

If Ovid, the Roman poet, was right when he complained that art is the tears that flow at the sight of reality, one might well add that applied art, such as porcelain, is supposed to decorationate this sad reality.

The plates that we take for granted when they appear on our tables today have a long prehistory. The fact that Rosenthal was able to achieve such success with them depended on the onset of the Industrial Revolution. During the German Biedermeier era [1815-1848] the living conditions of the middle class improved, and the middle class became so widespread that mass production and sales on a grand scale could take place. Just as the middle class took the nobility to be its model, so the middle class became the model for the working class.

Prestige and ornamentation were more important to him than utility--a viewpoint that is of great importance for porcelain. Porcelain dining services ideally unite beauty and utility, but the accent can be placed differently. The wish to show how high one had risen in the world was welcomed by the porcelain industry with its dining service styles of the 19th century, the historical baroque, rococo and pseudo-classic utensils.

Even the rising strata of the skilled worker placed more value on a prestigious living room--the best room--than on the furnishings of the bedroom or kitchen. Simple people, for example, collected discount tickets until they could afford at least a six-piece place setting, which then, as a well-protected family treasure, was used only on special occasions.

A complete assortment of dishes included dining, coffee, tea and chocolate services. There could also be special serviing plates for game, fish dishes, etc., and today for salads, noodle dishes, etc. In the 19th century, though, it was not yet possible to buy pieces of a set (plates, cups, bowls, etc.) individually, each according to what the customer could afford--that was only an achievement of the economic necessities of the twenties. One always had to buy a set complete, which even in the case of a simple set required a well-filled pocketbook. Naturally, one did not have to buy all one's tableware from the same pattern, but could combine various sets for meals, coffee, etc., according to one's own taste.

The custom of having twelve matching sets of plates, cups and utensils came from the royal courts where silver services for twelve existed before porcelain services appeared. The custom also was based on the traditions of product dealers, who ordered by the dozens until well into the 19th century. They both based their systems on the pattern of the ancient Greeks and Romans, which recommended the duodecimal (or the related sexagecimal) system to them, and which we still use today in our calculations of time and angles (as well as wine and egg boxes!).

Thus, in 1907, the Rosenthal tableware production appeared as follows:

Note that a cup and saucer counted as one, and that each plate, cup and saucer were ordered by the dozen.

Plates, flat, 25, 21, 19, 17, 15 and 13 cm. diameter; 25 cm. deep; soup tureen with two handles and cover; soup bowls large and small with plates underneath; ragout bowls, large and small; gravy boats; sauce bowls; salad bowls, with and without feet, 28 & 23 cm. diameter; platters, round 34 & 30 cm. diameter, flat and deep; oval platters 55, 50, 43, 38, 33, 28 & 24 cm. long; fish dishes with inserts; fruit bowls on high and low feet; butter dishes; salt and pepper cellars; mustard bowls; fruit dishes; butter plates; radish bowls; blueberry bowls on saucers; coffee cups; tea cups; tea plates; mocha plates; chocolate plates; breakfast plates; coffeepots in four sizes; teapots in three sizes; chocolate pots; sugar bowls in three sizes; cream pitchers in four sizes; cake plates; cookie jars and teapot bases.

In 1979 the "Century" service included:

flat plates, 26, 20, 16 cm. diameters, deep plates, 17 cm. diameter, soup (or fruit) bowls, ragout bowls, gravy boat, salad bowls, sizes 1 & 2 platters, 30 & 24 cm. diameters, oval platters, 38, 33 & 24 cm. diameters, butter dishes, salt and pepper shakers, egg cups, coffee, tea and mocha cups, coffee pots, sizes 2 & 3, teapots, sugar bowls, cream pitchers, dessert platters, 31 cm. diameter, dessert plates, candy dishes, 12 cm. diameter.

Over the decades, the differences in the pieces available indicate changes in technology and dining culture. Formerly, for example, butter dishes were round; now they are rectangular because butter is packed by machine and must fit into the space in the refrigerator. Some components have remained unchanged over the years: the coffeepot was pear-shaped from the beginning, the teapot round, and the chocolate pot oval.

But today, coffee and tea are often poured out of glass containers that fit into machines, and the espresso cup has long been more important than the chocolate cup (after chocolate was "demoted" to cocoa for women and children over 150 years ago). It is worthwhile to carefully compare different eating and drinking scenes.

"Rococo/Louis XIV"

see examples on page 35

The French King Louis XIV reigned from 1643 to 1715. Linking him with the Rococo style in the name of a table service is erroneous. The "Sun King," the founder of the palace of Versailles, is the embodiment of Baroque. His name has been linked with the greatest array of splendor, but, whether Baroque or Rococo, the hard reality behind it has never interested the latter-day observer of this opulence. What matters is that the middle class wanted to share this splendor.

The products listed for the Rosenthal firm's first year in business, 1891, is counted as the "Third Rococo." There are still no model numbers, and the products, like all earlier Rosenthal dishes, were made at the Selb factory. The original Rococo officially disappeared in the French Revolution in 1791 and the execution of King Louis XVI under the guillotine, but it lived on in the underground culture and awakened to new life in the twenties of the 19th century as the "Second Rococo" after the Bourbon family had been put back on the French throne.

Although this imitation (or continuation) was rejected again and again by the art and commercial critics, the Neo-Rococo reached its greatest height at the 1851 World's Fair in London and clearly showed that there was more to it than mere imitation. It obviously expressed the human desire for play and decorationation, for which porcelain was an ideal medium. And the displays at the fair resulted in making it international, as well as announcing its entry into the Industrial Revolution.

The fact that the Neo-Rococo soon faded away again shows that porcelain is closely linked not only with styles but also with fashion trends. In Germany, for example, neo-rococo was dislodged because of the "modern" anti-French attitude and replaced by the more patriotic Neo-Renaissance. Soon, though, it was remembered that the Rococo--hanging on tenaciously in the "underground" this time too--was more comfortable and picturesque. The castles of Linderhof (begun 1868) and Herrenchiemsee (begun 1878), built by King Ludwig II of Bavaria, are the most famous examples of this. At the 11th World's Fair in Paris in 1889, the "Third Rococo" reigned once more unchallenged, and prevailed until Art Nouveau began in the nineties.

Yet the Rococo never completely disappeared. It still lives on today, even, for example, in the "Rosenthal Classic" assortment of "Monbijou" dishes of 1896 (130, Selb factory) and the "Sanssouci" of 1926 (480 and 490, Selb factory), as well as, one might say, under cover and in disguise, in the "Studio Line" in reflections and quotations, such as the decoration by Björn Wiinblad for the "Zauberflöte" (Magic Flute) design of 1968 (1260, Plössberg factory) and the form of Paul Wunderlich's "Mythos" design of 1991 (9000, Rotbühl factory).

Eternal Rococo? The cultural historian Siegfried Giedion wrote about the reason for its popularity: "The shell ornament of the Rococo gives the objects, with its precise reproduction of forms that occur in nature, the free but structured lines of living organisms." And: The Rococo forms a "unity of cool planning with a wealth of organic shapes." For example, a twig might provide the pattern for a Rococo chair's leg.

A design like the "Rococo/ Louis XIV" lives--like all Neo-Rococo dishes--through imitation, or in the jargon of the field, "replication." The arsenal of every artistic style is, thanks to its variations, nearly inexhaustible. At Rosenthal alone, dozens (!) of "Louis XIV" dishes are reproduced that can be subsumed under the Rococo. The most demanding and imaginative in terms of technology and skill is probably the "Moliere" tea service (300, Kronach factory), which probably was created just before the turn of the century.

"Louis XVI" was developed from the "Madeleine" dishes first made in 1889 by Haviland & Co. of Limoges, at that time France's leading porcelain manufacturer, and "Madeleine" in turn had its roots in the second and first Rococo. Some of the changes from the forerunners probably came about more or less automatically through the steady progress made in the technology of porcelain production, often in minute details, and from the desire not to be regarded as mere imitators. Today the patent, competition and copyright laws require more obvious originality. But the original Rococo style has not been lost.

Historically based tableware designs have a quality that can be a disadvantage as well as an advantage: They can not be bought simply as tableware, for they go better with certain decor, though they can not be decorated themselves. A Rococo shape almost always looks best only in a Rococo decor. A Bauhaus service, on the other hand, can blend with several different decors, as can many other modern services. Perhaps it is because of this that a modern design looks more interesting in a modern industrial cafeteria than a historical style of tableware, for like a chameleon, it can more easily harmonize with quickly changing public taste.

"Botticelli" and "Donatello"

see examples of Botticelli on page 39 and of Donatello on page 38

The Art Nouveau was already flourishing when Rosenthal issued two renowned services, "Botticelli" (239, Selb factory, coffee, tea and dining services) in 1902 and "Donatello" (250, same factory, same extent) in 1905.

What may have impelled the firm to give these names to Art Nouveau services can only be assumed. The painter Sandro Botticelli and the sculptor Donatello were outstanding exponents of the Florentine Early Renaissance, and Philipp Rosenthal, a true connoisseur of Italian art, may have wanted to transpose the first rebirth of European art onto the hopes that Europe devoted to Art Nouveau in general and which Rosenthal applied particularly to his representative services.

These were not Rosenthal's first Art Nouveau services. They had already been preceded by "Flora" in 1899 (175), "Pâte sur Pâte" in 1899 (181), "Iris" in 1900 (190), "Pensée in 1901 (201), all with definite echoes of Art Nouveau, which was *floral* in its initial phase and, so to speak, introduced flowers into coats of arms. An eventual part of Art Nouveau was the "Secession" movement of 1901 (200), as this style was called in Austria. (All these dining services came from the Selb factory.) "Donatello" and "Botticelli," as far as we know, were designed by Hans Gunther Reinstein of the "United Commercial Artists of Darmstadt," a center of Art Nouveau. In "Donatello" the firm's owner collaborated, and it is thus more highly regarded today than "Botticelli," which many admirers nevertheless regard as more beautiful today. In both examples, the flowing forms of floral Art Nouveau have given way to the strictly geometrical abstract forms of the second phase.

The real problems for the porcelain makers, which were linked to Art Nouveau artists, cannot be seen in the dining services. Until that time, the manufacturers trained most of their designers, modelers and decorationators in their own factories. Now for the first time, they turned to a great degree to artists outside their factories, in order to make contact with modern art, and these independent artists cooperated because they thought they saw a great chance to develop their art. In the end, the purpose of Art Nouveau was to bring life and art back together, and applied art was supposed to be the medium for doing so.

But the independent artists of that time were dedicated to the rediscovered ideal of handicraft and thus were more convinced of their own value than their "colleagues" in the factory, the commercial artists. As an investigation into the archives of the Meissen porcelain factory shows, the conflicts were planned in advance.

A porcelain factory is a highly organized and technological entity based on strict business-economical controls. The artists, though, who were supposed to, and wanted to, work for a business, generally had no idea of the work processes, could or would not understand them, and often were not ready to come into the factory and get more closely involved. Often, in spite of their programmed statements, they produced luxury goods and not trade goods.

As far as is known, no artist came to Selb on his own at that time, nor in the twenties, to work for Rosenthal. This threshhold was crossed, at first gradually, thanks to the organizations Dürerbund (from 1901, progressive at first), the Deutsche Werkbund (from 1907), and the "Bauhaus" (from 1919), from which time artists willingly agreed to meet the requirements of industrial production without decreasing quality.

In addition, the manufacturers were accustomed to paying off the artists with a one-time honorarium. They regarded later modifications to the form or decoration as their business alone and were amazed that they now had to at least consult the artists. Besides, they were opposed to allowing the artist's name to appear next to their trademark on the bottom of the piece--until they realized that many artists were every bit as renowned as their brands, and that many customers began to look not for the trademark but for the artist's name. But at first the manufacturers were not willing to combine an honorarium with a contract for a service design, even for the sake of copyright protection. On the other hand, the artists did not want to accept a contract without being rewarded for it.

Tea Service "Hella"
Model no. 1120, Kronach works
First made 1929, designed by Friedrich Fleischmann
Teapot ht. 18.9/12.8 cm, sugar bowl ht. 14.2/9.3 cm.
Museum der Deutschen Porzellanindustrie, Hohenberg/Eger

Coffee Service "Ideal"
Model no. 560, tableware dept., Selb works
First made 1931. designed by Friedrich Fleischmann
Coffeepot ht. 26.2/20.1 cm, cream pitcher ht. 9.3 cm, sugarbowl 14.2/9.3 cm.
Museum der Deutschen Porzellanindustriem Hohenberg/Eger

Along with this, it turned out that large portions of the public wanted nothing to do with "modern" porcelain. Thus internal strife was often accompanied by sales failure, although even a large minority of interested customers would have been enough to make the work profitable. But at least it was a start, and Rosenthal was involved. "Donatello," perhaps more harmoniously formed than "Botticelli," is still in production today, using various modern decorations. New editions of these dishes can be recognized, besides by the trademark, by the fact that the cherry decoration lacks a three-dimensional form.

In 1905 Rosenthal offered a special crab tureen, with the knob of the lid shaped like a crab (936, Kronach factory). Five years later, a fish service (18, Selb factory, art department) was developed out of the "Donatello" design. The knob on the lid of the tureen has been shaped like a carp, and various food fish have been portrayed on the platter and plates, and the rims decorationated with fish-scale patterns. Both are reminiscent of the "services parlantes" of the Baroque era, which used their shapes and decorations to tell what foods they were intended for.

The dilemma that a leading porcelain factory like Rosenthal always faces anew with the development of a modern product requiring investment of capital [p. 13] is thus: How far dare one proceed ahead of the taste of a broad spectrum of customers when one has already set styles, without failing?

"Maria"

see example on page 58

Coffee, tea and dining service, 1914 (430, Selb factory).

The "Maria" service was designed, or at least inspired, by Philipp Rosenthal himself whose second wife was the attractive French Countess Maria des Beurges. The world is full of things--for example, Adelaide and Alice Springs--that are meant to remind one of a lovely lady.

This is the Rosenthal firm's most successful service. By now, "Maria" has sold in the millions. It is still in the "Rosenthal Classic" offerings today, although what with its stylistic uniqueness, it is not easy to combine with other "modern" Rosenthal pieces. By 1932 it had grown to over 100 pieces, some 70 of which are available now.

This is one of the services that was also put on sale undecorated as whiteware, and that truly justify this "economy." The colorful decoration, though, was changed several times over the years. The modern versions of "Maria" can be recognized by the whiter material and the less clear reliefs, as well as by the trademark.

The "Maria" service is anything but "modern." When Art Nouveau ended around 1910, large areas of applied art ceased to be developed further and dropped back into historicism--perhaps understandably in view of the problems noted above. The hollow octagonal shapes and the rims with raised borders

Coffeepot "Vera"
Model no. 1105, Kronach works
First made 1927, designed by Friedrich Fleischmann?
Ht. 28.7/20.4 cm.
Museum der Deutschen Porzellanindustrie, Hohenberg/Eger

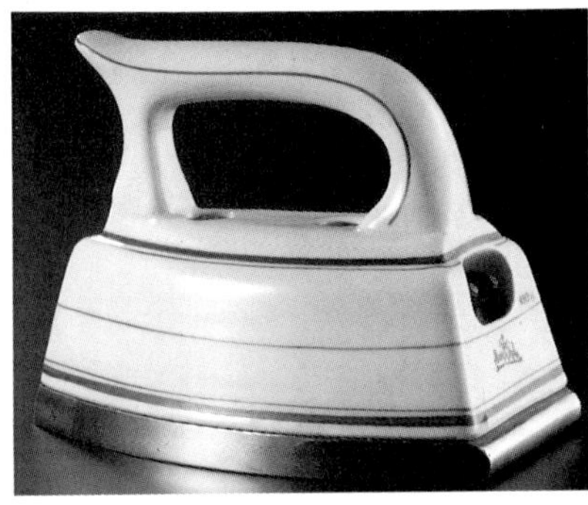

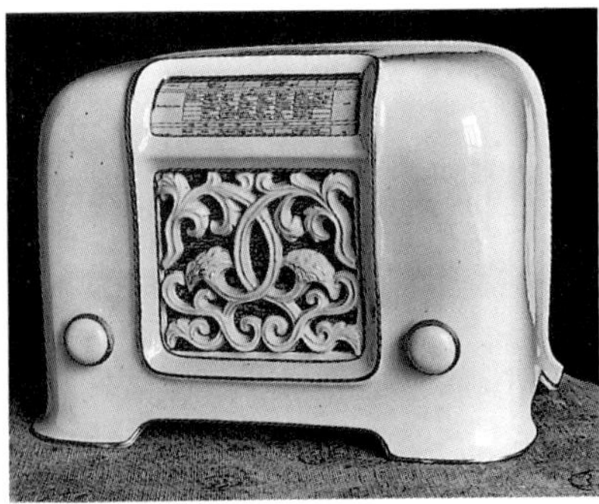

As of 1936, the Rosenthal-Isolatoren GmbH, within the parameters of the Four-Year Pian, produced grille covers, coffee makers, bed-warmers, irons, cigarette lighters and radio casings, some in charming forms, and some produced until 1948.

were probably inspired by silverwork of the Classic and Biedermeier times.

The border does not represent stylized roses, as is said today, but rather pomegranates and olive branches, and thus suggested the Roman goddess of fruitfulness, Ceres, after whom it was originally to be named.

This shows us how fragile and questionable our division of art into stylistic eras and the "dictates" of good taste can be. Why did the customers not prefer the "Canova" service (390, Selb factory), likewise designed by Philipp Rosenthal in 1913 and improved circa 1919. If one wants Classicism, "Canova" offers it in purer form. But it may have been the stylistic mixture of "Maria" that allowed the customer to get a more personal feeling with it.

Philipp Rosenthal was one of the few businessmen who also stood out as a designer. A number of good decorative objects were designed, or at least inspired, by him personally, including not only "Donatello," "Canova," and "Maria," but also "Isolde" (320, Selb, 1909). "Else" (1080, Kronach, 1913), and "Barock" (50, Plössberg, 1919. The firm's archives preserve a number of his designs in color.

"Li" or "Tirana"

see example on page 73

Until World War I, the names of the designers were known only in a few cases, but this situation changed afterward. To be sure, there was a long pause in the development of new patterns after 1918, until about 1925. But then a truly hectic activity began. The best-known designer of Rosenthal services in the epoch of Art Deco was Friedrich Fleischmann. Among his many designs, "Li," of 1926 (520, Selb factory), which includes a coffee, tea and dining service, is perhaps the most striking. In all the Rosenthal firms combined there were seventeen (!) definitely signed with his name, and he presumably collaborated on an unknown number of others as well.

"Li" displays almost everything that characterizes Art Deco porcelain: the shape of the pot is conical, the wall stepped, the spout attachment has multiple curves, and the handle is sharply angled. More could scarcely have been added. Or could it? The artist also dreamed up individualistic knobs for the lid, resembling Chinese writing, by which anyone could recognize the pieces from afar. Too much? A stylized, geometrized, colorful decoration and gold borders to accentuate the rims were added, and yet the service makes a unified, harmonious impression. "Li" was intended as "everyday dishes"--according to the Rosenthal advertising--and was very successful. Today, in the age of dishwashers (the principle of which had already been invented in the USA in 1865, but which came into general use in Europe only after World War II) one can no longer understand the use of "good" versus "everyday" dishes.

The original name of the dishes, "Li," provides an opportunity to speculate on the often puzzling names given to porcelain. Is the knob the simplified Chinese symbol for "Li": weight? Surely not. A hint may be given by Fleischmann's parallel services 530 and 540, La and Lu, the three being advertised together at first. The lyrics of the Dadaists at the time, and of their successors, are full of poems that play with these syllables; for instance, those by Richard Morgenstern, Kurt Schwitters and Karl Valentin. Porcelain linked with nonsense verse? That would not have been foreign to Art Deco. (Heinz Rühmann's famous lullaby,

"La, li, lu, only the man in the moon is watching," was written years later.) "Tirana" is a later name for this service.

"Helena"

see example on page 89

This service (660 white, 670 ivory, Selb factory), first made in 1936, was developed by Wolfgang von Wersin, who had formerly worked in the same way for the Nymphenburg porcelain factory. It included a coffee, tea, and dining service, and, in its simplicity as undecorated whiteware, was typical of Rosenthal dishes of the thirties, and in fact, of the porcelain of that time. After the manneristic Art Deco, designers discovered the simple, the modest again; the appropriate terms for this style from art history include Bauhaus, Neue Sachlichkeit, International Classicism. In 1938, von Wersin designed "Ariadne" (3130, Thomas factory, Marktredwitz) for Rosenthal in the same spirit. Another series from the thirties, the "Aida" (320 white, 360 ivory, Plössberg factory), is livelier in comparison. It was created in 1937 by Otto Koch, a Rosenthal factory director, and is still offered in the "Rosenthal Classic" series today.

The shapes of dishes were not to be changed at will if they were to remain useful. In addition, so much capital was needed for their development that the company could resist demands from outside the world of porcelain--in this case, everything that "smelled" of the "art of the Third Reich," of Hitler and National Socialism. An affinity with Classicism could be seen on an international scale. In "Helena," the effect of the "Bauhaus," now regarded as obsolete, and of related tendencies could be sensed. This is even true of Rosenthal products like the "Beauty of Work" pattern which was contracted for by the office of the same name in the similarly directed "Strength through Joy" organization. This office was particularly responsible for workplace designs, and the dishes were intended for factory cafeterias.

From these dishes, which were, if anything, decorated with a one-color border, usually red, a direct line leads to those of the fifties by Loewy/Latham and others. For example, the 1956 "Fontana" dining, coffee and tea service of the German-Russian Elsa Fischer-Treyden (650, Plössberg factory) and the "TAC I" and "TAC II: by Walter Gropius, the founder of the Bauhaus, made in 1969. Later versions of "Fontana" without good-luck symbols correspond more to their original intentions; Fischer-Treyden also designed various vases and glassware for Rosenthal.

"2000"

see example on page 92

Raymond Loewy (1893-1986) became world-famous in the fifties for his best-selling book *Ugliness Does Not Sell Well.* He states in it that he invented the profession of the industrial designer and made it socially acceptable. Be that as it may, he was at least one of the best-known and most talented designers of this century. Even if the present-day reader may be surprised at his belief in progress and lack of interest in environmental problems, the book is still quite readable.

Loewy came into contact with Rosenthal through the importer who hired him to design a service especially for the American market (1951, "E/Easterling," by Richard S. Latham, 3140, Thomas Works, Marktredwitz). Out of this design developed a direct contact with the Rosenthal firm and a fruitful cooperation, for which his partner Latham was probably responsible. For that reason, Latham and Loewy are always named together now. (Latham himself designed additional services for Rosenthal--"Exquisit" 90, Krister-Thomas Works, Landstuhl, in 1953, and "Form T," 1460, Thomas Works, Speichersdorf, in 1974.)

The most renowned result of this collaboration was the "2000" service of 1954 (2000, Selb factory), which included a coffee, a tea and a dining service. It was produced from 1954 to 1978, within the "Studio Line" from 1961 on, and experienced a minor renaissance from 1986 to 1990 in the "Rosenthal Classic" line. By 1961, two million sets had already been sold. It ranks among the most successful Rosenthal services, and was also effective as whiteware--as many modern services have been since the thirties, which would have been unthinkable without the influence of the "Bauhaus." With "2000," Rosenthal introduced the "New Look" in porcelain. With this same term, Christian Dior had introduced a new concept in women's clothing fashions (characterized by wasp waists and full skirts) in 1947.

The shape of "2000" is so radically different that one does not know just how to begin to describe it, because one reaches the end so quickly. It is conical, the walls are smooth, and the handles and knobs are somewhat thicker where one grasps them. It was suitable for a fantastic array of various decorations, applied by machine or by hand. Those who know it well say that there are at least 200, at most 400, different decorations. A probable total is 265--quite enough. The most famous are probably the "Seidenbast" decoration by Margret Hildebrand, that is amazingly like the contemporary style of kitchen furniture, the calligrpahic gold spout by J. Gallitzendörfer, and the gentle, colorful leaf pattern that many also ascribe to Margret Hildebrand.

In 1959, the "Berlin" dinner, coffee and tea service by Hans Theo Baumann also appeared; its straightforward character was especially effective in contrast to the warm-hearted, playful design by Raymond Peynet (Kronach 3000). He also designed, aside from a few services of doubtful origin, the equally extensive "Bettina white" (1959, Kronach 1210) and especially "ABC" (1965, Krister-Thomas Works, Landstuhl) services.

Timo Sarpaneva

Walter Gropius

"Magic Flute"

see example on page 104

In 1968, Rosenfeld introduced a service with a very different emanation in the Studio Line, "Magic Flute" (1260, Plössberg factory), which is a creation of the Danish stage designer Björn Wiinblad and includes coffee, tea and dinner services. If you imagine for a moment that the decoration is not there, it can be seen that Wiinblad developed a remarkably simple, modern shape.

The basis was an egg shape, which was more or less strongly adapted as needed. The handles appear to bend outward strikingly far; the spouts, as counterweights, are mounted noticeably high and point almost horizontally. The real identifying mark, though, is provided by the knobs of the lids, made high and pointed and ending in a small ball. They give the shape an exotic look, as if Upper Bavarian onion-domed churches had been moved to the Orient. In fact, towers of orthodox churches were the model. Elsa Fischer-Treyden, who comes from Moscow, had made the first designs of this type while under contract to the firm.

The decoration and theme also add their bit to the exotic air. So that nobody remains in the dark about it, one can read gilded quotations from the libretto in Wiinblad's handwriting on the pots and plates. The gold decoration in particular, especially on the "Shah Service" of 1971, strengthened this impression. If the decoration patterns are reminiscent of early Oriental art, then the luxurious ornamentation and fantasy hints at the Rococo, from which the theme was taken.

Wiinblad also developed for Rosenthal, among other things, four other services: In 1959-60, along with Hans Wohlrab, the modern Baroque-style "Romance" (1250, Plössberg factory); in 1967, along with Tapio Wirkkala, the "Lotus" (800, Plössberg factory); in 1971, the mocha service "Little Flower" (Petit Fleur, 4000, Rotbühl works, Selb); and in 1985, "Asymmetry" (8500, Rotbühl works).

"Variation"

see example on page 103

"Magic Flute" was, to be sure, designed by a Dane [Wiinblad], yet it does not necessarily follow the strict Scandinavian line that began for Rosenthal in 1957 with the "Finlandia" service (3180, Thomas Works, Marktredwitz), designed by Finnish designer Tapio Wirkkala, who had great influence on the line that continues to this day. Wiinblad came from Loewy's studio in New York. This simultaneous production of different styles was already one of the founder's principles, and was deliberately continued by his son. Thus, alongside the strict simplicity of a Wirkkala design there was the fanciful, playful style of Wiinblad; along with the undecorated was luxurious opulence--to mirror the condradictions of real life.

Wirkkala developed not only many vases and the like, but also several other services for Rosenthal:

"Variation" (2500, Selb works, 1962)

"Composition" (1350, Plössberg works, 1963)

"Tea for Two" tea service (7094, Selb works, 1964)

"Rotunda" (1440, Thomas works, Speichersdorf, 1966), designed with Richard Scharrer

"Lotus" (800, Plössberg works, 1967), with Wiinblad

"Modulation" (3400, Rotbühl works, Selb, 1967), with Scharrer

"Perlband" (710, Thomas works, Waldershof, 1967), again with Scharrer, and reissued in wholesale form in 1970 as 720

"Assam" tea service (7253, Selb works, 1968)

"Lanzette" (1450, Thomas works, Speichersdorf, 1969), with Werner Exner

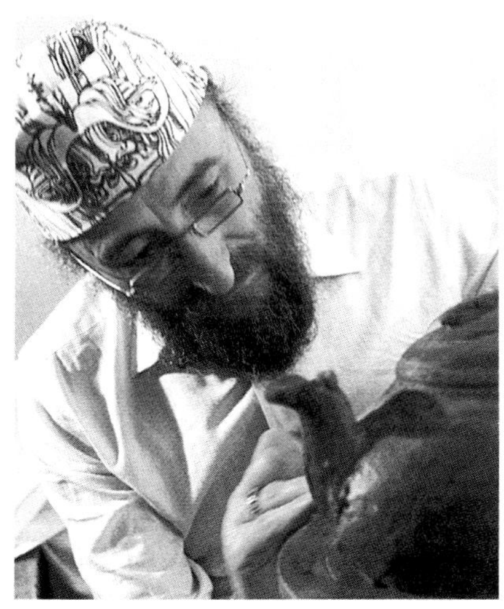

Ernst Fuchs working on the "Magic Sea" tea service, see page 128.

"Polygon" (6000, Rotbühl works, Selb, 1973)

"Century" (8000, Rotbühl works, Selb) in 1979.

Of them, "Polygon" and "Century" are still offered in the Studio Line. There were not many artists who influenced the development of the firm so long or so successfully.

The most well known of the services (along with the thin-walled "Century," with its rice-grain effect that was meant to be reminiscent of Chinese porcelain) was "Variation." The irregularly vertical reliefs on the walls of "Variation" hollow pieces, which made any further decoration all but impossible, also served to characterize this service. Walter Gropius, the founder of the Bauhaus, was so impressed by it that he took this concept into his design repertoire and applied it to the facades of the Rotbühl works, which he designed. Like Gropius, Wirkkala also applied the use of Black Porcelain--which, strictly speaking, consists not of porcelain, but of a ceramic that is particularly hard to produce--for several pieces of the "Variation" service and the "Pollo" vases. Gropius used this concept in the "TAC" service.

Here we must also take note of the "Drop" tea service of 1971, by the renowned German designer Luigi Colani, though it bears the low number 1282 (Rotbühl works, Selb). As usual with Colani, the simple "hydro-dynamic" form subordinates itself exactly to the function. He also designed the "seated landscape," "Pool," for Rosenthal.

"Suomi"

see examples on pages 114-116

A recent success in the Scandinavian line was created in 1976 by Timo Sarpaneva with the dinner, coffee and tea service "Suomi" (7000, Rotbühl works, Selb), which took four years to develope, since the artist had no previous experience with porcelain. He introduced the metal iron at the Rosenthal firm. But how was one to attach metal pieces securely to the smooth outer surface of a pot that resembled a block of porcelain?--that was one of the many questions he raised. The pot is still one of the most challenging tasks for the modeler. Sarpaneva tried to use the square of the circle, namely rounding a cubic hollow body so that the shape was pleasant enough for the dinner table.

The result was so successful that "Suomi" received the highest awards of any Rosenthal service, and is still available today, decorationated or as whiteware, in the Studio Line. It has also been decorated by several artists as "Suomi-objects" in the "limited art editions;" the artists include Otmar Alt, Salvador Dali, H.A.P. Grieshaber, Eduardo Paolozzi, Otto Piene, Ivan Rabuzin and Victor Vasarely.

"Cupola"

see examples on pages 121 and 123

In international commercial art, the Scandinavian style was followed by the Italian, and for Rosenthal the two Finns Tapio Wirkkala and Timo Sarpaneva were followed in 1985 by the Italian Mario Bellini with his "Cupola" service (8600, Rotbühl works). One can disagree as to whether the extremely rounded shapes with the usually broken black-white and dark gray lines reflect the style of Mannerism or, which is more probable, that of Art Deco. "Cupola" already points to the strict fantasies of the Post-modern style.

The cups from the "Cupola" service have led a life of their own for years in the form of "collector cups," of which there are now over twenty. Every cup was decorationated by a different artist, including Otmar Alt, Marcello Morandini, Gilbert Portanier, Salomé, Björn Wiinblad and Yang. Anyone can recognize these collector cups immediately from all the firm's other offerings, thanks to their diagonally mounted, semicircular, grooved handles, which find their pendants in the ring of the saucer and have astounded many users. How on earth does one grasp such a cup? It is best not to. Collector cups are not necessarily intended for use.

Additional collector cups are found in the present Rosenthal program in the form of about ten espresso cups, which were taken from the "Mythos" service by Paul Wunderlich. Also, there are more than thirty "artist cups" that were not only decorated but designed originally, if not downright extremely, by the most varied artists. Within these parameters, every artist who collaborates with Rosenthal can leave a small token. Every style, every trend, and every fashion is represented here with typical examples.

"Flash" and "Scenario"

In closing, here is a brief look at two noteworthy services. In the eighties, Rosenthal introduced for the first time services that were made not of porcelain but of ceramic, and that did not belong to the traditional style trends but to the post-modern.

"Flash" (4500, Kronach works, 1985), designed by the American Dorothy Hafner, and "Scenario" (2800, Kronach works, 1991), by the German Barbara Brenner, showed in their very names that they were aimed at the mature citizens of the large cities. Their wealth of color expressed the joy of beautiful moments. In terms of form, though, these post-modern ceramics are related to Art Deco. These ceramic pieces were not created in the newest style of art, but rather exploited tendencies of modern art commercially.

In all, there are about 210 services produced in the four Rosenthal factories: at (1) Selb, (2) Rotbühl-Selb, (3) Kronach, and (4) Plössberg (Bahnhof-Selb). In addition, some 160 services are made at (5) the Rosenthal Thomas works at Marktredwitz, (6) Thomas works at Speichersdorf, (7) Krister in Waldenburg, (8) Krister-Thomas in Landshut, (9) Haviland in Waldershof, and (10) Thomas in Waldershof, *which do not bear the Rosenthal trademark and therefore are not covered here.*

The limited art services, pots and the like by Lichtenstein, Morandini, etc., are introduced in the framework of the limited objects.

Two Dragon-dogs as Candlesticks
Bahnhof-Selb works, first made in the twenties, designed by FR (Rochard Förster?)
Museum der Deutschen Porzellanindustrie, Hohenberg/Eger

Figurines

All model numbers in the following text always refer, unless expressly stated otherwise, to the Selb works.

Animals

Animals are considered especially "suited to porcelain," and thus thousands of animals are made in porcelain by all the manufacturers

Two Toucans
Bahnhof-Selb works
First made in the twenties
Ht. 3.2 cm, lg. 3.8 cm
Privately owned, photo from the Museum der Deutschen Porzellanindustrie, Hohenberg/Eger

Tiger Drinking
Model no, 942, Art Dept., Selb, first made 1927, designed by Hermann Geibel
Ht. 12.5 cm, lg. 25 cm.
Museum der Deutschen Porzellanindustrie, Hohenberg/Eger

and factories. Rosenthal makes everything from stag beetles (such as 387) to elephants (such as 335). The portrayal of animals is a real job for every porcelain maker. The character of many animals can be captured well in porcelain.

Yet there are limitations to be made. The fact that a stag beetle can be made life-size or even bigger is beyond doubt. Yet what about the elephant, who has to be trimmed down to fit into a living room? The advantage of porcelain of being able to reproduce everything in a handy size simultaneously means a reduction. "Size," in the real or transposed sense, is not necessarily its strength.

When one looks at the Rosenthal animal figures, one notices that the large, dominant creatures that are often used in coats of arms and tavern signs, [and that were the pride of old-school hunters, such as bears, elephants, and lions] were portrayed fairly seldom, and the eagle even more rarely. Those that stand out instead are all the domestic animals, and the dog most of all. The considerably larger horse follows, some distance behind. What the porcelain maker felt like portraying in his material is made clear by the unending numbers of flying creatures, particularly the birds, native as well as exotic, of which one could make great flocks, and smaller, more fragile butterflies.

Whether the preference for certain animals in certain decades is typical only of Rosenthal, or of certain trends of the times, can only be speculated on here. Although Philipp Rosenthal was an enthusiastic hunter and rider, European game animals have appeared among his products in large numbers only since the thirties. Horses appeared mainly in the fifties, when he was already dead. Typical of the time, though, was the "Hereditary Farm Horse" (1601, Rottmann) of 1936. (Had this nag proved its arian ancestry?) The American birds that were missing before were modeled at the end of the fifties (as of 1959, between 5197 and 5243), perhaps partly as a result of requests from America.

It is striking that, in the course of the five decades (from 1910 to 1960) in which Rosenthal modeled animals in large numbers, the program became more and more specialized. At first there was a "Grazing Donkey" (144, 1912, Zügel), and in the end it had to be a "Somali Wild Ass Foal, Lying" (1845, 1954, Heidenreich). But hand in hand with this "scientification," this downright encyclopedic portrayal of animals, came a trend toward the familiar, the homey and lovable. This was no longer done by a "Playing Dachshund" (77, 1910); now and then there were still dachshunds, "Batzel," "Hexel" or "Axel" by name (1625-1626, 1936 and 1964, 1954). It is rewarding to find out exactly which modelers made these animals. There are surprises and new connections to be found.

As in all factories, animal specialists essentially determine the offerings and their quality at Rosenthal. In the first decade, not much happened. Still, one should take note of the small-scale sculptor *Karl Himmelstoss*. He worked for Rosenthal from 1912 until the thirties and created many animals, even though he was really not an animal specialist, but rather had created more significant figures. For animals, *Willy Zügel*, son of the renowned animal painter Heinrich Zügel (1850-1941), was somewhat superior to him. He also worked for the Meissen and Nymphenburg porcelain factories, and worked for Rosenthal from 1911 to 1926.

In the twenties, several new names emerged. The animals of *Theodor Kärner*, who also worked for Nymphenburg, created noteworthy animals for Rosenthal from 1918, working for the art departments at both Selb and Bahnhof-Selb. He carried on the Baroque style tradition. Equally important was *Grete Zschäbitz*, who came to Rosenthal from the Fürstenberg factory and worked from 1924 to 1933. In that period, *Gustav Oppel* also deserves mention; he worked for Rosenthal from 1924 to 1936, but also for the oldest porcelain factory, Volkstedt. Every Rosenthal enthusiast will encounter Oppel and his high-quality work in every area.

For the sake of completeness, it must be mentioned that such noteworthy sculptors such as *August Gaul* and *Richard Scheibe* worked individually for Rosenthal. In 1928 and 1929, the firm obtained twelve unpublished designs by Gaul and produced them in porcelain or stoneware in the art departments at Selb or Bahnhof-Selb. Scheibe was represented with animals in 1925 and 1950. *Gerhard Schliepstein* began with naturalistic animals, but in the latter half of the twenties he concentrated on human figures.

From the thirties on, the animal products were dominated by a single modeler, *Fritz Heidenreich*, who worked for Rosenthal from 1919. He attained a virtuosity in the combination of whole groups that probably has remained unmatched. His fish group "Scalare" (1636), made in 1937, was assembled from some forty individual parts but looked like a single casting, and was introduced at the Paris World's Fair that year. It was in production until 1991.

Today, Rosenthal offers only one bird by Wirkkala--too few, in the opinion of the seller as well as the buyer, to satisfy the unbroken interest in animal figures.

Human Figurines

Porcelain, at least when glazed, is capable of simulating scales or feathers. Scales and feathers can even be formed three-dimensionally, so that one can count every single one. But whoever sees porcelain birds or fish will still not have

Canary
Model no. 633, Selb art dept.
First made 1923, designed by Theodor Kärner
Ht. 17 cm.
Privately owned, photo from the Museum der Deutschen Porzellanindustrie, Hohenberg/Eger

the feeling of seeing real scales or feathers. It is always "only" porcelain. Porcelain animals share this fate with those of bronze or marble. Even the naturalistic painter may paradoxically employ the means of illusion to illustrate the differing consistency of the "surface," revealing more of its visual qualities than the porcelain artist.

On the other hand, porcelain can reflect all the more of the erotic quality of human skin. Porcelain has a lot in common with human beings. If one can take the Bible literally, man is also made of clay. Both actually consist of a very sensitive, transitory material. Breakability, in the literal sense for porcelain and more figuratively for mankind, is one of their main attributes, which depends greatly on the form and flexibility of the material. Movement and liveliness result from it. It is not by accident that one of man's earliest "activities," the dance, is one of porcelain's main themes.

The quality of natural "skin" was formerly created essentially by the whiteness, and now more by the purity and "shimmer" of its lucidity. Pimples and the like are a fault in both people and porcelain. In France it is still a compliment to tell a woman that she has a particularly clear skin, one of the loveliest things that man can create. Today the fear of pollution and its dangers is more and more important for the purity of skin.

The terms "purity" and "white quality" hint at a closer relationship between skin and porcelain: both can be color and decoration themselves, and at the same time ideal carriers of color and ornament, whether through (stylish) clothing, hair styles, jewelry, make-up, etc.

Trends of the Times

A connection between a figure and its time of origin is practically always given, and is most one-sided for subjects that are closely linked to historical events, such as the patriotic motifs of World War I, 1914-1918, which even appeared on plates a year earlier, in 1913. It is noteworthy that the Rosenthal firm made use of this theme for only two years, 1914-1915, mainly with portrayals of soldiers (381 to 423, A. Caasmann, Karl Himmelstoss, etc.) and a nurse (382, Berthold Boess). The "Landsturmmann" (399), who is obviously carrying a load of champagne bottles in his arms, is noteworthy.

Whoever is surprised that harmless soldier figures were made in wartime should remember that in Germany, soldiers were objects of admiration for centuries, from the "brash lieutenant" to the "chocolate soldier" of operettas and pop songs.

In 1915, a rarity (410, Gsell?), "Uncle Doctor" appeared, the caricature of a man with stovepipe hat, umbrella, and fur-lined coat. The coat hangs open, and the figure is naked under it. But it is not meant to be an exhibitionist, but presumably John Bull, the symbol of England. In any case, thus was England symbolized at the time in papers such as "Simplicissimus." The inspiration was probably the unfortunate Dardanelles offensive. The figure would then comment: "Outside gooey, inside phooey!"

The Hitler Era

The historical connection between some figures of the Hitler era is similar. Portraying the "Führer" himself was presumably the duty of every porcelain factory (1250). The bust with the title "Hitler as Drummer," by *Heinrich Moshage*, from 1933, is nevertheless noteworthy, because it does not stick to the prescribed iconography, which Hitler, along with the photographer Heinrich Hoffmann, had already worked out almost completely at that time. The drummer is still indebted to *Neue Sachlichkeit*, and anyone who does not know that Hitler is depicted will scarcely recognize him.

Autumn
Model no. 983, Selb art dept.
First made 1928, designed by Gerhard Schliepstein
Ht. 17.8 cm.
Museum der Deutschen Porzellanindustrie, Hohenberg/Eger

Also of note are models from history, such as Frederick the Great (1242, 1529, inspired by the Classicist *Louis Tuaillon*, 1584), his cavalry general Seydlitz (1563), though the otherwise indispensible Bismarck is missing, and military figures (1544-45, 1548-49). Several heroic titles must not be lacking, such as "Youthful Strength" and "Toward the Sun" (1240-41), likewise apparently "Arian" figures like the "Bamberg Rider," "Uta of Naumburg" and "Barbara of Strassburg" (1564, 1569, 1635).

The clever porcelain artist mounted his subject on a horse when possible, took a beautiful woman as his model, or a sporting appearance, to make the task more bearable. As porcelain figures these models cannot be bad, as a sort of deliberate Neoclassicism, often more pale coloring than style, was internationally popular at that time. The "most significant" sculptor of the "Thousand-year Reich," *Josef Thorak*, made only one Rosenthal figure, and oddly enough, "Das Licht" (5113) did not appear until 1958.

Dance and Dancers Figurines

All other thematic groups were naturally not so directly typical of their times. The dance has belonged to the classic themes of all epochs since the invention of Meissen porcelain. Rosenthal's art departments have profited from the enormous upsurge in the international dance scene, thanks to Diaghilev's "Ballets russes," the German expressive dance from Mary Wigman to Harald Kreutzberg (who was portrayed himself in 1951, 1864 and 1867), etc., the popularity of the revue (on film as well!), and the increasing interest in the dances of "exotic" peoples, often enough just European dancers in exotic costumes. Names like Loie Fuller (serpentine or veil dancer), Isadora Duncan and Vaslav Nijinsky were subjects for all kinds of portrayals. Celly de Rheydt (Cäcilie Schmidt) made nude dancing popular even before Josephine Baker and her bananas. But the public itself was wild about dancing in the entire decade.

In the twenties, two artists in particular must be noted: the Viennese *Constantin Holzer-Defanti*, who worked for both art departments from 1918 to 1927 and applied his personal interest in the dance scene, and the Russian *Dorothea Charol*, a member of the large colony of Russian emigrés in Berlin, who worked for the Schwarzburg Workshops for Porcelain Art, the Oldest Volkstedt Porcelain Factory and, in the twenties, for the art department of Rosenthal's Bahnhof-Selb factory.

Dorothea Charol's figures are characterized by elegance and the "unnatural" lengthening of limbs, very widespread then for portrayals of dancers, that reminds one of Expressionist forerunners like Wilhelm Lehmbruck. A dancer named "Spring," standing in a basket with flower decoration (Bahnhof-Selb), became especially popular. It has been shown that such figures were often based on photos. This is not meant negatively, for many great painters have made use of the advantages of photography since the latter half of the 19th century. Constantin Holzer-Defanti also worked from photos, although many of his dancers were modeled after well-known performers. Even his renowned coloration was not invented by him, but taken from models.

Thanks to their quality, the dancers of *Berthold Boess, Karl Himmelstoss, Ferdinand Liebermann, Rudolf Marcuse* and *Gustav Oppel*

also deserve special mention. From the thirties on, not only the titles were often paler and more neutral (the figures are just called "Dancer," "Dancing" or "Largo," "Finale," "Tango"), but the dancers also lacked the strong fascination of the past. Nor did any artists stand out any more, except, perhaps, for the Klimsch student Lore Friedrich-Gronau.

Theater, Fashion, and Music Figurines

Several other groups are related to the dance theme. They include particularly lovely figurines, but on account of their small numbers, they do not get much notice. In considering them, we must repeat some of the previously mentioned artists' names. Now and then portrait figures or busts attract attention, such as Enrico Caruso in 1913 (299) and Giuseppe Verdi in 1960 (5232). It is worth taking a close look at them, even if the choice seems to be accidental. For Goethe's 200th birthday in 1949, a bust (1794) was made, accompanying the characters from "Hermann und Dorothea" and "Wilhelm Meister" (832-838).

Fashion is a favorite theme for porcelain. In 1915 *Ludwig Vierthaler* created two ladies, one with a muff and one with a dog (426-427), who stand out from the crowd for their quality. Vierthaler had worked for Tiffany & Co. in New York and with Bruno Paul in Berlin, as well as in numerous ceramic studios. Unfortunately, he made only these two figures for Rosenthal. Artists seldom succeeded in transposing fashionable elegance into a completed, flowing porcelain form so differently and yet so true to the material.

The previously mentioned *Karl Himmelstoss* created a whole series of splendid caricatures of musicians over the years, for example, the shawm [an early double-reed woodwind instrument] player of 1910 ("Spring's Awakening," 96), the bass violinist and hunting-horn player in 1913 (196-197), the cellist of 1917 (487), and the clarinetist, guitarist, bass player and fiddler of 1956 (5039-42). The first three are said to be Selb originals. Unfortunately, no complete orchestra has been made. But it can safely be said that choirs could be made up of the Rosenthal angels and cherubs. In 1956 Himmelstoss was still alive, but it is not known whether the later musicians were modelled by the artist a long time before they first appeared. Solving this could explain many a perplexing question of dating.

Just as interesting is the lively, colorful figure "Überbrettl" [Cabaret] (328), designed by the sculptor *Rudolf Marcuse* in 1913 and finished in subdued underglaze painting. Marcuse worked for the Schwarzburg workshops, for the Royal Porcelain Factory in Berlin roughly between 1911 and 1913, and from 1913 to about 1919 for Rosenthal. The name "Überbrettl" was that of a famous Berlin cabaret founded in 1901. A similarity with a member of it has not been established, but it is impossible that Marcuse, a Berliner, could have come up with the name by chance.

From the early thirties are the figures of the Hungarian sculptress *Claire Weiss* (Klara Herczeg), who also worked for Bing & Gröndahl and Hutschenreuther. In 1932-33 she worked for the Selb and Bahnhof-Selb works. With her, Rosenthal once again had found an artist with a sense of refined, fashionable elegance. For her group "The Seasons" (1149-52, 1932), she obviously had mannequins in mind and turned the subject into a fashion show. One can hardly imagine that someone who created such high-style figures also "decorated" the squares of Hungary with colossal Stalinistic monuments after 1945.

Sports Figurines

If all the variations of games and shows seem made for porcelain figures, then sports should also rank among the preferred themes. When in 1851 a Briton, Charles-Frederick Worth, and a Swede, Bobergh, founded the first fashion house in Paris and thus set the victory march of haute couture in motion, the first special sport clothing had already been invented. For example, in 1811 the first street clothes in which one could do gymnastics were designed by "Turnvater" Jahn. Around 1830, the first bathing suit was designed by the Duchess de Berry, and it remained obligatory for women for a good hundred years. In 1838, the first mountain-climbing clothes were designed by a French woman. It soon was proved that sports were an ideal medium for the emancipation of women.

In addition, the proprietor [Philipp Rosenthal] was an enthusiastic sportsman. In the very first year of Rosenthal figurines, 1910, *Ferdinand Liebermann* created a "Tennis Player" (85). In all, the firm produced four female tennis players, one by *Philipp Kittler* in 1926 (852), by *Ernst Wenck* in 1932 (1171), and by *Fritz Klimsch* in 1936 (1586), but only one male tennis player, by Kittler in 1925 (782). Only equestrians and swimmers have been represented about this often, but most of them have been women too. The types of sports chosen and the combination of woman and fashion with sport tells something of where the modelers generally saw charm. For some figures, children were the models (1170-1172, 1932, by Claire Weiss).

One should take a longer look at the three "swimmer figures" of the sculptor *Rudolf Marcuse* (293, 294, 316), made in 1913. Such swimsuits were extremely modern for women then. The normal fashion was still the the two-piece suit designed by the Duchess de Berry eighty years before. But not only that: Could one not suspect that the figures were created in the twenties? In fact, in the years before World War I, circa 1912, there were already individual elements of Art Deco to be seen (just as elements of the "New Look" of 1947 had appeared in Paris in 1938-39). One could assume that these designs were only "resting" during the war years.

"Normal" sports were portrayed by *Philipp Kittler*. His usual assignments were monuments and structures; he only worked with Rosenthal for two years, 1925 and 1926. What was unique about his figures (756, 758, 780-782, 839, 843, 852) was that, according to the firm's advertising, they had been approved by the "Reich Sport Teacher" Waitzer. It is surprising, perhaps, to see a boxer (781, 1925). But why not? A good boxer has to "dance" in the ring, and Max Schmeling even sang in the film "Love in the Ring." The sportingly correct tennis player does exactly what one calls "löffeln" in German (843, 1926).

Gymnast
Model no. 724, Bahnhof-Selb works, first made in the twenties
Ht 22 cm, lg. 32 cm.
Jugendstilmuseum Reissmüller, Brühl; photo from the Museum der Deutschen Porzellanindustrie, Hohenberg/Eger

Allegorical and Mythololological Figurines

The rise of the Rosenthal firm in the realm of porcelain figurines is linked with the name of the naturalistic professor and sculptor *Ferdinand Liebermann*. He created three-dimensional structures, fountains, and monuments, but also worked for the Royal Porcelain Factory in Berlin. From 1909, he was chiefly responsible for mythological and allegorical subjects at Rosenthal. Following the lead of Alfred Böcklin, bacchantes, fauns, nymphs and silenes became his favorite subjects. When he first tried to use animals in 1910, he created a real "Theater of Apes" (3-7, 38-40).

Julius Meier-Graefe, the ruler of art in his time (who rediscovered the German Romanticists and Realists and made them French impressionists and their successors known in Germany, but was not exactly a friend of Böcklin) spoke of such figures as the "Munich Mardi Gras Renaissance." When Liebermann began to work for Rosenthal, Art Nouveau had already come to an end. In the masterful dominance of underglaze painting one can perhaps still see his influence, but the subject matter was determined by the Historicism that began around 1910.

The fact that his figures are still so popular today is attributable to their dynamicism and "humor," so atypical of porcelain. Liebermann seems to have been putting on a play with his figures, with himself as their "director," as in the faun bust "Terror" (74) of 1911, and in the extremely stretched "Straussenritt" (75) of 1910, where he creates a piece of tehcnical bravura. It may also be that hidden drives are revealed in these nature deities.

Working simultaneously with Liebermann but in a different style were, among others, the already noted *Karl Himmelstoss*

and *A. Caasmann*, about whom nothing is known except that he worked for Rosenthal from 1912 to 1923. The "Pearl Seeker" (446), made by Himmelstoss in 1917, became famous, as a similar work in bronze had already been exhibited at the Munich Glass Palace in 1906 under the title "Crouching Girl with Shellfish." A typical example of Caasmann's work is perhaps the "Faun with Grape Basket" (175) of about 1912.

All these allegorical and mythological portrayals vanished after World War I as if by magic. Since the subject was so successful, attempts were made to revive it now and then, but not much came of them. If anything, ancient deities were portrayed, such as "Europa" (603) by *Adolf Opel (?)* in 1921, "Leda" (753) by *Ernst Wenck* in 1924, or "Aurora" (1795) by *Fritz Klimsch* in 1949. A last venture by *Bele Bachem* and *Raymond Peynet* appeared at the end of the fifties, and then again in service motifs by, for example, *Björn Wiinblad* and *Paul Winderlich*. Attempts to portray deities of other cultures were rare ("Parvati," 696, by *Karl Himmelstoss* in 1923, "Miao Pudso." 940, by *Gustav Oppel* in 1927).

Christian motifs appeared from Rosenthal in greater numbers in the thirties--perhaps as an opposing reaction to National Socialism?--and then again in the fifties, in which the cultural historians like to see contradictions between modern and reaction. The firm could not attain a profile of its own with them.

Genre Figurines

In place of the allegories and mythologies, "genre scenes" of all kinds appeared after World War I. This change of subject can also be seen in Meissen porcelain beginning in 1902. Women and children naturally played a major role. A great many children appeared in the thirties, when the fecundity of the state was specifically demanded. All other subjects were divided more or less evenly. Portrayals of actions were never specified as such in titles, with the single exception of "Longing" of 1938 (1702), based on a figure by the Neo-baroque sculptor Reinhold Begas (1831-1911). Yet there were dozens of action figures in production, though one did not select them from the catalog. Feminine action figures in porcelain--without any allegorical or other significance--only became widely available to the general public in the twenties.

In the genre scenes, there occasionally appeared satirical figures, whether irritating or harmless. Exotic themes turned up too, such as the "Little Moor" of 1925 (760) by *Grete Zschäbitz*

or the "Dalmatian Farmer with Donkey" of 1928 (1019) by *Christian Metzger*. Portrayals of modern occupations must be emphasized: "Newsboy" by *Gustav Oppel* in 1930 (1081), and male and female "Telephoners" by *Klaus Backmund* in 1952 (5023, 5025).

Among the artists there were many old acquaintances, such as

Karl Himmelstoss, Constantin Holzer-Defanti, Gustav Oppel, and *Gerhard Schliepstein*. In addition, special attention was attracted by figures by *Bele Bachem, Fritz Klimsch, Raymond Peynet, Hans Stangl, Milly Steger* and *Ernst Wenck*.

The sculptor *Gerhard Schliepstein* is of particular interest, as he also created large constructions, cast bronzes and grave monuments. He worked for the State Porcelain Factory in Berlin, for Rosenthal from 1925 to 1937 and exclusively from 1929 on, specifically for the art departments at Selb and Bahnhof-Selb. His style, developed after a naturalistic beginning, consisted of elegantly practical cubistic components and very expressive elements.

Milly Steger, a sculptress and graphic artist, worked for Rosenthal only in 1925. Six of her designs were produced. They were exclusively action figures. Her contemporaries already noticed that "it is all soulfulness and internalization" (J. Grell). She was a student of Georg Kolbe, Aristide Maillol and Auguste Rodin, though her figures are more similar to those of Käthe Kollwitz. It is regrettable that the collaboration did not last longer.

Success came to *Ernst Wenck*, originally a woodcarver, whose small figures were produced by the State Porcelain Factory in Berlin, and who worked for Rosenthal, at Selb and Bahnhof-Selb, from 1925 until his death in 1929. Rodin proved to be a difficult model for porcelain artists because of his torn-up surfaces, yet remained the great model of the time. Wenck, following Maillol's lead, was able to capture the shimmering Mediterranean atmosphere in his action figures.

In 1935 Rosenthal was able to hire one of the classic sculptors of the time, *Fritz Klimsch*. His action figures and portraits, true to the Classic tradition, were always lively and harmonious and thus sold very well. He still worked for Rosenthal in the fifties.

A very individual case is that of sculptor *Hans Stangl*, who-- following Henry Moore, perhaps without realizing it--created the first "hol-

Hexagonal Covered Vase
Model no. 515, Selb art dept.
First made 1913
Ht. 31.7/25.9 cm.
Museum der Deutschen Porzellanindustrie
Hohenberg/Eger

Perfume Atomizer
Model no. 1105, Selb art dept.
First made 1930, designed by Hans Küster
Ht. 14 cm.
Thomas Ullrich Collection, Spielberg; photo from the Museum der Deutschen Porzellanindustrie, Hohenberg/Eger

low three-dimensional" figures as early as 1938 and had great success with them for Rosenthal in the fifties. The two men together formed a basis of biomorphism that carried on elements of Art Nouveau. Hans Stangl's figures looked well on the kidney-shaped tables of his day. Henry Moore's monumental style was never seen in Stengl's work.

The figures that *Bele Bachem* and *Raymond Peynet* created for Rosenthal in the fifties and sixties are reminiscent of the satyr plays with which the ancient Greeks ended their tragic dramas. Mankind's amorous entanglements were portrayed once more ironically--it is noteworthy that both artists were successful as illustrators and stage decorators-- and then the Rosenthal firm slowly ended its splendid production of figures. Instead, they sought connections with modern art in a completely new form. Cost and market factors probably had an effect on Rosenthal's withdrawal from figure production.

Figures as illustrative elements, though, are still found, if almost exclusively in decorative form, in Rosenthal products, such as in the services by Björn Wiinblad. His great success probably was gained in part by these elements.

Older figures were still introduced by Rosenthal until 1991. When they were first produced, after the Classic Rose or Rosenthal Classic brand was introduced, that trademark could be found on the bottom. Then Rosenthal stopped figure production completely. In all, the firm produced 2356 figures, animals and decorationative objects at the Selb works through the end of the eighties, according to modelers. There were also a few "a-numbers." At the Bahnhof-Selb and Plössberg works, approximately 1150 pieces were made. There are also a few pieces from the Kronach works, so that the total is about 3500 numbers.

Ornamental Porcelain

The pictures in this book offer a look at the kinds of decorationative porcelain that were produced and what was popular in which decades. Even before the founding of the art department in the first decade of the 20th century, the offerings were varied, though vases dominated it all. This changed as soon as the art department was founded at the Selb works in 1910. The offerings became more varied; along with the vases, various containers, lamps and bowls were offered in particular. In the third decade, the vases almost completely vanished, while the three other categories blossomed.

As for the 1930s, the lists that remain do not allow us to say for sure; the catalogs of the art department at Selb consist almost exclusively of the figures of 1934. Decorationative porcelain had formerly been and was then, according to employees' statements, produced more often in the tableware department, and probably was catalogued in special lists, which apparently have not survived. There could be unexpected omissions in the numbering of the objects, to say nothing of the numbering of the objects made by the art department at Bahnhof-Selb, which operated from about 1920 to 1969-70.

To what extent the assortment of objects was typical of the time and/or of Rosenthal can only be speculated on within limits.

Vases

In the beginning, the Rosenthal production emphasised vases, which had an appealing appearance even without flowers or other contents. The increasing numbers of lamps after 1900 corresponded to the growing use of electricity and resulting urge to turn the night to day and drive the shadows out of

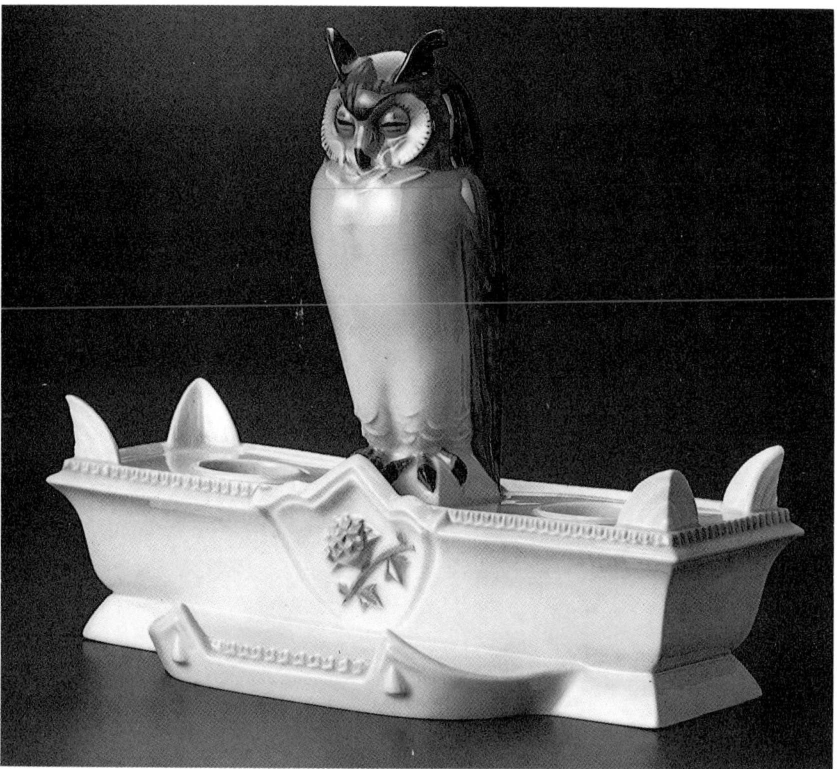

Owl Desk Set
Model no. 1025, Selb art dept., first made 1929, designed by Gustav Oppel, ht. 21 cm, lg. 25 cm. Thomas Ullrich Collection, Spielberg, photo from the Museum der Deutschen Porzellanindustrie, Hohenberg/Eger

"Marlene" Fruit Dishes
Decoration no. 1438, Kronach works, first made ca. 1930, Walter Garbs Collection, Hannover, photo from the Museum der Deutschen Porzellanindustrie, Hohenberg/Eger

the farthest corner. Rosenthal's dwindling variety of flowerpots is surprising after Art Nouveau brought living plants into the living room, but the demand for vases was probably met better by cheaper ceramics. Rosenthal's expansion of offerings corresponded to the trend of Art Nouveau of making a total work of art out of the entire dwelling.

In studying the catalogs, one often gets the impression that Rosenthal was constantly looking for gaps in the market. They produced charming writing equipment, which, to be sure, vanished from the writing desk after the thirties--like everything else that had to be cleaned constantly--in part, probably, because Hitler ordered servant girls to work in the armament factories in 1938.

On what should one's interest be concentrated in all this extensive array? First of all, probably on objects that were combined with three-dimensional figures of all kinds. Here one meets all the artists again who were singled out before, and who now let the same figures--or at least the ideas for them--"wander" from one decorationative ornament to another. Along with the vases, one must particularly note the lamps and clocks, whose shapes are ideal places for further adornment--where the functionality of time in itself would have required a lack of ornamentation.

Along with the figural decorations, the decoration on ornamental porcelain is also very important. The growth of the art department began in 1909 with the move of the Danish painter

Julius-Vilhelm Guldbrandsen from the Royal Porcelain Factory in Copenhagen to Rosenthal, where he directed the art department at the Selb works from 1910 to 1924. His underglaze painting, with its soft,

Container on Three Feet
Selb art dept., first made in the twenties, width 9.6 cm, ht. 8.6/7.1 cm. Museum der Deutschen Porzellanindustrie, Hohenberg/Eger

Covered Bowl, Cover also serves as bowl
Rosenthal, first made ca. 1930, diam. 18.3 cm, ht. 9.5/5.2 cm. Museum der Deutschen Porzellanindustrie, Hohenberg/Eger

flowing colors that were so inherent to Art Nouveau, and especially his "Rosari Decorations" that were inspired by the Viennese Art Nouveau, won him deserved fame.

The term "Rosari-Decorations" refers to a geometric-ornamental flower decoration in underglaze painting, which was done mainly in cobalt blue with gold trim. There were 25 such vase designs, plus corresponding designs for bowls, boxes and writing implements, each of which was limited to 25 pieces, plus the "Maria" service with decoration no. 601. The limitations were probably abolished in the twenties, but Rosari-Decorations were continued, with interruptions, until 1946-47, though marked only with the design number then. Guldbrandsen probably did not design all the Rosari-Decorations himself, and most of them were completed by *Max Wesp*.

Guldbrandsen also designed Christmas and Easter plates with typical Art Nouveau landscapes--probably the only place where a landscape, not inherently suited to porcelain, can look well.

In the twenties, two other painters, *Kurt Severin* and *Kurt Wendler*, joined the staff. They practiced not only underglaze but also overglaze painting, in order to follow the trend of the times for glowing, contrasting, sharply defined colors. Wendler worked for Rosenthal from 1920 to 1930. Along with his renowned "Indra" decorations, he also produced designs for lamps (1059, 1061), writing implements (1058, with a box as no. 1072), and a figure ("Till Eulenspiegel," 1060) in 1929. Indra was the war god of Indian mythology, who killed the dragon and thus made life possible. This was an era when the exotic was popularized and, going back to Paul Lincke's operetta "In the Kingdom of Indra" in 1899, was misused. Wendler's glowing colors, especially his flaming red, were reminiscent of Indian legends, and at the beginning of the twenties he was already anticipating many elements of Art Deco. His "Indra" decorations were hand-painted, signed with his last name, and according to the information in the catalog, limited at one time to a hundred pieces.

Kurt Severin was a pattern painter for Rosenthal from 1924 to 1928. He created designs not only for animals (such as 772, 941), but also for clock casings (such as 776) and especially for services (such as "Fatima," 120, and "Safia," no. 844). His fairy-tale "Indian" flower motifs from "Indian" painting, which he adapted into Art Deco elements, still enchant the eye today. "Indian" (also known as "Japanese") flowers, as they were called out of ignorance of India and East Asia, and confusion with Amerindians, were actually exotic Chinese flowers such as the chrysanthemum, lotus and peony, as opposed to the native "European" (also called "German") flowers. Along with Wendler and Severin, other artists also worked in Art Deco style for Rosenthal, including the architect *Friedrich Fleischmann, W. Gress, Walter Mutze* and *Tono Zoelch*.

The twenties, and especially Art Deco, were an incredibly fruitful era for Rosenthal. Art Deco also required the setting of the individual object in a suitable ambience. The idea of the total work of art, originally developed by Richard Wagner and Gottfried Semper, became a decorative fashion, though not for the man in the street, but rather for luxurious living which, as the cultural historian Siegfried Gideon ironically noted, could live only in dwellings of this style with the support of artists. This quality was often intensified by succeeding artistic styles, even when they, like the "Bauhaus," strove to attain exactly the opposite.

Between 1932 and 1940, *Fritz von Stockmayer* emerged. He had already lived a busy life as an export merchant when he turned to porcelain painting as a way to live with a war wound, and he worked for Arzberg, Fürstenberg and Schönwald before he came to Rosenthal, where he directed the art department at the Selb works as of 1935. He not only brought hand painting back to life, but also created a new style of decoration, using Japanese models to create plant motifs that, in turn, required new glazing techniques.

Vases in particular experienced a new upswing after World War II, and it has lasted to this day. To begin, let us cite the vases of *Beate Kuhn* and the decorations of *Klaus Bendixen*.

The ceramicist Beate Kuhn, who worked for Rosenthal from 1953 to 1962, designed vases that, like the works of Hans Stangl, were created of biomorphic elements of modern art. They are round, gently curved shapes that lead back into themselves, reminiscent of microscopic animals or even of the works of, for example, Hans Arp. A particularly typical example is the "Kummet Vase" (2644) of 1952.

The painter and graphic artist Klaus Bendixen was a master student of Wilhelm Baumeister. His decorations are unimaginable without the model of his master, as well as those of Joan Miro or Vassili Kandinsky. This is also true of the famous and frequently imitated "Pregnant Luise," an asymmetrical orchid vase (2593) made by *Fritz Heidenreich* in 1950. Along with the kidney-shaped table, it became a symbol of an entire style of home furnishing.

Fruit Bowl and Lampshade
No model no., Selb art dept. First made 1953, designed by Wilhelm Wagenfeld, Rosenthal Archives, Selb

But the days of asymmetrical and biomorphic vases at Rosenthal were numbered; people made fun of the "second Art Nouveau." The strict style of the "Bauhaus" followers came to dominate, although a few "Bauhaus" teachers (such as Vassili Kandinsky and Paul Klee) themselves were among the chief exponents of biomorphic trends in modern art.

Beyond vases, the path taken by Rosenthal led into the world of modern art. In this respect, the vases of *Hans Theo Baumann* ("Puzzle Vases"), *Elsa Fischer-Treyden, Johan van Loon* ("Pergament Vases"), *Timo Sarpaneva, Alev Siesbye, Alan Whittaker* and *Tapio Wirkkala* ("Bag Vases," etc.) were of prime importance. Their shapes were not limited, other than "Tissu" by Whittaker. Any limitations that took place almost always involved the combination of a decoration with a vase, as with Fischer-Treyden and Sarpaneva.

Limited Edition Art Objects

Limited issue alone does not guarantee the artistic value of an object. Along with the enormous technical expenditure, demand and commercial, psychological effects are involved; in short, marketing considerations result in limitation and thus in shortages and higher prices. Nor does the artist's name alone determine the artistic value. The question of whether a porcelain object has an artistic value can only be answered in terms of the individual object.

At first everything seemed to be simple. In 1964, Arnold Bode, the founder of the "Documenta" show in Kassel, urged modern artists, most of whom were not acquainted with the particulars of porcelain, to design reliefs for porcelain. It was no longer the case, as it had been in Art Nouveau or in the twenties, that porcelain utensils or decorations were to be designed by independent artists, but instead that objects that were more than just decorative porcelain should be created. It was no longer to be commercial art, but "pure" art, whatever that may be.

In 1968, within the parameters of the Relief Series, Rosenthal presented 33 porcelain works of art that had been developed since 1964, in editions of from six (Henry Moore, "Moonhead") to at most a hundred pieces. Their designers included some of the best-known names on the scene, from Emil Cimiotti to Fritz Wotruba, and they were--corresponding to an old Rosenthal principle--exponents of the most varied artistic trends. Among these works, the designs of Lucio Fontana and Henry Moore stand out clearly.

It is probably not by chance that this relief edition was developed between 1964 and 1968. In the history of art, the year 1968 forms a dividing line. Dissatisfaction with the events of the postwar [World War II to Vietnam] years led to revolutions in many areas. Students took to the street, men became stylishly colorful, the miniskirt, the Beatles (rock music) and "pop art" conquered the world, the concept of environment and concern for it developed. The concept of art was very much expanded as a result: for example, "land art," "process art," "happening," "fuxus," "environment," etc. On the other hand, pop art followed the road to tangible things, everyday consumer goods.

Reliefs were soon left in the lurch, since one could speak of reliefs in the traditional sense only in a few cases, even if the artist himself chose this designation for his work. To be sure, there were objects involved that were so technically complex that many examples could not be sold because of various faults. Everything that the milieu offered was represented, from the Surrealist Salvador Dali to the "Bauhaus" representative Werner Bayer and the former pop artist Eduardo Paolozzi, plus Post-historicists like Alexander von Weizsäcker. Other materials besides porcelain were used, as long as they were rigid. Joseph Beuys with his grease and felt was missing from this collection, but metal, glass, ceramics, wood and such were represented.

The decorations used by modern artists for utilitarian and ornamental porcelain cover a wide range. For instance, the Gropius pots of the "TAC I" service alone come in limited editions of twelve different designs by modern artists such as Sandro Chia and Rainer Fetting. The espresso cups from the "Cupola" service by Mario Bellini were decorationated by Marcello Morandini, Salome, Yang and the like. The artists not only decorated the cups, but also designed their forms. Thus the Rosenthal "Artist Cup" program was born, with, for example, Barbara Brenner, Dorothy Hafner, Gilbert Portanier and Ambrogio Pozzi represented. These cups are not meant for everyday use, but are often charming as witty rejections of everyday objects.

In addition, artist plates (such as place setting plates) have come back into fashion. They have typical plate shapes, of course, and are made in relatively large numbers, but in spite of that they are, as always, collectibles; items, not utilitarian objects. There are unlimited plates, time-limited plates such as the one by Jörg Immendorf issued in 1991, or limited editions, such as a plate by Elvira Bach in an issue of 2000 pieces. Containers, clocks and such were taken back into the program.

Along with them, objects of art have appeared which are not reminiscent of either utilitarian or ornamental porcelain in either shape or decoration, and many artists, such as Otmar Alt, Ernst Fuchs, H.A.P. Grieshaber, Otto Piene, Natale Sapone, Victor Vasarely, Björn Wiinblad and Paul Wunderlich, have obviously become both successful and famous. Yet the further development of modern art did not take place in porcelain. The technical and economic prerequisites are much too high for that, and young artists would become much too dependent on it. Therefore modern artists in general have only been represented at Rosenthal when they have already made a name for themselves in simpler, more basic materials.

In other words, the work of art in porcelain is always, if at all, a "late" work of art. It is also noteworthy that the choices from the broad spectrum of modern art have become limited. Under this name one finds much that has never been represented at a "documenta" or a "biennial" show, because they were basically intended for porcelain, ceramics or glass. They are made by designers rather than "artists." This restriction, though, can improve the quality of the work.

As always, the Rosenthal firm continues to offer a broad spectrum of objects for the collector with artistic standards, and to offer them gratefully.

Living and Dining Room Objects

The Rosenthal firm evolved from a porcelain factory that set the table to one that decorated the dining room in the same style, and finally, to a certain degree, included the living room and office. The furnishings were all supposed to come "out of the same mould," or at least the customer was supposed to be linked exclusively to one firm that could satisfy all his requirements in the realm of interior design in various ways, but always with high quality.

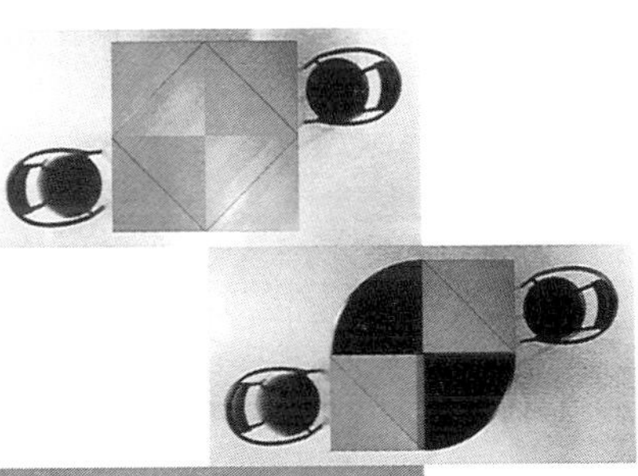

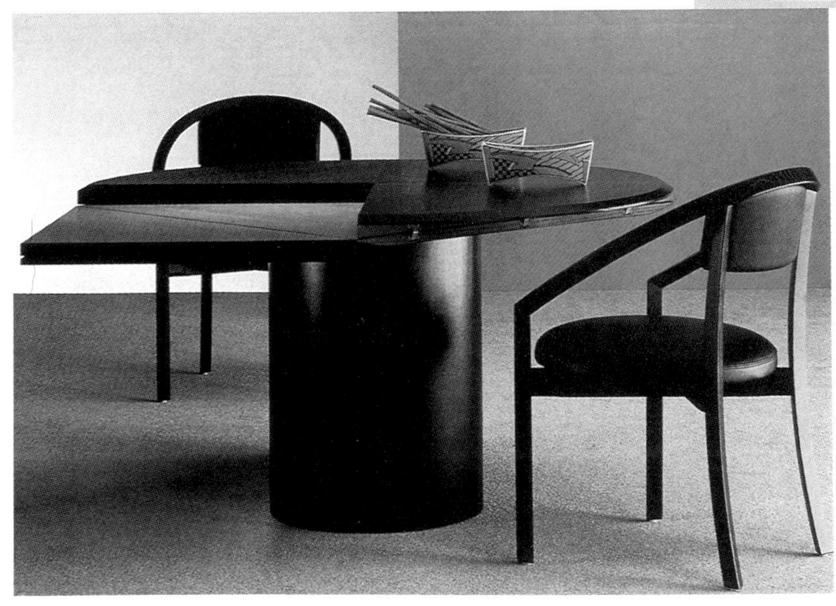

Utensils
Above: Giro, design, Tile Geismar
Below: Concave, design, Claudia Plikat/Carola Zwick

Glassware
Above: Cupola, design, Michael Boehm/Mario Bellini
Center and below: Fuga, design, Eals Fischer-Treyden

Furniture
Above: Quadrondo, design, Erwin Nagel
Lower left: Lettera, design, Günther Uecker
Lower right: Corner, design, Marcello Morandini

Coffee Service "Gladstone"
No model no., Kronach works, first made ca. 1900
Coffeepot ht. 27.4/24.2 cm, cream pitcher ht. 15.9 cm, cup ht. 8.6 cm, saucer diam. 13.7 cm. Rosenthal Archives, Selb

Abbreviations in the photo captions
diam.=diameter
dp.=depth
ht.=height
lg.=length
wd.=width.
A diagonal line between two measurements (/) indicates height with and without lid on.

Coffeepot, "Moliere" Service
Model no. 300, dish dept., Kronach works. first made ca. 1900,
ht. 26/23.2 cm.
Rosenthal Archives, Selb; photo by Rudolf Majonica, Munich

Coffee Service "Monbijou"
Model no. 130, decoration no. 2485, Selb dish dept. First made 1896.
Coffeepot ht. 23.8/21 cm, sugarbowl ht. 12/9 cm, cream pitcher ht. 12.8 cm, cup ht. 7 cm, saucer diam. 13.6 cm, fruit bowl diam. 21.2 cm. Walter Garbs Collection, Hannover; photo from Rosenthal Archives, Selb.

Dining Service "Versailles"
Model no. 120, Selb dish dept. First made 1894
Ragout bowl ht. 16.2/9.3 cm, lg. 28.1 cm.
Rosenthal Archives, Selb

Dining Service "Monbijou"
Model no. 130, decoration no. 495/74, Selb dish dept. First made 1896. Ragout bowl 15.6/9.5 cm, gravy bowl ht. 9.5 cm, lg. 22.5 cm. Walter Garbs Collection, Hannover; photo from Rosenthal Archives, Selb

Coffee Service "Rococo/Louis XIV"
No model no., Selb dish dept. First made 1892. Coffeepot ht. 21.5/17.5 cm, pitcher ht. 13.8 cm, cup ht. 5.8 cm, saucer diam. 13.5 cm. Rosenthal Archives, Selb, photo by Rudolf Majonica, Munich

Mocha Cup and Dessert Plate "Iris"
Model no. 190, Selb dish dept. First made 1900. Cup ht. 5.5 cm, saucer diam. 10.7 cm, plate diam. 15 cm. Giorgio Silzer Collection, Hannover; photo from Rosenthal Archives, Selb

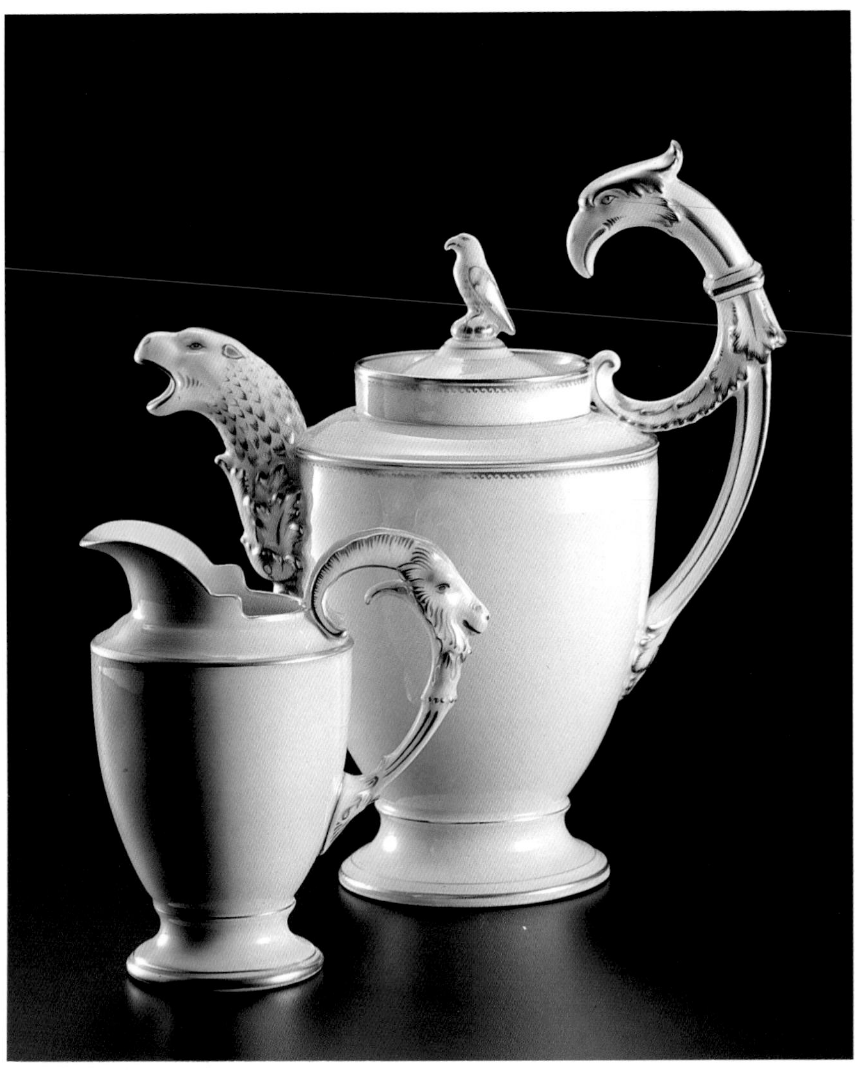

Coffee Service "Empire"
Model no, 110, Selb dish dept. First made 1894, designed at Selb works. Coffeepot ht. 27.6/26.5 cm, cream pitcher ht. 19.4 cm. Rosenthal Archives, Selb

Coffee Service "Empire," new, checkered decoration
Model no. 470, Selb dish dept. First made 1918. Teapot ht. 15.5/11.5 cm, pitcher 12 cm, sugarbowl ht. 9/7 cm, lg. 16.8 cm, cup ht. 5.5 cm, saucer diam. 14 cm.
Rosenthal archives, Selb, photo by Rudolf Majonica, Munich

Coffee Service "Secession"
Model no. 200, Selb dish dept. First made 1901. Coffeepot ht. 24/20.4 cm, pitcher ht. 11/5 cm, sugarbowl ht. 10.5/6.4 cm, lg. 16.5 cm, cup ht. 5 cm, saucer diam, 14.6 cm. Rosenthal Archives, Selb, photo by Rudolf Majonica, Munich

Dining Service "Hertha"
Model no. 217, Selb dish dept. First made ca. 1902, form and decoration designed by Hermann Friling. Tureen ht. 12.9/9.8 cm, pitcher ht. 11.1 cm, lg. 21.7 cm. Walter Garbs Collection, Hannover, photo from Rosenthal Archives, Selb.

Breakfast Service "Donatello", Cherry Relief Decoration
Model no. 250, Selb dish dept. Made ca. 1910, design without relief by Hans Günther Reinstein & Philipp Rosenthal, relief decoration by Julius V. Guldbrandsen. Coffeepot ht. 23.3/19.7 cm, teapot ht. 12/8.4 cm, sugarbowl ht. 10.4/6/5 cm, cream pitcher ht. 8.5 cm, coffee cup ht. 5.7 cm, saucer diam. 14.3 cm, teacup 5.1 cm, saucer diam. 14.3 cm, butter dish ht. 9 cm, lg. 19.3 cm, cake plate lg. 30 cm, bread basket ht. 6.2 cm, lg. 32.8 cm, egg cup ht. 6.5 cm. Coffee cup, cream pitcher, Walter Garbs Collection, Hannover, photo from Rosenthal Archives, Selb; bread basket, egg cup, Giorgio Silzer Collection, Hannover, everything else from Rosenthal Archives, Selb.

Fish Service
Model no. 18, Selb art dept. First made 1910, designed at Selb works (see "Donatello" service), relief decoration by Julius V. Guldbrandsen. Tureen ht. 14.1/7.8 cm, platter lg. 59.5 cm, pitcher ht. 9.3 cm, lg. 22.6 cm, plate 22 cm. Rosenthal Archives, Selb

"Botticelli" Coffee Cups in six decorations
Model no. 230, Selb dish dept. First made 1902. Designed by Hans Günther Reinstein. Cup ht. 5.8 cm, saucer diam. 14 cm. Rosenthal Archives, Selb, photo by Rudolf Majonica, Munich.

Tea Service "Pâte sur Pâte"
Model no. 181, decoration no. 2065, 2632, Selb dish dept. First made 1899. Teapot ht. 20.1/15.7 cm, cup ht. 5 cm, saucer diam. 13.2 cm. Cup: Kestner Museum, Hannover, photo from Rosenthal Archives, Selb, pot from Rosenthal Archives, Selb.

Coffee Service "Botticelli," heart-shaped leaf decoration
Model no. 230, Selb dish dept. First made 1903, form and decoration designed by Hans Günther Reinstein. Coffeepot ht. 21.9/19 cm, sugarbowl 9.2/6.1 cm, cream pitcher ht. 11.9 cm, cup ht. 7.2 cm, saucer diam. 13.7 cm, cake plate diam. 27.2/25.2 cm.
Cup and cake plate, Kestner Museum, Hannover, photo from Rosenthal Archives, Selb, everything else from Rosenthal Archives, Selb

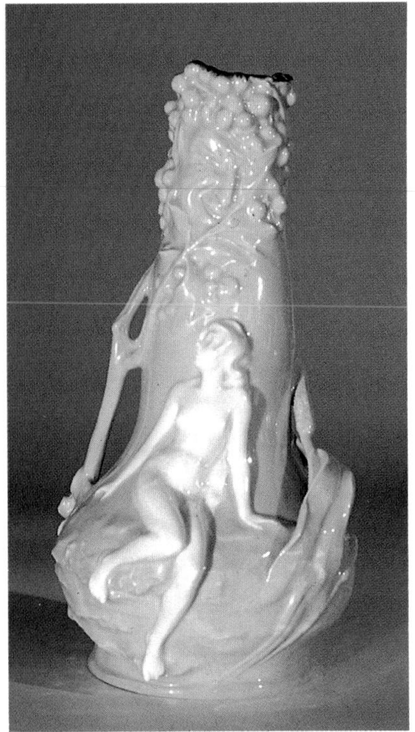

Relief Vase
No model no., Kronach dish dept. First made ca. 1900. Ht. 25 cm. Rosenthal Archives, Selb, photo by Rudolf Majonica, Munich.

Vase
Kronach works, first made 1913, design by Adolf Opel, ht. 35.4 cm. Rosenthal Archives, Selb

Vase
Bauer, Rosenthal & Co. KG, Kronach, first made after 1900, designed by Hermann Hidding, 1900. Ht. 43.5 cm. Water Garbs collection, Hannover, photo from Rosenthal Archives, Selb

Four-section Vase
(left) No model no., first made ca. 1907, ht. 20.3 cm. Art Auction House Ahlden Castle, Catalog no. 79/80/1992

Vase
(center) No model no., first made ca. 1907, decoration designed by Kriesch, ht. 18.4 cm. Art Auction House Ahlden Castle, Catalog no. 79/80/1992

Vase
(right) Model no. 61, Selb art dept., first made 1910, monogram HK, ht. 14.5 cm. Art Auction House Ahlden Castle, Catalog no. 81/2/1993

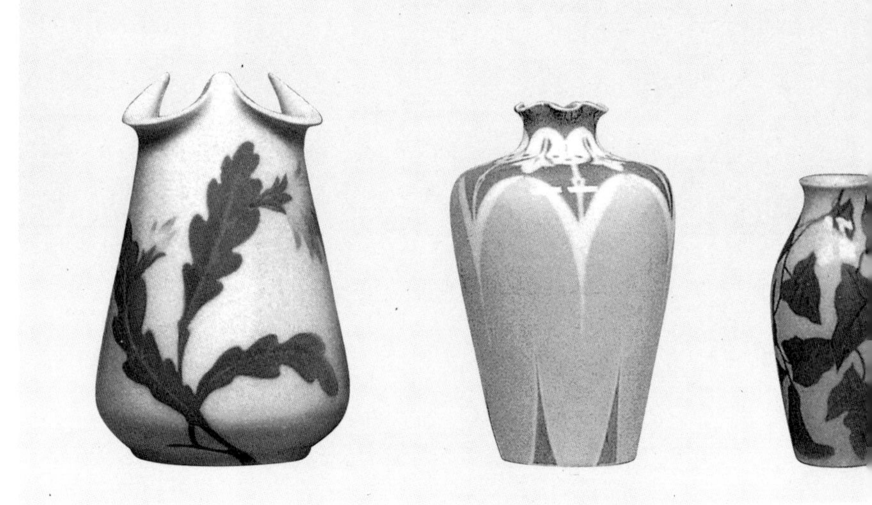

Vase
No model no., Kronach works, first made ca. 1900, design by Adolf Opel? Ht. 18 cm, diam. 17 cm. Monika Berg Gallery of 20th-Century Porcelain and Glass, Munich, photo by Rudolf Majonica, Munich

Vase
Model no. 51, Selb dish dept. First made ca. 1900, relief designed by F. Meder, ht. 22.6 cm, Giorgio Silzer Collection, Hannover, photo from Rosenthal Archives, Selb

Vase
(left) No model no., first made ca. 1910, signed S.S. Clark? Ht. 26.5 cm. Art Auction House Ahlden Castle, Catalog no. 79/80/1992

Vase (Medallion with picture after Antonio de Pollaiuolo)
(center) No model no., first made 1910, monogram R.O., ht. 43.8 cm. Art Auction House Ahlden Castle, Catalog no. 70/1991

Vase
(right) No model no., first made ca. 1907, ht. 29.3 cm. Art Auction House Ahlden Castle, Catalog no. 91/1994

Storage Pot
Model no. 165, decoration no. 1077, Selb art dept. First made ca. 1910, form and decoration designed by Julius V. Guldbrandsen ca. 1910. Ht. 16.6 cm, diam. 21 cm. Rosenthal Archives, Selb

Vase
Model no. 61 old, Selb art dept. First made ca. 1910, decoration designed by Julius V. Guldbrandsen, ht. 32.6 cm. Rosenthal Archives, Selb

Vase
Model no. 149, Selb art dept. First made 1910, form designed at Selb art dept., decoration by Julius V. Guldbrandsen ca. 1910, ht. 33.5 cm. Rosenthal Archives, Selb

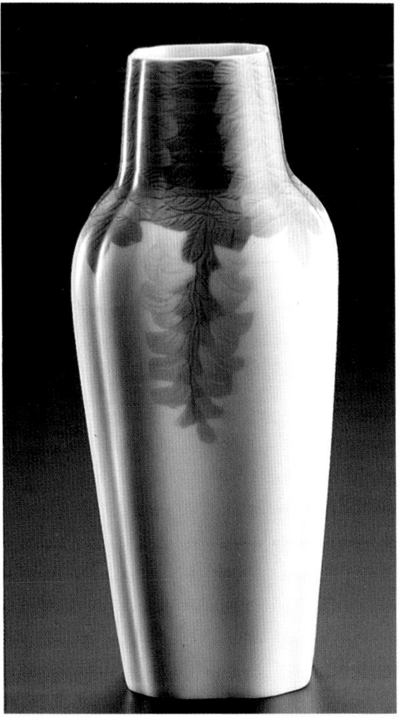

Vase
Model no. 109 old, decoration no. 1207, Selb art dept. First made ca. 1901, decoration designed by Julius V. Guldbrandsen ca. 1912, ht. 22.5 cm. Rosenthal Archives, Selb

Vase
Model no. 109 old, Selb art dept. First made 1901, decoration designed by Julius-V. Guldbrandsen ca. 1913, ht. 23 cm. Rosenthal Archives, Selb.

Vase
Model no. 145, Selb art dept. First made 1910, form and decoration designed by Julius V. Guldbrandsen, ht. 13.6 cm, Munich City Museum, photo from Rosenthal Archives, Selb

Vase with Mouse
Model no. 55a, decoration no. 1071, Selb art dept. First made ca. 1900, form designed by Karl Gross?, decoration by Julius V. Guldbrandsen, ht. 16 cm. Rosenthal Archives, Selb

Four-footed Vase with "Rosari" Decoration
Model no. 454, decoration no. 351, Selb art dept. First made 1917, decoration designed by Julius V. Guldbrandsen, ht. 12 cm, Rosenthal Archives, Selb, photo Rudolf Majonica, Munich

Lamp Base
Model no. ? Selb art dept. First made 1914, decoration designed by Julius V. Guldbrandsen? Ht. 22 cm, diam, 12 cm. Monika Berg Gallery of 20th-Century Porcelain and Glass, Munich, photo by Rudolf Majonica, Munich.

Covered Pot with "Rosari" Decoration
Model no. 229, "Rosari" decoration no. 1/ 23, Selb art dept. First made 1912, decoration designed by Julius V. Guldbrandsen, 1917, ht. 20.7/18 cm. Rosenthal Archives, Selb

Pair of Covered Vases with "Rosari" Decoration
Model no. 542, Selb art dept. First made 1919, form designed by Norvill?, "Rosari" decoration by Julius V. Guldbrandsen, painted by Max Wesp, ht. 32 cm. Art Auction House Ahlden Castle, Catalog no. 71/1991

Caught
Model no. 538, Selb art dept.
First made 1919,
Designed by Ferdinand Liebermann
Ht. 22.5 cm. Art Auction House Ahlden Castle,
Catalog no. 91/1994

Cellist
Model no. 342, Selb art dept.
First made 1914,
Designed by Ferdinand Liebermann
Ht. 11.7 cm. Art Auction House Ahlden Castle,
Catalog no. 91/1994

Teasing
Model no. 523, Selb art dept.
First made 1918
Designed by Ferdinand Liebermann
Ht. 22 cm. Art Auction House Ahlden Castle,
Catalog no. 71/1991

Faun with Grapes
Model no. 298, Selb art dept.
First made 1913,
Designed by Ferdinand Liebermann
Ht. 8.8 cm. Art Auction House Ahlden Castle,
Catalog no. 85-86, 1993

Cherub "Congratulations"
Model no. 234, Selb art dept.
Designed by Ferdinand Liebermann
Ht. 16.7 cm. Art Auction House Ahlden Castle,
Catalog no. 87, 1994

Latin
Model no. 72, Selb art dept.
First made 1910,
Designed by Ferdinand Liebermann
Ht. 15 cm, Art Auction House Ahlden Castle,
Catalog no. 79-80/1992

Dancer, large
Model no. 44 new, Selb art dept.
First made 1910,
Designed by Ferdinand Liebermann
Ht. 19.6 cm. Art Auction House Ahlden Castle,
Catalog no. 91/1994

Two Princesses
Model no. 537, Selb art dept.
First made 1919,
Designed by Ferdinand Liebermann
Ht. 14 cm. Art Auction House Ahlden Castle
Catalog no. 91/1994

High School
Model no. 41, Selb art dept., first made 1910, form designed by Ferdinand Liebermann. Ht. 23 cm. Rosenthal Archives, Selb

Capriccio
Model no. 68, decoration no. 1160, Selb art dept., first made 1911, form designed by Ferdinand Liebermann. Ht. 62 cm. Rosenthal Archives, Selb

Philosophical Dispute
Model no. 35, decoration no. 1080, Selb art dept.
First made 1911, form designed by Ferdinand Liebermann
Ht. 17.4 cm, lg. 39 cm. Rosenthal Archives, Selb

Faun Bust: Horror
Model no. 74, decoration no. 1159, Selb art dept.
First made 1911, dorm designed by Ferdinand Liebermann
Ht. 39.5 cm. Rosenthal Archives, Selb

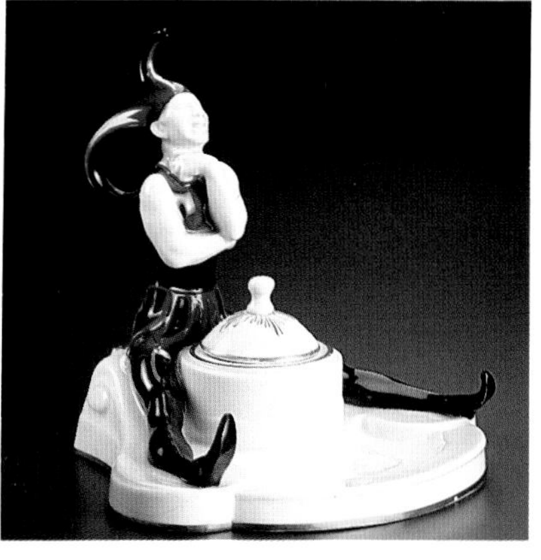

Harlequin with Inkwell
Model no. 592, Selb art dept.
First made 1921, designed by Ferdinand Liebermann
Ht. 16 cm, lg. 17.4 cm. Thomas Ullrich collection, Spielberg, photo from Museum der deutschen Porzellanindustrie, Hohenberg/Eder

From Faraway Lands
Model no. 536, Selb art dept.
First made 1919, designed by Ferdinand Liebermann
Ht. 23 cm, Monika Berg, Gallery of 20th-Century Porcelain and Glass, Munich, photo by Rudolf Majonica, Munich

Storming Bacchantes
Model no. 190, decoration no. 1421, Selb art dept. First made 1912, form designed by A. Caasmann. Ht. 21 cm. Rosenthal Archives, Selb

Musical Clown (Pierrot with Accordion)
(outside left) Model no. 436, Selb art dept., first made 1916, designed by A. Caasmann. Ht. 18.7 cm. Art Auction House Ahlden Castle, Catalog no. 91/1994

Playmates
(inside left) Model no. 355, Selb art dept., first made 1914, design by A. Caasmann. Ht. 11.6 cm. Art Auction House Ahlden Castle, Catalog no. 91/1994

Faun's Flight
(inside right) Model no. 208, Selb art dept., first made 1913, design by A. Caasmann. Ht. 14 cm. Monika Berg Gallery of 20th-Century Porcelain and Glass, Munich, photo by Rudolf Majonica, Munich

Herald of Spring
(outside right) Model no. K 657, Selb art dept., first made 1923, designed by A. Caasmann. Ht. 11 cm. Monika Berg Gallery of 20th-Century Porcelain and Glass, Munich, photo by Rudolf Majonica, Munich

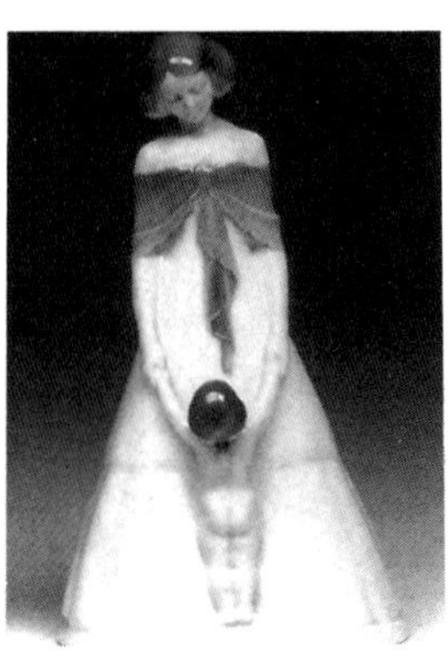

Ariadne
(far left) Model no. 346, Selb art dept., first made 1914, designed by A. Caasmann. Ht. 15 cm. Art Auction House Ahlden Castle, Catalog no. 71/1991

Magic of Love
(near left) Model no. 304, Selb art dept., first made 1913, designed by A. Caasmann. Ht. 25 cm. Art Auction House Ahlden Castle, Cayalog no. 71/1991

Tyrolean Girl, Tyrolean Boy
Model no. 168 new & 112, Selb art dept.
First made 1912, designed by Karl Himmelstoss
Ht. 18.8 and 17.5 cm.
Art Auction House Ahlden Castle
Catalog no. 83-84/1993

Faun with Butterfly (in love)
Model no. 124, decoration no. 1262. Selb art dept.
First made 1911, designed by Karl Himmelstoss.
Ht. 12.4 cm, base lg. 13.5 cm.
Walter Garbs Collection, Hannover
Photo from Rosenthal Archives, Selb

Round Dance
Model no. 210, Selb art dept.
First made 1912, designed by Karl Himmelstoss
Ht. 63.5 cm.
Rosenthal Archives, Selb

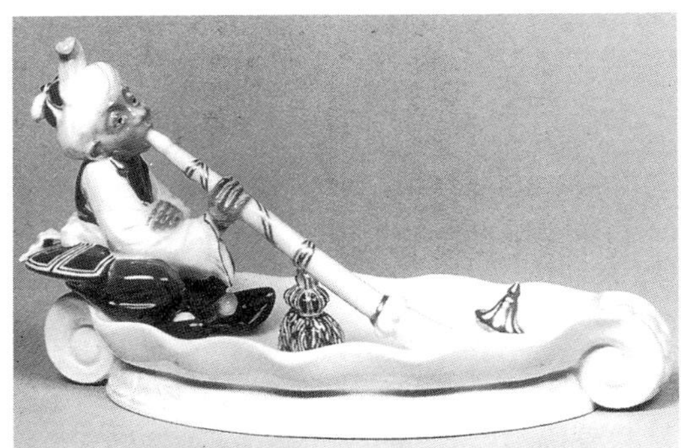

Ashtray with Turk
Model no. 628, Selb art dept.
First made 1923, designed by Karl Himmelstoss
Ht. 16 cm. Art Auction House Ahlden Castle,
Catalog no. 81-82/1993

Bass Violinist, Hunting Horn Player (Weiss Ferdl)
Model no. 196, 197, Selb art dept. First made 1913, designed by Karl Himmelstoss
Ht. 19.7, 19.6 cm. Rosenthal Archives, Selb, photo by Rudolf Majonica, Munich

Amazon
Model no. 519, Selb art dept.
First made 1918, designed by Anton Grath
Ht. 36.7 cm. Art Auction House Ahlden
Castle, catalog no. 91/1994

Bagpiper
Model no. 194, Selb art dept.
First made 1913, designed by M. E. Beyrer
Ht. 17.4 cm. Art Auction House Ahlden
Castle, catalog no. 91/1994

Faun with Nymphs
Model no. 198, decoration no. 1517, Selb art dept.,
First made 1913, form designed by Walter Schott, 1901
Ht. 43 cm. Rosenthal Archives, Selb

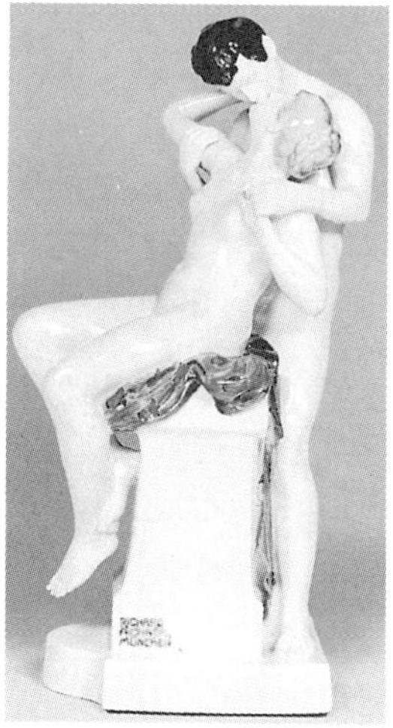

"Empire" Dancer
Model no. 206, Selb art dept.
First made 1913,
designed by Erna Langenmantel-Reitzenstein
Ht. 24.5 cm. Art Auction House Ahlden
Castle, catalog no. 92/1995

Lovers
Model no. 295, Selb art dept.
First made 1913, designed by Richard Aigner
Ht. 26 cm. Art Auction House Ahlden
Castle, catalog no. 92/1955

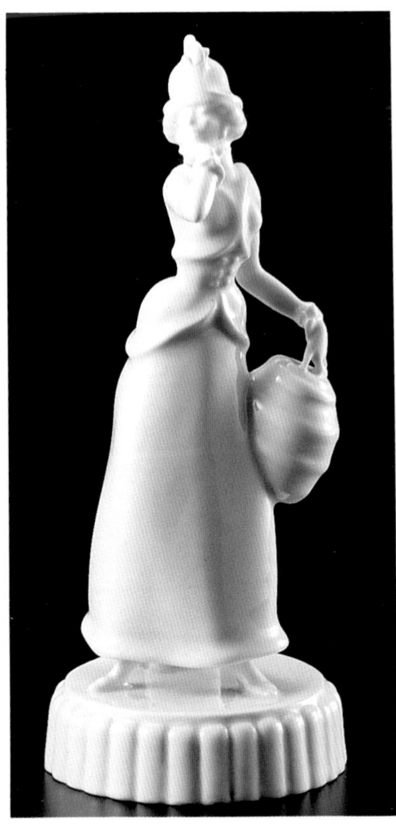

Lady with Muff
Model no. 426, Selb art dept.
First made 1915, form designed by Ludwig Vierthaler. Ht. 21.7 cm.
Annette Vierthaler Collection, Hannover, photo from Rosenthal Archives, Selb

Lady with Dog
Model no. 427, Selb art dept.
First made 1915, form designed by Ludwig Vierthaler
Ht. 21.2 cm. Kunstgewerbemuseum, Berlin, photo from Rosenthal Archives, Selb

Tilla Durrieux
Model no. 343, Selb art dept.
First made 1914, designed by Thekla Harth-Altmann, ht. 20.6 cm.
Rosenthal Archives, Selb, photo by Rudolf Majonica, Munich

Soldier on Skis, Nurse, and Advance Guard
Model nos. 423, 382, 397, Selb art dept.
First made 1915, 1914, 1914, designed by Ferdinand Liebermann, Berthold Boess, ?
Ht. 15 cm, lg. 27 cm; ht. 20.4 cm; ht. 14 cm, lg. 16.5 cm.
Rosenthal Archives, Selb, photo by Rudolf Majonica, Munich

Indian Snake Charmer
Model no. 202?, Bahnhof-Selb art dept.,
First made in the twenties
Ht. 8 cm. Monika Berg Gallery of 20th-Century Porcelain and Art, Munich, photo by Rudolf Majonica, Munich

Lily
Model no. 430, Bahnhof-Selb art dept.
First made in the twenties, designed by Adolf Opel?
Monika Berg Gallery of 20th-Century Porcelain and Glass, munich, photo by Rudolf Majonica, Munich

Snake Dancer
Model no. 442, Selb art dept.
First made 1916, designed by Berthold Boess
Ht. 18.9 cm. Monika Berg Gallery of 20th-Century Porcelain and Glass, Munich, photo by Rudolf Majonica, Munich

Ionian Dancer
(left) Model no. 201, Selb art dept.
First made 1913, designed by Berthold Boess
Ht. 21 cm. Art Auction House Ahlden Castle, catalog no. 92/1995

Enrico Caruso
(center) Model no. 299, Selb art dept.
First made 1913, designed by Thekla Harth-Altmann
Ht. 20.5 cm. Art Auction House Ahlden Castle, catalog no. 70/1991

Venus with Parrott
(right) Model no. 288, Selb art dept.
First made 1913, designed by Adolf Opel
Ht. 17 cm. Art Auction House Ahlden Castle, catalog no. 70/1991

Drake
Model no. 352, Selb art dept.
First made 1914, designed by Willy Zügel
Ht. 16.5 cm. Art Auction House Ahlden Castle, catalog no. 81-82/1993

Drake
Model no. 250, Selb art dept.
First made 1913, designed by Willy Zügel
Ht. 20.2 cm.
Rosenthal Archives, Selb, photo by Rudolf Majonica, Munich

Duck (Protest)
Model no. 1302, Selb art dept.
First made 1934, designed by Karl Himmelstoss
Ht. 19.5 cm. Art Auction House Ahlden Castle, catalog 92/1995

Pair of Chickens
(above left) Model no. 218, Selb art dept.
First made 1913, designed by Karl Himmelstoss
Ht. 14 cm. Art Auction House Ahlden Castle, catalog no. 77-78/1992

Greyhound
Model no. 200, Selb art dept.
First made 1913, designed by Max Valentin
Ht. 11.5/16.8 cm. Art Auction House Ahlden Castle, catalog no. 91/1994

Duck
Model no. 172, Selb art dept.
First made 1912, designed by Karl Himmelstoss
Ht. 6.7 cm. Art Auction House Ahlden Castle, catalog no. 89-90/1994

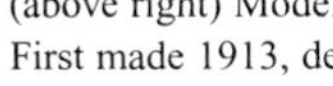

Budgies, large
(above right) Model no. 257, Selb art dept.
First made 1913, designed by A. Caasmann
Ht. 18.3 cm. Art Auction House Ahlden Castle, catalog no. 91/1994

Young Magpie
Model no. 127, Selb art dept.
First made 1912, designed by Willy Zügel
Ht. 12 cm, lg. 24.5 cm.
Rosenthal Archives, Selb, photo by Rudolf Majonica, Munich

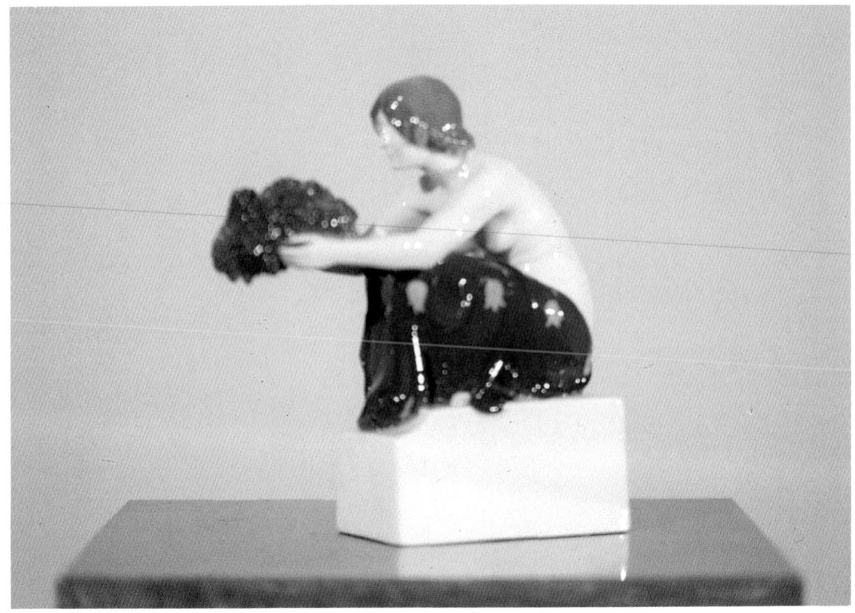

Snake Dancer
Model no. 497, Selb art dept.
First made 1917, designed by Rudolf Marcuse
Ht. 39 cm.
Rosenthal Archives, Selb, photo by Rudolf Majonica, Munich

Grape Carrier
Model no. 477, Selb art dept.
First made 1917, designed by Rudolf Marcuse
Ht. 16 cm, Monika Berg Gallery of 20th-Century Porcelain and Glass, Munich, photo by Rudolf Majonica, Munich

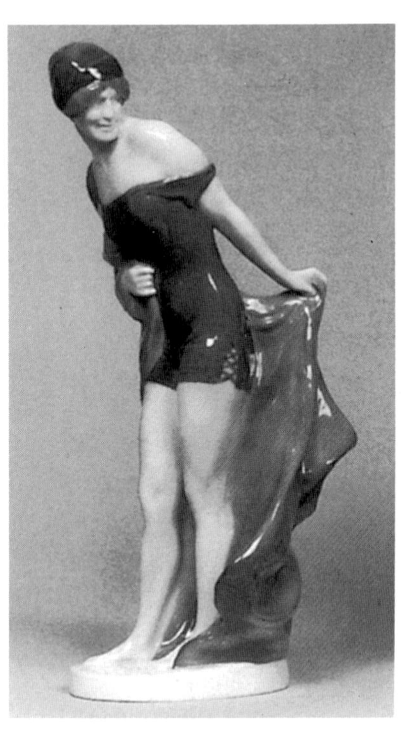

In the Wind (Swimmer)
Model no. 293, Selb art dept.
First made 1913, designed by Rudolf Marcuse
Ht. 35 cm. Art Auction House Ahlden Castle, catalog no. 92/1995

Duet, large and small
Model no. 311, Selb art dept.
First made 1913, designed by Rudolf Marcuse
Ht. 35 cm, Art Auction House Ahlden Castle, catalog no. 92/1995

Cabaret
Model no. 328, decoration no. 1636, Selb art dept.
First made 1913, form designed by Rudolf Marcuse
Ht. 41.7 cm. Rosenthal Archives, Selb

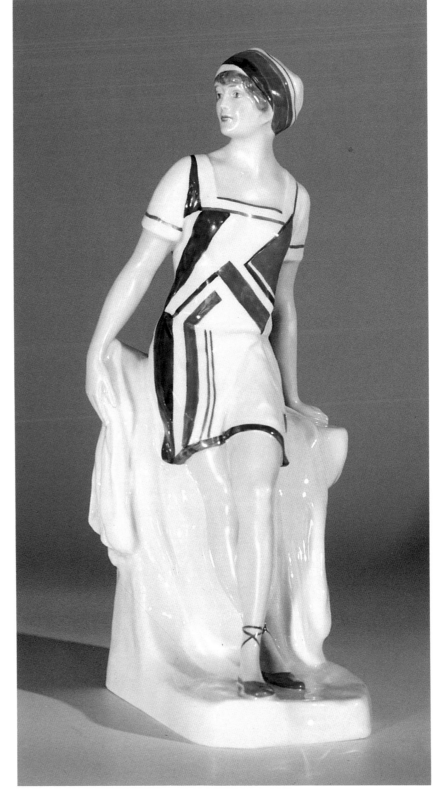

On the Beach (Swimmer)
Model no. 294, Selb art dept.
First made 1913, designed by Rudolf Marcuse
Ht. 28 cm. Rosenthal Archives, Selb,
photo by Rudolf Marcuse, Munich

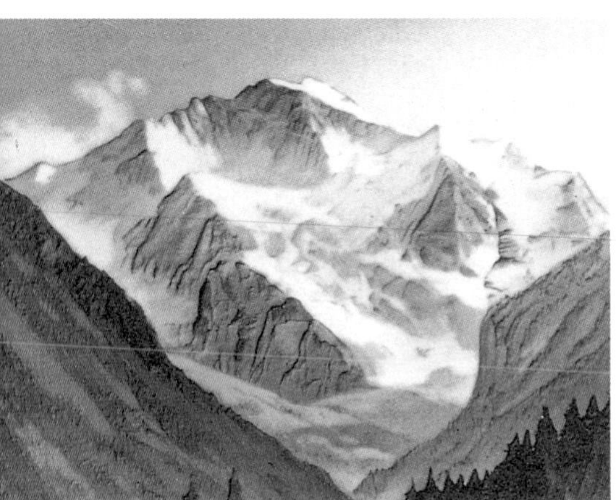

Porcelain Picture
Decoration no. 115/1115. first made ca. 1910
Diam. 23 cm. Art Auction House Ahlden Castle,
catalog no. 79-80.1992

Fruit Plate
No model no., Selb art dept., made 1927
Diam. 21 cm. Rosenthal Archives, Selb, photo by Rudolf Majonica, Munich

Plate with Silhouette
No model no., Selb art dept., first made 1917
Diam. 21 cm. Rosenthal Archives, Selb, Photo by Rudolf Majonica, Munich

Easter Plate
No model no., Selb art dept., first made 1914, designed by Julius V. Guldbrandsen. Diam. 21 cm. Rosenthal Archives, Selb, photo by Rudolf Majonica, Munich

Art déco Plate
No model no., Selb dish dept., first made latter twenties.
Diam 21.5 cm. Rosenthal Archives, Selb, photo by Rudolf Majonica, Munich

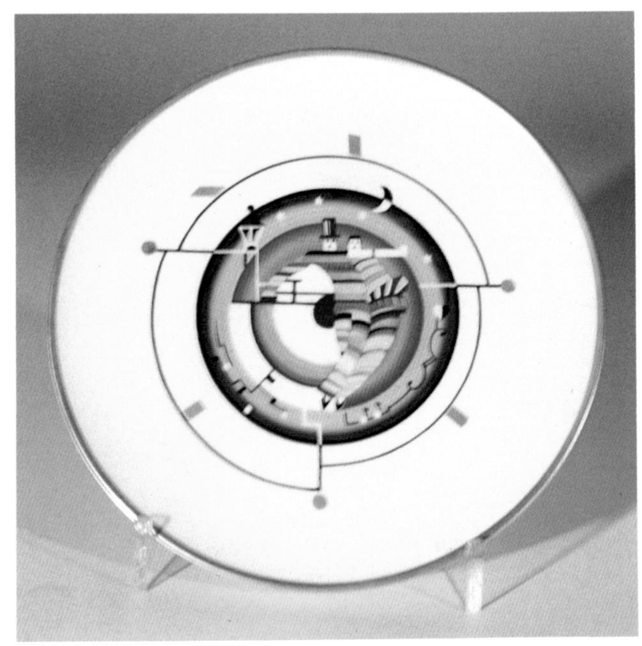

Christmas Plate
No model no., Selb art dept.
First made 1926, designed by Theo Schmuz-Baudis
Diam 21.8 cm. Rosenthal Archives, Selb, photo by Rudolf Majonica, Munich

Memorial Plate, 100th Anniversary, Battle of Nations, VDI
(lower left) No model no., Selb art dept., first made 1913
Diam 24.5 cm. Rosenthal Archives, Selb, photo by Rudolf Majonica, Munich

Christmas Plate
(lower right) No model no., Selb art dept.
First made 1911, designed by Heinrich Vogeler
Diam. 21.1 cm. Rosenthal Archives, Selb, photo by Rudolf Majonica, Munich

Classic Dining Services

Coffee Service "Maria", white
Model no. 430, Selb dish dept.
First made 1914, designed by Philipp Rosenthal
Coffeepot ht. 23 cm, sugarbowl ht. 13.3 cm, cream pitcher ht. 13.5 cm, cup ht. 6.3 cm, saucer diam. 14.1 cm.
Rosenthal Archives, Selb

Selected Additions to the "Maria" Service
Model no. 430, Selb dish dept., designed by Philipp Rosenthal
Napkin holder ht. 11 cm, lg. 23 cm, fruit press ht. 10 cm, lg. 19.5 cm, with top ht. 12.5 cm, onion box ht. 9.8/5.8 cm, lemon squeezer ht. 7 cm, lg. 16 cm, matchbox ht. 5 cm.
Rosenthal Archives, Selb, photo by Rudolf Majonica, Munich

Tea Service "Isolde"
Model no. 320, decoration no. 1574, Selb dish dept.
First made 1909, form and decoration designed by Philipp Rosenthal
Teapot ht. 15.5 cm, sugarbowl ht. 10.7 cm, pitcher ht. 13.6 cm, cup ht. 5.8 cm, saucer diam. 14 cm. Rosenthal Archives, Selb

Tea Service "Antique"
Model no. 410, Selb dish dept.
First made ca. 1914, form designed by Bruno Paul, silver decoration by Hans Schiffner, ca. 1919
Teapot ht. 15.7 cm, sugarbowl ht. 10 cm, pitcher ht. 11.2 cm, cup ht. 5.8 cm, saucer diam, 13.8 cm. Rosenthal Archives, Selb

Coffee Service "Canova", Apple Blossom decoration
Model no. 390, Selb dish dept., first made 1913-19, designed by Philipp Rosenthal
Coffeepot ht. 23/20 cm, pitcher ht. 12 cm, sugarbowl ht. 9.5/7 cm, cup ht. 5 cm, saucer diam. 14.5 cm. Rosenthal Archives, Selb, photo by Rudolf Majonica, Munich

Chinese (Tschaokiun Sword Dancer)
Model no. 533, Selb art dept.
First made 1919, form and (1921) decoration designed by Constantin Holzer-Defanti
Ht. 37 cm. Privately owned, Bernsmann, photo from Rosenthal Archives, Selb

Korean Dancer
Model no. 566, decoration no. 206n, Selb art dept.
First made 1919, form and (1921) decoration designed by Constantin Holzer-Defanti
Ht. 40 cm. M. & M. Wulff Collection, photo from Rosenthal Archives, Selb

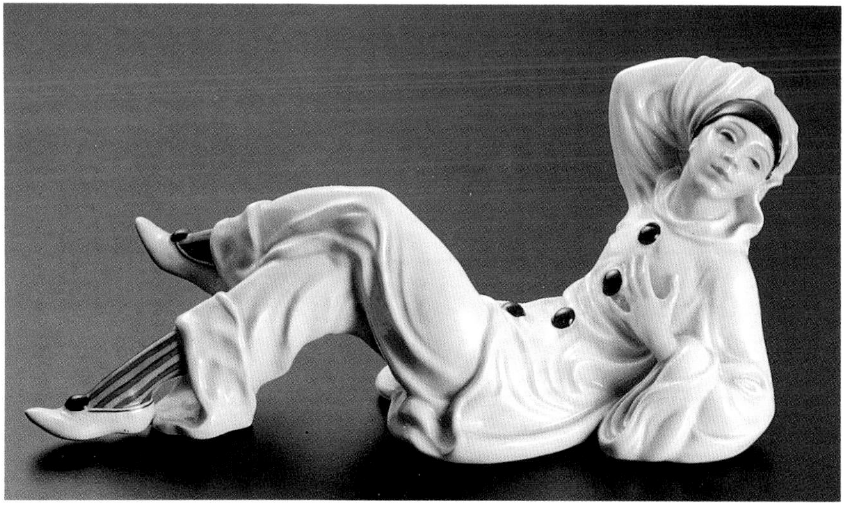

Pierrot (Ash Wednesday)
Model no. 549, Selb art dept.
First made 1919, form designed by Constantin Holzer-Defanti
Ht. 15.5 cm, lg. 29.5 cm, Museum für Kunsthandwerk, Frankfurt am Main, photo from Rosenthal Archives, Selb

Pierrette (Anita Berber)
Model no. 579, Selb art dept.
First made 1920, form and (1921) decoration? designed by Constantin Holzer-Defanti
Ht. 32 cm. Kunstgewerbemuseum, Berlin, photo from Rosenthal Archives, Selb

Dancer Lo Hesse
Model no. 53, Bahnhof-Selb art dept.
First made early twenties, design by Constantin Holzer-Defanti
Ht. 31 cm. Monika Berg Gallery of 20th-Century Porcelain and Glass, Munich, photo by Rudolf Majnnica, Munich

Pierrette with Guitar
Model no. 78, Bahnhof-Selb art dept.
First made early twenties, designed by Dorothea Charol
Ht. 16 cm, lg. 28.6 cm.
Rosenthal Archives, Selb, photo by Rudolf Majonica, Munich

Ashtray with Pierrette
Model no. 48, Bahnhof-Selb art dept.
First made early twenties, designed by Constantin Holzer-Defanti
Ht. 7.2 cm, lg. 15.2 cm, width 12 cm. Monika Berg Gallery of 20th-Century Porcelain and Glass, Munich, photo by Rudolf Majonica, Munich

Rococo Dancer
no model no., Bahnhof-Selb art dept.
First made 1921-22? Designed by Constantin Holzer-Defanti
Ht. 15 cm. Art Auction house Ahlden Castle, catalog no. 92/1995

Chinese (Tschaokiun Dancer)
Model no. 534, Selb art dept.
First made 1919, designed by Constantin Holzer-Defanti
Ht. 34 cm. Art Auction House Ahlden Castle, catalog no. 92/1995

Mocha Cup
Model no. 249, Selb dish dept.
First made 1905, decoration designed by Walter Mutze? ca. 1920
Cup ht. 4.8 cm, saucer diam. 10.5 cm.
Rosenthal Archives, Selb

Mocha Cup
Model no. 712, Selb dish dept
First made 1914, decoration designed by Kurt Severin, 1924.
Cup ht. 5.5 cm, saucer diam. 10.9 cm.
Rosenthal Archives, Selb

Mocha Cup with underglaze painting
No model no., Selb art dept.
First made ca. 1910, decoration designed by Dora Krahe
Cup ht. 5 cm, saucer diam. 10.8 cm.
Rosenthal Archives, Selb, photo by Rudolf Majonica, Munich

Two Mocha Cups
Model no. 250, basic form "Donatello", and 656, basic form, twenties decorations
Monica Berg Gallery of 20th-Century Porcelain and Glass, Munich, photo by Rudolf Majonica, Munich

Two Mocha Cups with silver trim
Model no. 230 Winifred and 230 Chippendale, Selb and Bahnhof-Selb dish depts.
First made 1933, 1951, designed by Friedrich Fleischmann, Otto Koch
Cup ht. 4.5, 4.2 cm, saucer diam. 12.2, 11.5 cm.
Rosenthal Archives, Selb, photos by Rudolf Majonica, Munich

Two Mocha Cups
No model no. Selb dish dept. First made 1918 (left cup), 1946 (saucer), 1910 (right)
Cup ht. 5 cm, 5.4 cm, saucer diam. 11.9 cm, 11.2 cm.
Rosenthal Archives, Selb, photo by Rudolf Majonica, Munich

Three Mocha Cups
No model no., Selb dish dept. First made 1943, 1910, 1928
Cup ht. 5 cm, saucer diam. 10.7 cm.
Rosenthal Archivesa, Selb, photo by Rudolf Majonica, Munich

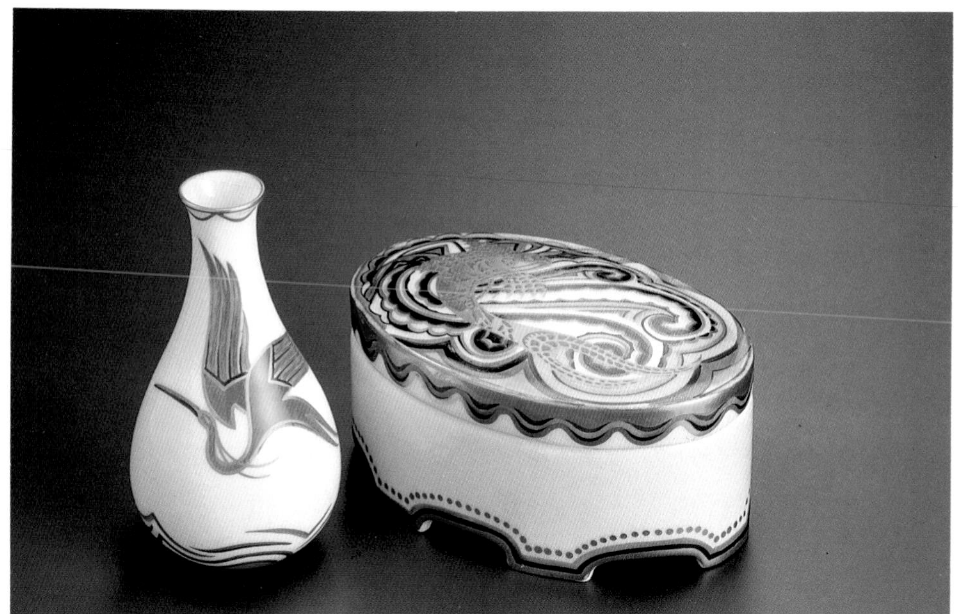

Vase and box
Model no. 11 ?, Selb art dept.
First made 1910, 1921, decoration designed by Kurt Wendler, 1921
Container ht. 5/2 cm, museum; vase privately owned, photos from Museum der Deutschen Porzellanindustrie, Hohenberg/Eger

Covered Bowl on foot
Selb art dept. First made ca. 1921. Designed by Kurt Wendler
Ht. 11.8 cm. Museum der Deutschen Porzellanindustrie, Hohenberg/Eger

Three Bracelets and one Ring
No model no., Selb art dept.
First made ca. 1923, decoration designed by Kurt Wendler?
Bracelet diam. 6.8-7.9 cm. Thomas Ullrich Collection, Spielberg, photo from Museum der Deutschen Porzellanindustrie, Hohenberg/Eger

Two Bracelets
Wendler decoration no. 90, Selb art dept.
First made ca. 1923, decoration designed by Kurt Wendler, ca. 1923
Left diam. 6/8-7/9 cm, right diam. 8.2-9.2 cm.
Rosenthal Archives, Selb

Bowl on six feet with "Indra" Decoration
Model no. 595, "Indra" decoration no. 32, Selb art dept.
First made 1921, decoration designed by Kurt Wendler, 1921
Ht. 7.7 cm, lg. 24.9 cm, width 16.6 cm.
Rosenthal Archives, Selb

Covered Jar with "Indra" Decoration
Model no. 229, "Indra" decoration no. 15, Selb art dept. First made 1912, decoration designed by Kurt Wendler, 1921
Ht. 20.5/18.3 cm. Rosenthal Archives, Selb

Vase with "Indra" Decoration
Model no. 42, "Indra" decoration no. 31, Selb art dept.
First made ca. 1900, decoration designed by Kurt Wendler, 1921
Ht. 16.5 cm. Rosenthal Archives, Selb

Four Cactus and Flower Pot Covers
No model no., Bahnhof-Selb art dept., first made twenties
Ht. left & center front 13 cm, diam. 14 cm, Walter Garbs Collection, Hannover; center rear and right, and photo, Museum der Deutschen Porzellanindustrie, Hohenberg/Eger

Bowl and Two Vases in different sizes
Model no. 119, 117, 119, Bahnhof-Selb works, first made twenties
Designed by Philipp Rosenthal. Vases ht. 19 cm, 13 cm.
Museum der Deutschen Porzellanindustrie, Hohenberg/Eger

Two Vases and one Cactus Pot
(right) Model no. 119, 117, 104, Bahnhof-Selb works
First made twenties, designed by Philipp Rosenthal
Ht. 19 cm, 13 cm, 6 cm. Monika Berg Gallery of 20th-Century Porcelain and Glass, munich, photo by Rudolf Majonica, Munich

Covered Bowl
Model no. 847, Selb art dept.
First made 1926, decoration designed by Prof. Hennig's class, State Ceramic School, Bunzlau?
Ht. 16.5/8.5 cm. Rosenthal Archives, Selb

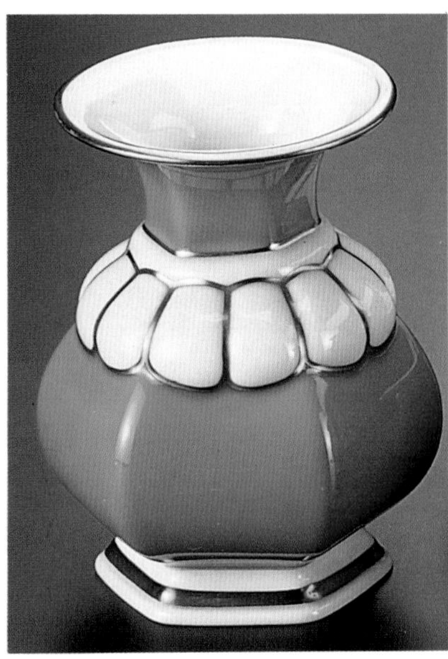

Vase
Model no. 255/1, Selb art dept.
First made 1913, designed by Philipp Rosenthal
Ht. 12 cm. Museum der Deutschen Porzellanindustrie, Hohenberg/Eger

Covered Box
Model no. 227, Selb art dept.
First made 1912, decoration designed by Tono Zoelch, 1929
Ht. 4.4/3.5 cm, diam. 10.2 cm.
Water Garbs Collection, Hannover, photo from Rosenthal Archives, Selb

Covered Vase
Model no. 873, Bahnhof-Selb dish dept.
First made 1926, form designed by Hans Küster, decoration by Röder? Ht. 28.5/19.8 cm.
Monika Berg Gallery of 20th-Century Porcelain and Glass, Munich, photo by Rudolf Majonica, Munich

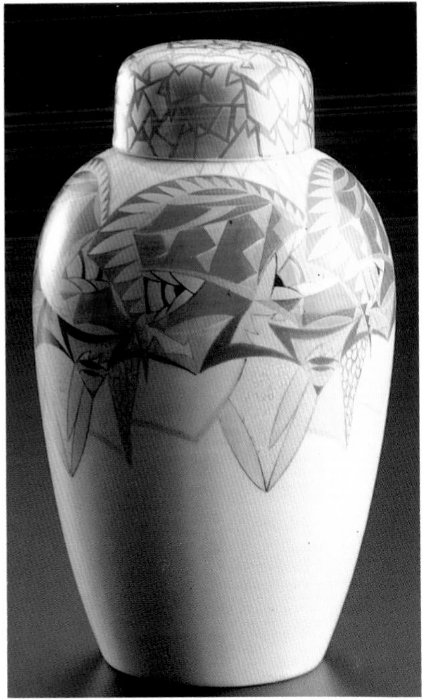

Covered Jar
Model no. 167, Selb art dept.
First made 1911, decoration designed by W. Gross, 1924
Ht. 21.4/20.6 cm, Rosenthal Archives, Selb

Covered Vase
Model no. 873, Selb art dept.
First made 1926, form designed by Hans Küster?, decoration by Walter Mutze? Ht. 28/20.1 cm. Rosenthal Archives, Selb

Orchid Vase in two decorations
Model no. 179, Selb dish dept. First made twenties
Ht. 18 cm. Monika Berg Gallery of 20th-Century Porcelain and Glass, Munich, photo by Rudolf Majonica, Munich

Vase
Model no. 424, Selb art dept. First made 1916, decoration designed by W. Gross, 1925, ht. 11.8 cm. Rosenthal Archives, Selb

Covered Jar
Model no. 229, Selb art dept. First made 1912, decoration designed by Walter Mutze, 1927. Ht. 20.3/18.4 cm. Rosenthal Archives, Selb

Ashtray
Model no. 155 old, Selb dish dept. First made ca, 1896
Dimensions 12.4 x 12.4 cm. Rosenthal Archives, Selb

Candy Dish with figural base
Model no, 953, Selb art dept, first made 1927, designed by Gustav Oppel. Ht. 15.5 cm. Thomas Ullrich Collection, Spielberg, photo by Museum der Deutschen Porzellanindustrie, Hohenberg/Eger

Perfume Bottle and Powder Box on feet
Model no. ? and 208, Bahnhof-Selb art dept.
First made in 1920s.
Porcelain-Meyer, Hannover and Thomas Ullrich Collection, Spiellberg. Photo by museum der Deutschen Porzellanindustrie, Hohenberg/Eger

Perfume Bottle
Model no. 90, Bahnhof-Selb/Neustadt works, first made 1930
Ht. 4.6/6 cm. Rosenthal Archives, Selb

Small Clock
Model no. 37 new, Selb art dept. First made 1910, decoration designed by Mey. Ht. 14 cm.
Rosenthal Archives, Selb, photo by Rudolf Majonica, Munich

Two Small Clocks
Model no. 37 new and 38 new, Selb art dept. Decoration designed by Gustaf Oppel, 1927. No. 38 new ht. 13.8 cm, width 13.2 cm.
Thomas Ullrich Collection, Spielberg, and Walter Garbs, Hannover, photos from Museum der Deutschen Porzellanindustrie, Hohenberg/Eger

The Young Day
Model no. 776, Selb art dept. First made 1925, form designed by Gustav Oppel, decoration by Kurt Severin
Ht. 34.6 cm, lg. 26.7 cm, width 10.6 cm.
Walter Garbs Collection, Hannover, photo from Rosenthal Archives, Selb

Perfume Atomizer
Model no. 3064, Selb art dept. First made 1949, designed by Franz Karl. Ht. 11/4 cm, diam. 23.5 cm.
Rosenthal Archives, Selb, photo by Rudolf Majonica, Munich

Dish with Inkwell from Gentleman's Desk Set
Model no. 820, Selb art dept. First made 1926. Ht. 7.5/4.5 cm, lg. 26.5 cm. Rosenthal Archives, Selb, photo by Rudolf Majonica, Munich

Sea Horse *(Opposite page)*
(page 71) Model no. 941, decoration no. 489n, Selb art dept. First made 1927, form designed by Gustav Oppel, decoration by Kurt Severin. Ht. 31 cm, lit from inside. Rosenthal Archives, Selb

Bookend (Maraboo)
Model no. 1011, Selb art dept. First made 1928, designed by Hans Küster. Ht. 20.2 cm. Rosenthal Archives, Selb, photo by Rudolf Majonica, Munich

Lights with Pierrette and Pierrot Heads
Model no. 985, 986, Selb art dept., made 1928, designed by Theodor Kärner, Conatantin Holzer-Defanti. Ht. 17.2 ca, 14.5 cm.
Rosenthal Archives, Selb, photo by Rudolf Majonica, Munich

Teapot "Fatima"
(right) Model no. 120, Bahnhof-Selb dish dept. First made 1926, form designed by Philipp Rosenthal, decoration by Kurt Severin? Ht. 15/10.6 cm. Rosenthal Archives, Selb

Coffee Service "Safia"
Model no. 844, Selb art dept.
First made 1926, form designed by Hans Küster, decoration by Kurt Severin
Coffeepot ht. 29.9/22.4 cm, sugarbowl ht. 14.8/8.6 cm, cream pitcher 13.7 cm, cup ht. 7.2 cm, saucer diam. 15.1 cm.
Rosenthal Archives, Selb

Chocolate Service "Asra"
Model no. 841, Selb art dept. First made 1926, form and decoration designed by Kurt Severin
Coffeepot ht. 22.9/21.3 cm, sugarbowl 10.1/5.4 cm, cup ht. 11.1 cm, saucer diam. 12.9 cm. Rosenthal Archives, Selb

Dining Service "Li" or "Tirana" in two decorations
Model no. 520, Selb dish dept.
First made 1927, designed by Friedrich Fleischmann
Tureen ht. 14.9/11.2 cm, lg. 30.6 cm, pitcher ht. 7.3 cm, lg. 24.4 cm.
Rosenthal Archives, Selb, photo by Rudolf Majonica, Munich

Coffee Service "Madeleine"
Model no. 150, Bahnhof-Selb dish dept.
First made 1927, form and decoration? designed by Friedrich Fleischmann
Coffeepot ht. 24/18.8 cm, sugarbowl ht. 17.8/12 cm, cream pitcher 13 cm, cup 5.3 cm, saucer diam. 15.2 cm.
Rosenthal Archives, Selb, and Museum der Deutschen Porzellanindustrie, Hohenberg/Eger

Service "Maja"
Model no. 1650, Kronach dish dept. (also Thomas, Marktredwitz)
First made 1927, designed by Friedrich Fleischmann
Pot ht. 15.8/11.6 cm, cream pitcher ht. 5.4 cm, lg. 9.6 cm, cup ht. 4.1 cm, saucer diam. 11.2 cm, platter lg. 32.5 cm, width 21.8 cm, bowl diam, 7.4 cm
Museum der Deutschen Porzellanindustrie, Hohenberg/Eger

Ash Wednesday (Pierrot)
Model no. 1040, Selb art dept. First made 1926, form designed by Max Valentin. Ht. 38.2 cm. Rosenthal Archives, Selb

Pierrot
Model no. 79, Bahnhof-Selb art dept. First made ca. 1923, form designed by Dorothea Charol. Ht. 28.5 cm. Munich City Museum, photo from Rosenthal Archives, Selb

Snake Dancer
Model no. 138, Bahnhof-Selb art dept. First made twenties, design by Richard Förster. Ht. 20 cm.
Art Auction House Ahlden Castle, catalog no. 79-80/1992

Dream
Model no. 264, Bahnhof-Selb art dept. First made twenties, designed by Dorothea Charol. Ht. 31 cm.
Rosenthal Archives, Selb, photo by Rudolf Majonica, Munich

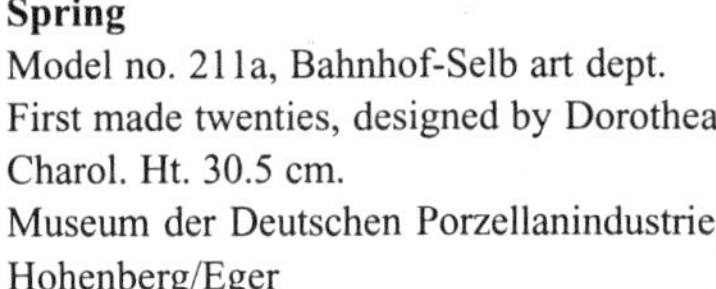

Spring
Model no. 211a, Bahnhof-Selb art dept. First made twenties, designed by Dorothea Charol. Ht. 30.5 cm.
Museum der Deutschen Porzellanindustrie, Hohenberg/Eger

Crouching Girl
Model no. 809, Selb art dept. First made 1925, designed by Milly Steeger
Ht. 30.2 cm. Rosenthal Archives, Selb

Kneeling Girl
Model no. 807, Selb art dept.
First made 1925, designed by Milly Steeger
Ht. 25 cm. Rosenthal Archives, Selb

Queen of Sheba
Model no. 126, Bahnhof-Selb art dept.
First made early twenties, designed by Richard Förster. Ht. 9.5 cm.
Art Auction House Ahlden Castle, catalog no. 91/1994

Drinking Girl
Model no. 752, Selb art dept.
First made 1924, designed by Ernst Wenck.
Ht. 17 cm.
Art Auction House Ahlden Castle, catalog no. 77-78.1992

Sleeping Girl
Model no. 969, Selb art dept.
First made 1927, designed by Ernst Wenck
Ht. 23.4 cm. Rosenthal Archives, Selb

Cake Eater, Newsboy
Model no. 1091, none, Selb art dept.
First made 1930, ca. 1930. Designed by Gustav Oppel
Ht. 23.8 cm, 21 cm.
Rosenthal Archives, Selb, photo by Rudolf Majonica, Munich

Ribbon Dancer
No model no., Bahnhof-Selb art dept. First made 1928? Designed by Lothar Otto
Ht. 13.2 cm. Monika Berg Gallery of 20th-Century Porcelain and Glass, Munich, photo by Rudolf Majonica, Munich

Newspaper Reader
No model no. Selb art dept.
First made 1925, designed by Karl Röhrig
Ht. 35.5 cm. Rosenthal Archives, Selb

Cherub with Flute
Model no. 997, Selb art dept.
First made 1928, designed by Edmund Otto
Ht. 12.6 cm. Art Auction House, Ahlden Castle, catalog no. 91/1994

Cherub with Whippet
Model no. 1282, Selb art dept.
First made 1934, designed by Max H.D. Fritz
Ht. 17 cm. Art Auction House Ahlden Castle, catalog no. 91/1994

Cherub with Kid
Model no. 1283, Selb art dept.
First made 1934, designed by Max H.D. Fritz
Ht. 20 cm. Art Auction House Ahlden Castle, catalog no. 70.1991

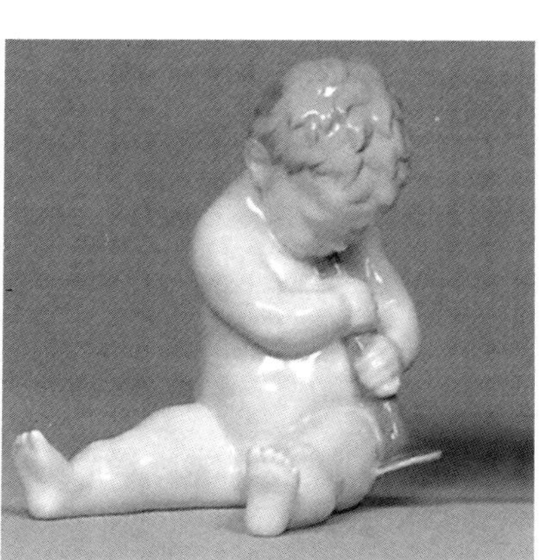

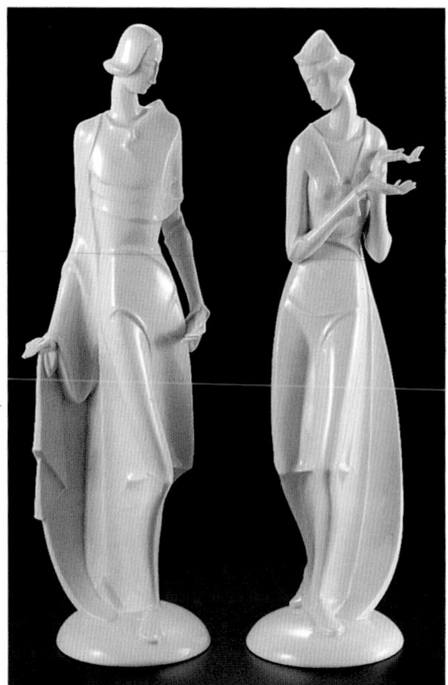

Resting (Sunning Herself)
Model no. 936, Selb art dept. First made 1927, designed by Gerhard Schliepstein
Ht. 23.4 cm, lg. 31.3 cm, width 14.5 cm. Rosenthal Archives, Selb

Prince, Princess
Model no. 826, 827, Selb art dept.
First made 1926, designed by Gerhard Schliepstein
Ht. 46 cm. Württemberg State Museum, Stuttgart, Fritz Klee Collection, photos from Rosenthal Archives, Selb

Music
Model no. 945, Selb art dept.
First made 1927, designed by Gerhard Schliepstein
Ht. 40 cm, base diam. 21 cm. Rosenthal Archives, Selb

Mountain Goat Clock
Model no. 977, Selb art dept. First made 1928, designed by Gerhard Schliepstein
Ht. 39.1 cm, lg. 59 cm. Rosenthal Archives, Selb, photo by Rudolf Majonica, Munich

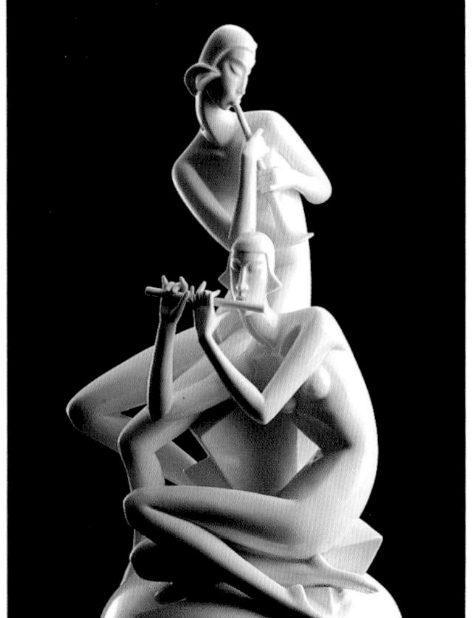

Hotel Dishes, Kaffee Hag
Model no. 380, Selb dish dept.
First made 1911
Coffeepot ht. 21/17 cm, pitcher ht. 8 cm, sugarbowl ht. 11/8 cm, cup 7 cm, saucer diam. 13.2 cm.
Rosenthal Archives, Selb, photo by Rudolf Majonica, Munich

Waldbaur Ashtray
No model no. Lg. 16.2 cm, width 8.2 cm.
Monika Berg Gallery of 20th-Century Porcelain and Glass, Munich, photo by Rudolf Majonica, Munich

Three Rosenthal Advertisements
No model no., Ht. 8.8, lg. 15.8 cm.; ht. 6.8 cm, lg. 11 cm.; ht. 4 cm, lg. 10.5 cm.
Monika Berg Gallery of 20th-Century Porcelain and Glass, Munich, photo by Rudolf Majonica, Munich

Sarotti Ashtray
No model no. lg. 17.2 cm, width 14.5 cm.
Monika Berg Gallery of 20th-Century Porcelain and Glass, Munich, photo by Rudolf Majolica, Munich

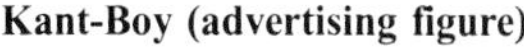

Kant-Boy (advertising figure)
Model no. 823, Selb art dept.
First made 1926, designed by Gustav Oppel
Ht. 30 cm. Rosenthal Archives, Selb, photo by Rudolf Majonica, Munich

China Boy (Riquet advertising figure)
Model no. 851, Selb art dept.
First made 1926, designed by Gustav Oppel
Ht. 38.5 cm. Rosenthal Archives, Selb, photo by Rudolf Majonica, Munich

Sarotti Moor
Model no. 1977, Selb art dept.
First made 1954, designed by Lauermann
Monika Berg Gallery of 20th-Century Porcelain and Glass, Munich, photo by Rudolf Majonica, Munich

Spring, Summer, Autumn, Winter
Model no. 1149-1152, decoration no. 2186, 2180, 2188, 2189, Selb art dept. First made 1932. Form designed by Claire Weiss
Ht. 24.3, 24.4, 21, 24.1 cm. Summer privately owned; others and photo from Rosenthal Archives, Selb

Looking, Torso
Model no. 1603, Selb art dept.
First made 1936, designed by R. Kaesbach
Ht. 24.6 cm, Art Auction House Ahlden Castle, catalog no. 88.1994

Sitting Girl
Model no. 1623, Selb art dept.
First made 1937, designed by Fritz Klimsch
Ht. 25 cm. Art Auction House Ahlden Castle, catalog no. 88/1994

Seated Feminine Act
Model no. 1040, Bahnhof-Selb art dept.
First made 1940? Designed by Otto Koch
Ht. 30.7 cm. Art Auction House Ahlberg Castle, catalog no. 77-78/1992

Dancer (Ursula Deinert)
Model no. 1714, Selb art dept.
First made 1939, designed by Lore Friedrich-Gronau
Ht. 30.5 cm. Art Auction House Ahlden Castle, catalog no. 91/1994

Crouching Girl
Model no. 1581, Selb art dept.
First made 1936, designed by Fritz Klimsch
Ht. 36 cm. Rosenthal Archives, Selb

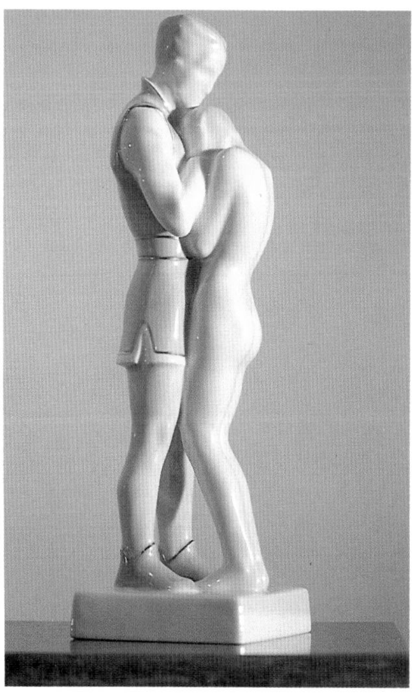

Refuge
Model no. 802, Bahnhof-Selb art dept.
First made thirties, designed by M. Schwartzkopff
Ht. 35 cm. Monika Berg Gallery of 20th-Century Porcelain and Glass, Munich, photo by Rudolf Majonica, Munich

Accordion Player
Model no. 1656, Selb art dept.
First made 1937, designed by Höfer-Kelling
Ht. 24.8 cm. Art Auction House Ahlden Castle, catalog no. 1987/1994

Round Dance
Model no. 681, Bahnhof-Selb art dept.
First made early thirties, designed by F. Bessom
Ht. 21 cm, lg. 26 cm. Rosenthal Archives, Selb, photo by Rudolf Majonica, Munich

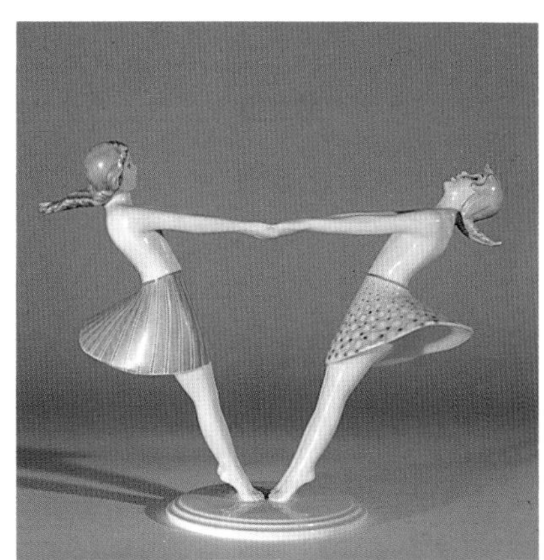

Small Moor
Model no. 760, Selb art dept.
First made 1925, designed by Grete Zschäbitz
Ht. 9.2 cm. Monika Berg Gallery of 20th-Century Porcelain and Glass, Munich, photo by Rudolf Majonica

Moor with Fruit Dish
Model no. 863, Bahnhof-Selb art dept.
First made thirties, designed by Hugo Meisel
Ht. 18 cm. Monika Berg Gallery of 20th-Century Porcelain and Glass, Munich, photo by Rudolf Majonica, Munich

Moor with Fish Plate and Jug
Model no. 866, Bahnhof-Selb art dept.
First made early thirties, designed by Hugo Meisel
Ht. 18.5 cm. Art Auction House Ahlden Castle, catalog no. 81-82.1993

Moor with Poultry Plate
Model no. 865, Bahnhof-Selb art dept.
First made thirties, designed by Hugo Meisel
Ht. 18.7 cm. Art Auction House Ahlden Castle, catalog no. 81-82/1993

Moor with Accordion
Model no. 1056, Bahnhof-Selb art dept.
First made thirties, designed by Hugo Meisel
Ht. 19.5 cm. Art Auction House Ahlden Castle, catalog no. 87/1994

Moor with Lute
Model no. 1057, Bahnhof-Selb art dept.
First made thirties, designed by Hugo Meisel
Ht. 19.5 cm. Art Auction House Ahlden Castle, catalog no. 79-80/1992

Moor with Dessert Bowl
Model no. 864? Bahnhof-Selb art dept.
First made thirties, designed by Hugo Meisel
Ht. 18.5 cm. Art Auction House Ahlden Castle, catalog no. 88.1994

Grotesque Duck (Fashion Show)
Model no. 1087, Selb art dept.
First made 1930, designed by Gustav Oppel
Ht. 11 cm. Monika Berg Gallery of 20th-Century Porcelain and Glass, Munich, photo by Rudolf Majonica, Munich

Fox (Fashion Show)
Model no. 1090, Selb art dept.
First made 1930, designed by Gustav Oppel
Ht. 7.8 cm. Monika Berg Gallery of 20th-Century Porcelain and Glass, Munich, photo by Rudolf Majonica, Munich

Foo Dog
Model no. 912, Selb art dept.
First made 1927, designed by Grete Zschäbitz
Ht. 25.2 cm. Rosenthal Archives, Selb, photo by Rudolf Majonica, Munich

Laughing Rabbits
Model no. 510, Bahnhof-Selb art dept.
First made thirties, designed by Max D. H. Fritz
Ht. 13.6 and 5 cm. Monika Berg Gallery of 20th-Century Porcelain and Glass, Munich, photo by Rudolf Majonica, Munich

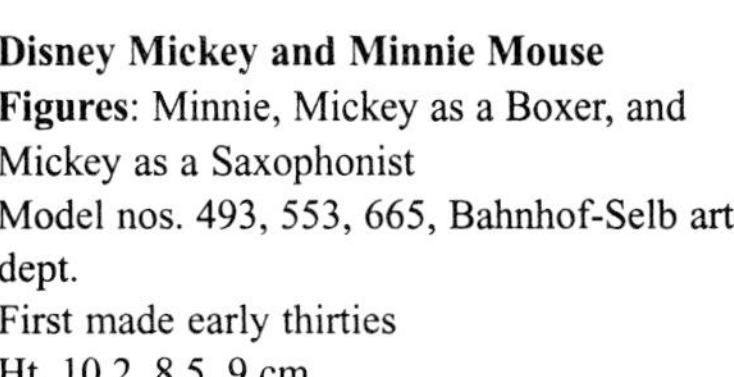

Disney Mickey and Minnie Mouse Figures: Minnie, Mickey as a Boxer, and Mickey as a Saxophonist
Model nos. 493, 553, 665, Bahnhof-Selb art dept.
First made early thirties
Ht. 10.2, 8.5, 9 cm.
Rosenthal Archives, Selb, photo by Rudolf Majonica, Munich

Imaginary Bird
Model no. 880, decoration no. 430n, Selb art dept.
First made 1926, form designed by Grete Zschäbitz, decoration by Kurt Severin?
Ht. 28 cm. Rosenthal Archives, Selb

Dog (Stretched Dachshund), Horse (Bucephalus), Grotesque Weasel and Marabou
Model no. 803, 799, 914, 918, Selb art dept.
First made 1925, 1927, designed by Hans Küster
Ht. 2 cm, lg. 13.8 cm, ht. 7 cm, 8 cm, 6.5 cm.
Rosenthal Archives, Selb, photo by Rudolf Majonica, Munich

Fish
Model no. 772, decoration no. 341n, Selb art dept.
First made 1925, form designed by Richard Scheibe, decoration by Kurt Severin?
Ht. 23 cm. Rosenthal Archives, Selb

Polar Bear
Model no. 1009, Selb art dept.
First made 1928, form designed by Hans Küster
Ht. 23.8 cm, lg. 34 cm, width 17.3 cm, Rosenthal Archives, Selb

Lying Sheep
Model no. 196, Bahnhof-Selb art dept.
Twenties, designed by Theodor Kärner
Ht. 10.2 cm. Art Auction House Ahlden Castle, catalog no. 91/1994

Rhinoceros Beetle
Model no. 764, Selb art dept.
First made 1925, designed by Grete Zschäbitz
Ht. 4.5, lg. 2.8 cm. Monika Berg Gallery of 20th-Century Porcelain and Glass, Munich, photo by Rudolf Majonica, Munich

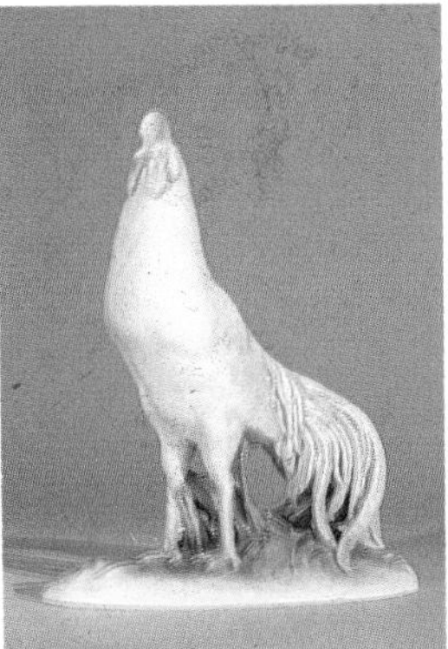

Rooster
Model no. 1008, Selb art dept.
First made 1928, designed by Hans Küster
Ht. 18 cm. Rosenthal Archives, Selb, photo by Rudolf Majonica, Munich

Greyhound
Model no. 80, Bahnhof-Selb art dept.
First made early twenties, designed by Theodor Kärner
Ht. 8 cm, lg. 16.5 cm.
Rosenthal Archives, Selb, photo by Rudolf Majonica, Munich

Heron
Model no. 1212, Bahnhof-Selb art dept.
First made 1950?, designed by Max D. H. Fritz
Ht. 26.4 cm. Art Auction House Ahlden Castle, catalog no. 91.1994

Guinea-fowl Group
No model no., Bahnhof-Selb art dept.
First made thirties, designed by Ottmar Obermaier
Ht. 19.5 cm. Art Auction House Ahlden Castle, catalog no. 92/1995

African Parrot
Model no. 22? Bahnhof-Selb art dept.
First made 1935? Designed by Dorothea Moldenhauer
Ht. 17 cm. Art Auction House Ahlden Castle, catalog no. 91/1994

Parrot
no model no., Bahnhof-Selb art dept.
First made 1940? Designed by Dorothea Moldenhauer
Ht. 17 cm. Art Auction House Ahlden Castle, catalog no. 71/1991

Exotic Bird
Model no. 446, Bahnhof-Selb art dept.
First made 1930? Designed by O. Eichwald
Ht. 23 cm. Art Auction House Ahlden Castle, catalog no. 71/1991

Siskin
Model no. 1653, Selb art dept.
First made 1937, designed by Fritz Heidenreich
Ht. 14.5 cm. Art Auction House Ahlden Castle, catalog no. 70/1991

Sparrow Group
Model no. 1531, Selb art dept.
First made 1934, designed by Karl Himmelstoss
Ht. 11.5 cm. Art Auction House, Ahlden Castle, catalog no. 70.1991

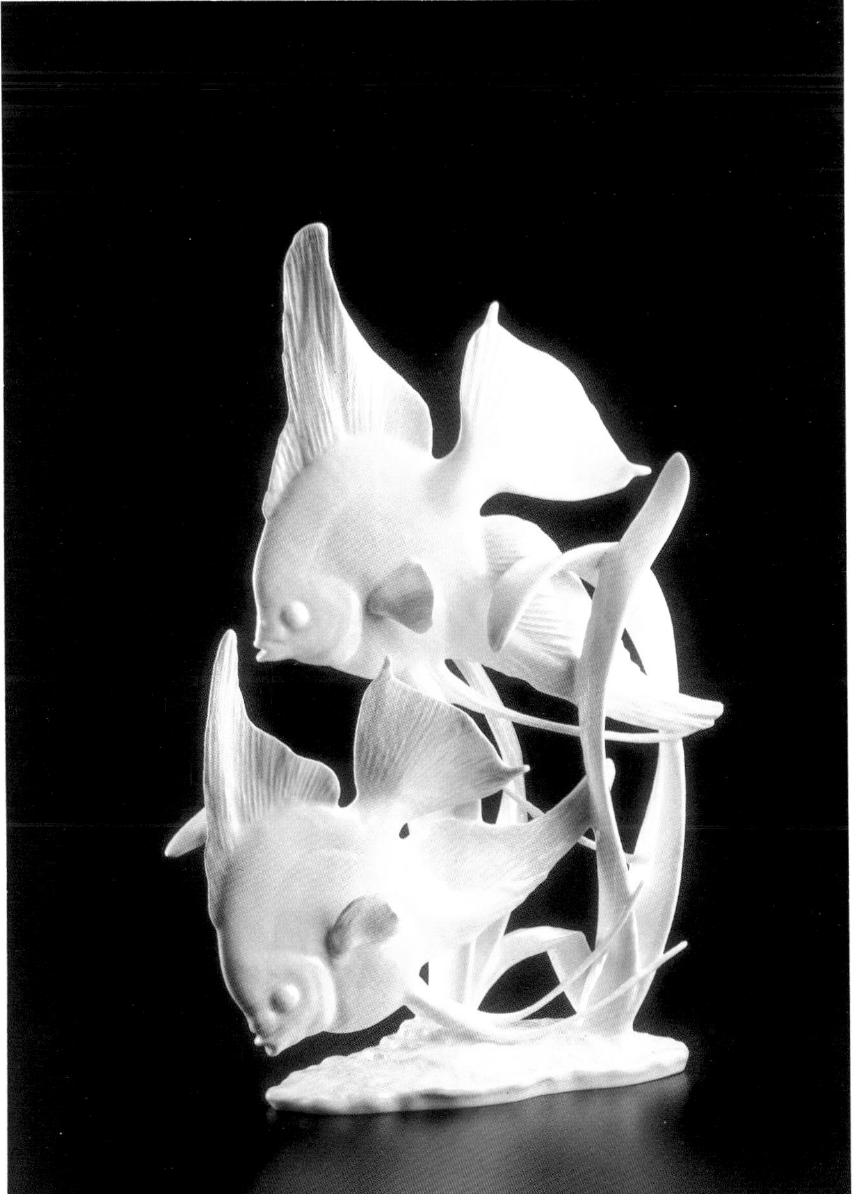

Scalare
Model no. 1636, Selb art dept.
First made 1937, designed by Fritz Heidenreich
Ht. 39.5 cm. Rosenthal Archives, Selb

Male Dove
Model no. 1589, Selb art dept.
First made 1936, designed by Fritz Heidenreich
Ht. 14.7 cm. Art Auction House Ahlden Castle, catalog no. 77-78/1992

Pair of Doves
Model no. 1591, Selb art dept.
First made 1936, designed by Fritz Heidenreich
Ht. 14 cm. Art Auction House Ahlden Castle, catalog no. 92/1995

Elephant (Wastl)
Model no. 1195, Selb art dept.
First made 1932, designed by Theodor Kärner
Ht. 15.5 cm. Rosenthal Archives, Selb, photo by Rudolf Majonica, Munich

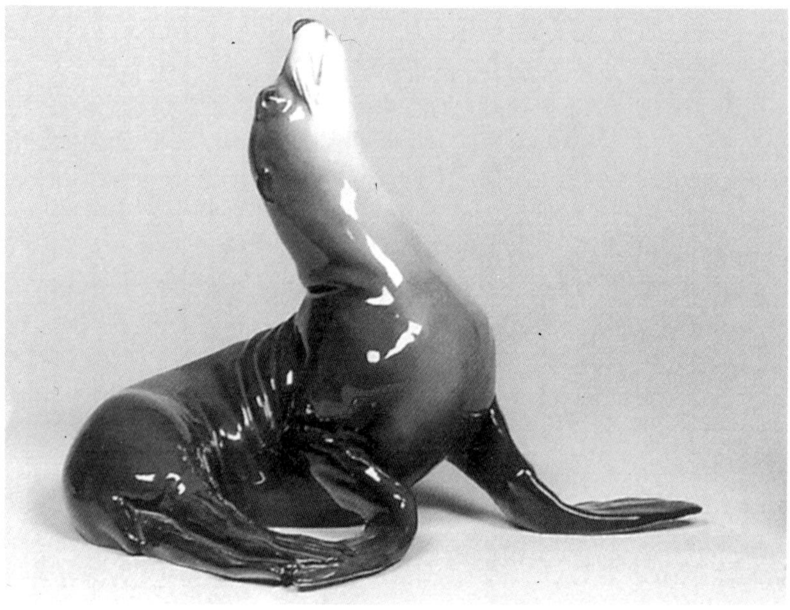

Sealion
Model no. 1289, Selb art dept.
First made 1934, design by Theodor Kärner
Ht. 20.5 cm. Art Auction House Ahlden Castle, catalog no. 91/1994

Sitting Rabbit
Model no. 801, Bahnhof-Selb art dept.
First made 1939, designed by Karl Röhrig
Ht. 12.5 cm. Art Auction House Ahlden Castle, catalog no. 92/1995

Coffee Service "Helena"
Model no. 660 white, Selb dish dept.
Made 1936-1960, designed by Wolfgang von Wersin
Coffeepot ht. 19.8/17 cm, sugarbowl ht. 8.5/5.4 cm, cream pitcher ht. 10.3 cm, cup ht. 5.3 cm, saucer diam. 13.8 cm.
Rosenthal Archives, Selb

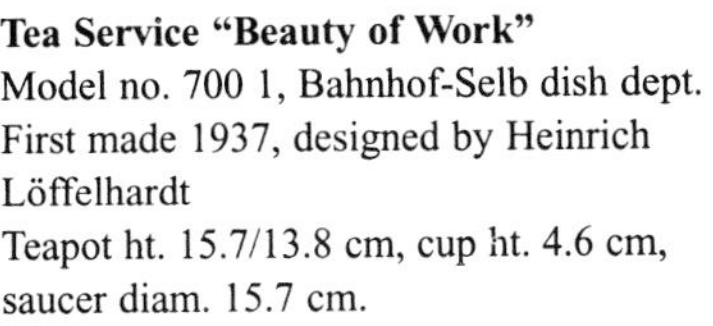

Tea Service "Beauty of Work"
Model no. 700 1, Bahnhof-Selb dish dept.
First made 1937, designed by Heinrich Löffelhardt
Teapot ht. 15.7/13.8 cm, cup ht. 4.6 cm, saucer diam. 15.7 cm.
Rosenthal Archives, Selb

Coffee Service "20:1"
Model no. 800, Bahnhof-Selb dish dept.
First made 1938, designed by Otto Koch
Ht. 22.7 cm. Rosenthal Archives, Selb

Partial Coffee Service
Model no. 760, Selb dish dept.
First made 1928, form designed by Georg A, Mathéy
Coffeepot ht. 19.9/11.4 cm, cup ht. 6 cm, saucer diam. 14.9 cm (cake plate diam. 19.6 cm)
Rosenthal Archives, Selb

Bank
No model no. Kronach dish dept.
First made 1934. Ht. 19 cm.
Rosenthal Archives, Selb, photo by Rudolf Majonica

Mocha Service
Model no. 3508, Selb art dept.
First made 1938, designed by Fritz von Stockmayer
Mocha pot ht. 18.5/16 cm, pitcher ht. 7 cm, lg. 10 cm, bowl ht. 4.5 cm, cup ht. 4 cm, saucer diam. 11 cm.
Rosenthal Archives, Selb, photo by Rudolf Majonica, Munich

Perfume Atomizer
No model no., Selb art dept.
First made latter thirties, designed by Fritz von Stockmayer
Ht. 11.5 cm, lg. 11.2 cm.
Rosenthal Archives, Selb, photo by Rudolf Majonica, Munich

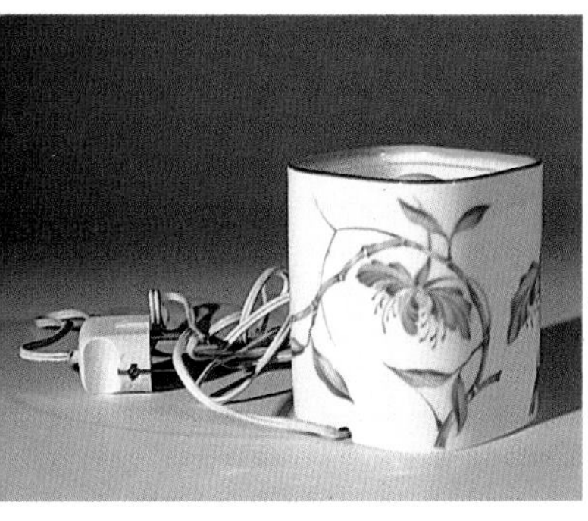

Vase
Model no. 2517, Selb art dept.
First made 1936, form and decoration designed by Fritz von Stockmayer
Ht. 13 cm, diam. 18.6 cm. Rosenthal Archives, Selb

Vase
Model no. 2518, decoration no. 11994? Aelb art dept.
First made 1936, form and decoration designed by Fritz von Stockmayer
Ht. 17.9 cm, diam. 18.2 cm. Rosenthal Archives, Selb

Dining Service "2000"
Model no. 2000, Selb dish dept., Rosenthal Studio Line
First made 1954, form designed by Richard Latham-Raymond Loewy, decoration by J. Gallitzendörfer, modeler Richard Scharrer
Ragout bowl ht. minus rack 12/8.3 cm, diam. minus rack 24.5 cm, gravy bowl ht. 6.3 cm, diam. 18.8 cm, soup bowl ht. 6.5 cm, saucer diam. 17.8 cm.
Rosenthal Archives, Selb

Coffee Service "2000," Tusser-silk Design
Model no. 2000, Selb dish dept., Rosenthal Studio Line
First made 1954, form designed by Richard Latham & Raymond Loewy, modeler Richard Scharrer, decoration by Margret Hildebrand 1954
Coffeepot ht. 23.3/20.8 cm, sugarbowl size 3 ht. 10.8/7.4 cm, cream pitcher size 3 ht. 9.3 cm, cup ht. 7.2 cm, saucer diam. 14.5 cm (plate 19.4 cm). Rosenthal Archives, Selb

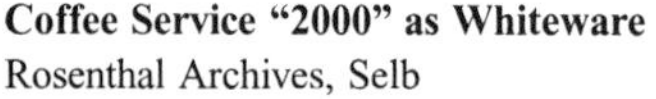

Coffee Service "2000" as Whiteware
Rosenthal Archives, Selb

Coffee and Tea Service "Berlin,"
left **Whiteware**, below **Carousel Decoration**
Model no. 1300, Kronach dish dept., Rosenthal Studio Line
First made 1959, form designed by Hans Theo Baumann, decoration below by Bele Bachem, 1961
Teapot ht. 15.2/12.7 cm, sugarbowl ht. 8.1/5.2 cm, diam. 9.1 cm, cream pitcher ht. 8.1 cm, cup ht. 5 cm, saucer diam. 14.3 cm, cake plate diam. 19.2 cm.
Rosenthal Archives, Selb

Coffee Service "2000," Grass Decoration
Model no. 2000, Selb dish dept. First made 1954, designed by Richard S, Latham-Raymond Loewy
Coffeepot ht. 23/20.3 cm, pitcher ht. 9 cm, sugarbowl 10/7.2 cm, cup ht. 7.2 cm, saucer diam. 14.6 cm.
Rosenthal Archives, Selb, photo by Rudolf Majonica, Munich

Mocha Service "Oval"
Model no. 1100, Bahnhof-Selb dish dept.
First made 1951, form designed by Rudolf Lunghard
Pot ht. 23.3/20.5 cm, sugarbowl ht. 10/5.6 cm, cream pitcher ht. 9.9 cm, cup 4.1 cm, saucer lg. 14 cm, width 10.7 cm.
Rosenthal Archives, Selb

Coffee Service "Fortuna"
Model no. 650, Bahnhof-Selb dish dept.
First made 1956, designed by Elsa Fischer-Treyden
Coffeepot ht. 20/18 cm, sugarbowl ht. 9/6.5 cm, cup ht. 7 cm, saucer diam. 14.5 cm.
Rosenthal Archives, Selb, photo by Rudolf Majonica, Munich**Coffee Service**

"Romanze," Four Color Decoration
Model no. 1250, Bahnhof-Selb dish dept., Rosenthal Studio Line
First made 1959, form and decoration designed by Björn Wiinblad, 1959, modeler Hans Wohlrab
Coffeepot ht. 23.4/18.4 cm, sugarbowl ht. 9.7/6.1 cm, cream pitcher ht. 8.7 cm, cup ht. 8.2 cm, saucer diam. 15.2 cm.
Rosenthal Archives, Selb

Eight Candlesticks in three sizes
Model no. 3256-58? Kronach works?
Ht. 29, 23 and 16.5 cm.
Monika Berg Gallery of 20th-Century Porcelain and Glass, Munich, photo by Rudolf Majonica, Munich

Vase "Bettina"
Model no. 1208? Kronach works
Ht. 20 cm. Monica Berg Gallery of 20th-Century Porcelain and Glass, Munich, photo by Rudolf Majonica, Munich

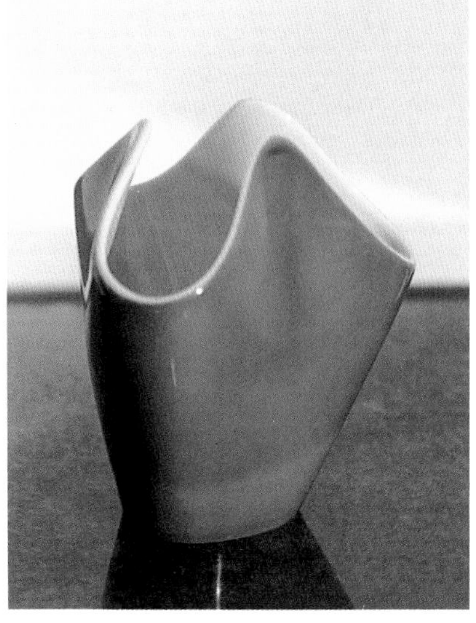

Small Triangular Vase with rounded corners
(far right) Model no. 2684, Selb art dept.
First made 1954, designed by Hans Stangl
Ht. 9.5 cm, dp. 9 cm. Monika Berg Gallery of 20th-Century Porcelain and Glass, Munich, photo by Rudolf Majonica, Munich

Brocken Hotel Dish
(top left) No model no.
Lg. 10.5 cm, width 7 cm.
Monika Berg Gallery of 20th-Century Porcelain and Glass, Munich, photo by Rudolf Majonica, Munich

Dish (sea shell)
(bottom left) Model no. 2149, Selb art dept.
First made 1952, designed by A. Klingler
Lg. 9 cm, width 8 cm.
Monika Berg Gallery of 20th-Century Porcelain and Glass, Munich, photo by Rudolf Majonica, Munich

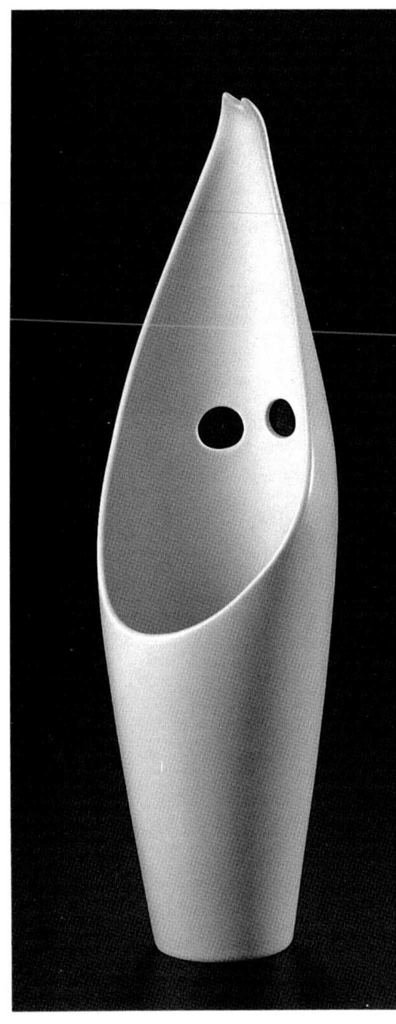

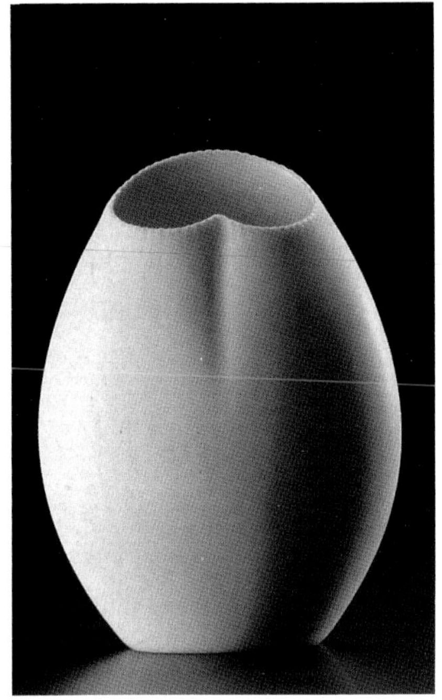

Vase
Model no. 2728, Selb art dept., Rosenthal Studio Line
First made 1956, designed by Tapio Wirkkala
Ht. 23.4 cm. Rosenthal Archives, Selb

Vase
Model no. 2739, Selb art dept., Rosenthal Studio Line
First made 1956, designed by Tapio Wirkkala
Ht. 17.6 cm. Rosenthal Archives, Selb

Vase
Model no. 2683, Selb art dept.
First made 1952, designed by Beate Kuhn
Ht. 43.4 cm. Rosenthal Archives, Selb

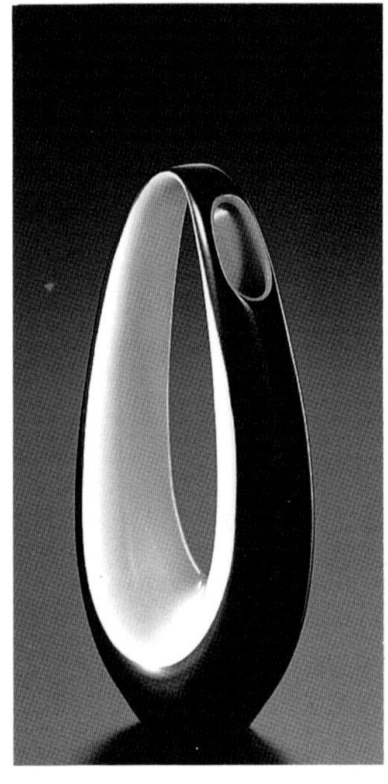

Kummet Vase
(near right)Model no. 2661, Selb art dept.
First made 1953, form and decoration designed by Beate Kuhn
Ht. 17 cm. Rosenthal Archives, Selb

Vase
(far right)
Model no. 2637, Selb art dept.
First made 1952, designed by Jan Bontjes van Beek
Ht. 23 cm. Rosenthal Archives, Selb

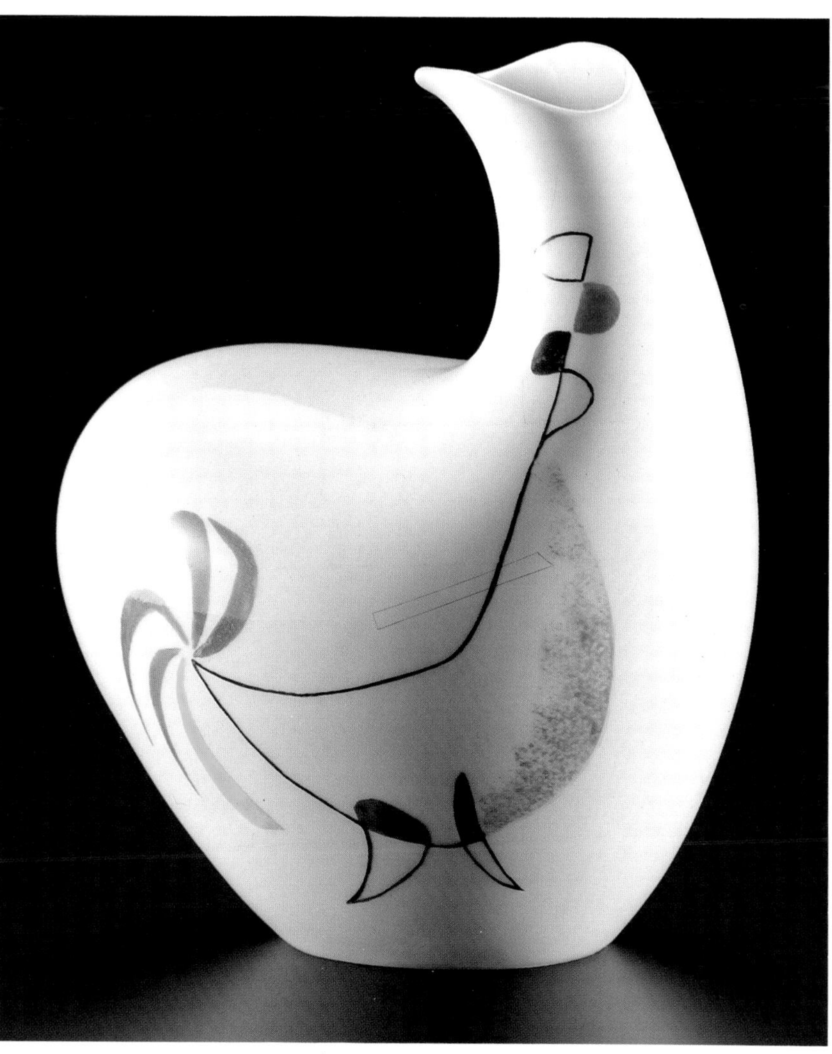

Vase
Model no. 2594, Selb art dept.
First made 1952, form designed by Fritz Heidenreich, decoration by Klaus Bendixen
Ht. 23.6 cm. Rosenthal Archives, Selb

Vase with narrow neck
(right) Model no. 2628, Selb art dept.
First made 1952, form designed by Hans Wohlrab, decoration by Klaus Bendixen
Ht. 19.5 cm. Rosenthal Archives, Selb

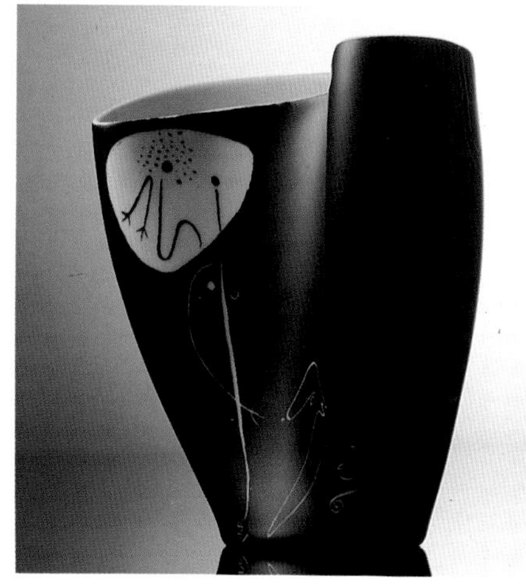

Asymmetrical Vase
(far left) Model no. 2690, Selb art dept.
First made 1955, designed by Fritz Heidenreich
Ht. 21 cm. Monika Berg Gallery of 20th-Century Porcelain and Glass, Munich, photo by Rudolf Majonica, Munich

Vase
(near left) Model no. 2644, Selb art dept.
First made 1952, form and decoration designed by Beate Kuhn
Ht. 19 cm. Rosenthal Archives, Selb

Four Orchid Vases "Pregnant Louise," in two sizes
Model no. 2592, Selb art dept.
First made 1950, designed by Fritz Heidenreich
Ht. 24 and 17.5 cm. Monika Berg Gallery of 20th-Century Porcelain and Glass, Munich, photo by Rudolf Majonica, Munich

Acropolis and Carnation Vases
Model no. 2722 and 2740, Selb art dept.
First made 1954, 1956, designed by Hans Wohlrab
Ht. 32.8 and 28.2 cm.
Monika Berg Gallery of 20th-Century Porcelain and Glass, Munich, photo by Rudolf Majonica, Munich

Box
Model no. 2002, Selb art dept.
First made 1954, form designed by Beate Kuhn. decoration by Max Weber
Ht. 6.4 cm, lg. 14.8 cm, wd. 13.8 cm.
Rosenthal Archives, Selb

Asymmetrical Bowl
Model no. 2169, Selb art dept.
First made 1953, designed by Hans Stangl
Ht. 18.5 cm, lg. 14.5 cm, wd. 10 cm.
Monika Berg Gallery of 20th-Century Porcelain and Glass, Munich, photo by Rudolf Majonica, Munich

Bowl with Peynet Decoration
Model no. 2179, Selb works
First made 1959, decoration designed by Raymond Peynet
Lg. 13 cm, width 9.5 cm.
Monika Berg Gallery of 20th-Century Porcelain and Glass, Munich, photo by Rudolf Majonica, Munich

Sea Star Vase
Model no. 2651, Selb art dept.
First made 1949, designed by Beate Kuhn
Ht. 15.2 cm, dp. 14.8 cm.
Monika Berg Gallery of 20th-Century Porcelain and Glass, munich, photo by Rudolf Majonica, Munich

Vase with Handle
Model no. 2736, Selb art dept.
First made 1956, designed by Hans Wohlrab
Ht. 17.8 cm.
Monika Berg Gallery of 20th-Century Porcelain and Glass, Munich, photo by Rudolf Majonica, Munich

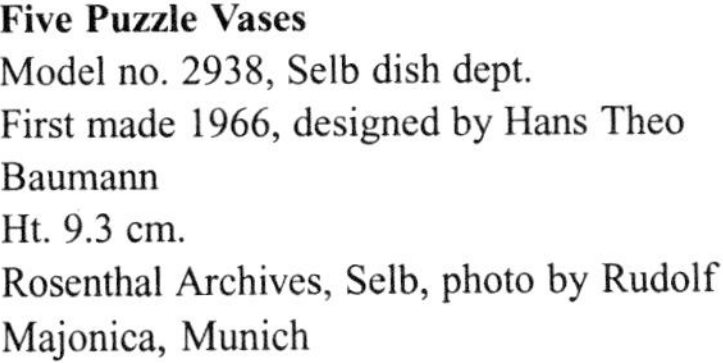

Five Puzzle Vases
Model no. 2938, Selb dish dept.
First made 1966, designed by Hans Theo Baumann
Ht. 9.3 cm.
Rosenthal Archives, Selb, photo by Rudolf Majonica, Munich

Donkey Driver, Daphne, Fountain Idyll, and Boy with Dog
Model nos. 1872, 1861, 1858, 1905, Selb art dept.
First made 1952, 1951, 1951, 1952, designed by Bele Bachem
Ht. 11.2 cm, lg. 17 cm; ht. 17.8 cm, 11 cm, 12 cm.
Rosenthal Archives, Selb, photo by Rudolf Majonica, Munich

Sabine
Model no. 1972, Selb art dept.
First made 1954, designed by Bidlingmaier
Rosenthal Archives, Selb, photo by Rudolf Majonica, Munich

Round Dance, Piggyback, and Boy with Book
Model nos. 5132, 5130, 5131, Selb art dept.
First made 1958, designed by Renate Rhein
Ht. 13 cm, 19 cm, 7.5 cm, lg. 10 cm.
Rosenthal Archives, Selb, photo by Rudolf Majonica, Munich

Centaur
(upper left)Model no. 5095, Selb art dept.
First made 1957, form and decoration designed by Raymony Peynet
Ht. 24 cm, lg. 20.2 cm, dp. 10 cm.
Rosenthal Archives, Selb

Cavalier with Heart, Girl with Heart, small versions
(upper right) Model no. 5121, 5120, Selb art dept.
First made 1958, designed by Raymond Peynet
Ht. 15.6 cm, 15 cm.
Rosenthal Archives, Selb, photo by Rudolf Majonica, Munich

Courtship, Romance with Book, and Lovers
Model nos. 5151, 5218, 5150, Selb art dept.
First made 1959, 1960, 1959, designed by Raymond Peynet
Ht. 23.4 cm; 12 cm, lg. 18.8 cm; ht. 21.5 cm.
Rosenthal Archives, Selb, photo by Rudolf Majonica, Munich

Smoker, Lady with Umbrella, Woman and Man Telephoning, Man with Folded Arm, and in front Girl Student
Model nos. 5017, 5024, 5025, 5023, 5016, front 5013, Selb art dept. First made 1955, designed by Klaus Backmund, front by Engel
Ht. 15, 14.6, 14.5, 14.2, 15.2 cm, front ht. 9.4, lg. 11 cm.
Rosenthal Archives, Selb, photo by Rudolf Majonica, Munich

Madonna, and Affection
Model nos. 1918 and 1919, Selb art dept.
First made 1953, designed by Hans Stangl
Ht. 27 cm, 27.4 cm.
Rosenthal Archives, Selb, photo by Rudolf Majonica, Munich

Shepherd and Muse
Model no. 1860, Selb art dept.
First made 1951, form and decoration designed by Bele Bachem
Ht. 15 cm, lg. 21 cm, width 13.3 cm. Rosenthal Archives, Selb

Coffee and Dining Service "Variation"
(right and below) Model no. 2500, with Porcelaine noire, Rosenthal Studio Line
First made 1962, designed by Tapio Wirkkala, modeler Richard Scharrer
Coffeepot ht. 21.8/20.5 cm, sugarbowl ht. 7.2/5.6 cm, cream pitcher ht. 9.3 cm, cup ht. 6.7 cm, saucer diam. 14.3 cm, ragout bowl ht. 10/7.5 cm, saucer ht. 4.3 cm, diam. 30.2 cm, shakers ht. 5.4 cm, diam. 4 cm.
Rosenthal Archives, Selb

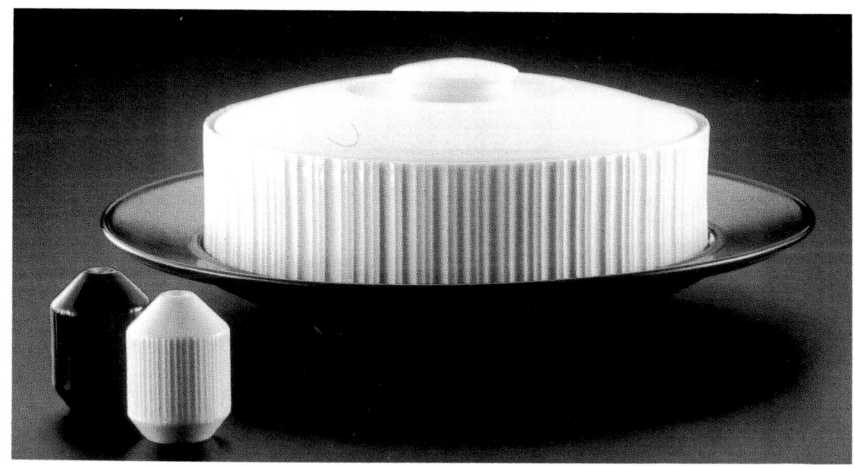

Vase
Model no. 3026, Rosenthal Studio Line
First made 1969, form and decoration designed by Martin Freyer
Ht. 15.3 cm. Rosenthal Archives, Selb

Coffee Service "Composition"
Model no. 1350, Rosenthal Studio Line
First made 1963, designed by Tapio Wirkkala, modeler Richard Scharrer
Coffeepot ht. 21.3/18.6 cm, sugarbowl ht. 9.1/7.3 cm, pitcher ht. 9.7 cm, cup ht. 7.8 cm, saucer diam. 12.5 cm.
Rosenthal Archives, Selb

"Shah" Dining Service
No model no., Rosenthal Studio Line, made only in 1971, form and decoration designed by Björn Wiinblad, relief modeler Hermann Bocek
Coffeepot ht. 23.6/15 cm, sugarbowl ht. 12.2/6.5 cm, cream pitcher ht. 6.3 cm, tablet lg. 31.3 cm, width 17.7 cm, cup ht. 6.5 cm, saucer diam. 16.3 cm, ragout bowl ht. 21.1/11 cm, saucer ht. 3.1 cm, diam 27.8 cm.
Photo, Rosenthal Archives, Selb

Mocha Service "Magic Flute"
Model no. 1260, Rosenthal Studio Line
First made 1968, form and decoration designed by Björn Wiinblad, modelers Hermann Bocek and Aldo Falchi
Mocha pot ht. 18.8/12 cm, cup ht. 4.4 cm, saucer diam. 12.1 cm.
Rosenthal Archives, Selb

Artist Service "Duo," Pastoral Decoration
Model no. 1270, Rosenthal Studio Line
First made 1968, form designed by Ambrogio Pozzi, decoration by HAP Grisehaber
Ragout bowl ht. 13.6/8.3 cm (soup cup ht. 5.3 cm, saucer diam. 15.6 cm). Rosenthal Archives, Selb

Coffee Service "Lotus"
Model no. 800, Rosenthal Studio Line
First made 1964, form and decoration designed by Björn Wiinblad, modeler Hans Wohlrab
Coffeepot ht. 18.8/17 ca, sugar bowl ht. 10.2/5.7 cm, cream pitcher ht. 7.7 cm, cup ht. 6.8 cm, saucer diam. 13.8 cm. Rosenthal Archives, Selb

Coffee Service "Duo"
Model no. 1270, Rosenthal Studio Line
First made 1968, designed by Ambrogio Pozzi
Coffeepot ht. 21/16.8 cm, sugarbowl 8.1/5.2 cm, diam 8.8 cm, cream pitcher ht. 8 cm, cup ht. 7.1 cm, saucer diam. 13.5 cm.
Rosenthal Archives, Selb

Tea Service "TAC I"
Model no. 1280 with black porcelain, Rosenthal Studio Line.
First made 1969, designed by The Architects Collaborative/Walter Gropius, Louis McMillen
Teapot ht. 12.3 cm, lg. 23.7 cm, sugarbowl ht. 7.7/5.1 cm, diam. 10.1 cm, cream pitcher ht. 7 cm, cup ht. 4.9 cm, diam. 10.1 cm minus handle, saucer diam. 15.8 cm, cake plate diam. 19.3 cm.
Rosenthal Archives, Selb

Hommage to Gropius, Artist Coffeepots, selection
Model no. 1290, Rosenthal Studio Line, first made ca. 1969, decorations 1994 by Sandro Chia, Sergei Bugaev
Ht. 21.2/20.2 cm. Rosenthal Archives, Selb

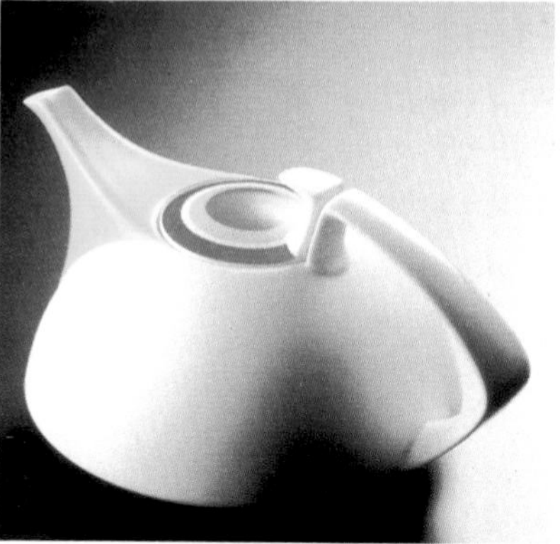

Artist Service "TAC I," Bauhaus Hommage I Decoration
Rosenthal Studio Line, first made 1969, form designed by TAC/Walter Gropius, Louis McMillen, decoration by Herbert Bayer, 1979
Teapot ht. 23.7 cm. Rosenthal Archives, Selb

Coffee Service "TAC II"
Model no. 1290, Rosenthal Studio Line
First made ca. 1969, designed by The Architects Collaborative/Walter Gropius, Louis McMillen
Coffeepot ht. 21.2/20.2 cm, sugarbowl ht. 6.7/5.6 cm, cream pitcher ht. 9.5 cm, cup ht. 7.3 cm, saucer diam. 13.5 cm.
Rosenthal Archives, Selb

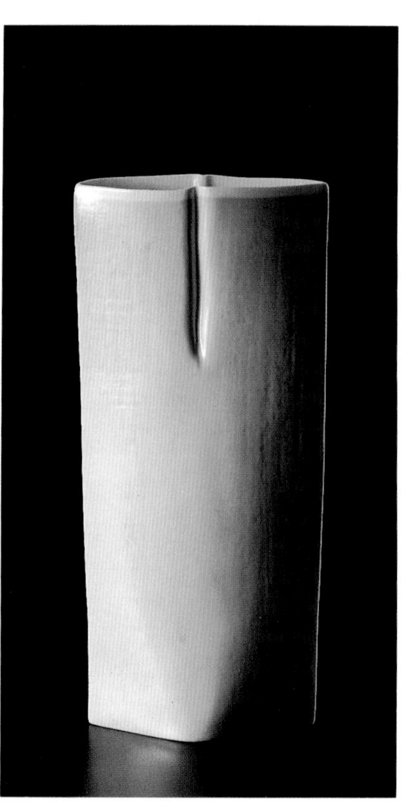

Osman Bowl, Black Porcelain, Milet Decoration
(above right) Model no. 3579, Rosenthal Studio Line
First made 1979, form and decoration designed by Alev Siesbye
Ht. 12 cm, diam. 15 cm. Rosenthal Archives,

SelbVase
(upper left) Model no. 2660, Rosenthal Studio Line, first made 1953, form designed by Elsa Fischer-Treyden, decoration by Emilio Pucci, 1973.
Ht. 32.3 cm. Rosenthal Archives, Selb

Vase
(far left) Model no. 3702, Rosenthal Studio Line
First made 1981, form and decoration designed by Johan van Loon
Ht. 24.7 cm. Rosenthal Archives, Selb

Candlestick
(near left) Model no. 1250, Bahnhof-Selb art dept.
First made pre-1961, designed by Bkörn Wiinblad
Ht. 14.2 cm. Monika Berg Gallery of 20th-Century Porcelain and Glass, Munich, photo by Rudolf Majonica, Munich

Vase, Black Porcelain
(upper right) Model no. 3527, Rosenthal Studio Line, first made 1972, form and decoration designed by Tapio Wirkkala
Ht. 22 cm. Rosenthal Archives, Selb

Chicken Vase, Black Porcelain
(below) Model no. 7209, Rosenthal Studio Line, first made 1970, form and decoration designed by Tapio Wirkkala
Nt. 10 cm, lg. 14 cm. Rosenthal Archives, Selb

Box, Black Porcelain
(bottom left) Model no. 7209, Rosenthal Studio Line, first made 1996, form designed by Elsa Fischer-Treyden, relief decoration by Margret Hildebrand
Ht. 10.7 cm, diam. 9.7 cm. Rosenthal Archives, Selb

Commedia dell'arte Bowl
Model no. 2116, Selb Porcelain Factory
First made 1984, decoration designed by Björn Wiinblad
Lg. 12.5 cm, width 12.5 cm.
Monika Berg Gallery of 20th-Century Porcelain and Glass, Munich, photo by Rudolf Majonica, Munich

Ball Bowl
Model no. 0081, Selb art dept., Studio Line
First made 1971, designed by Tapio Wirkkala
Ht. 10.8 cm, lg. 26.3 cm, width 21 cm.
Monika Berg Gallery of 20th-Century Porcelain and Glass, Munich, photo by Rudolf Majonica, Munich

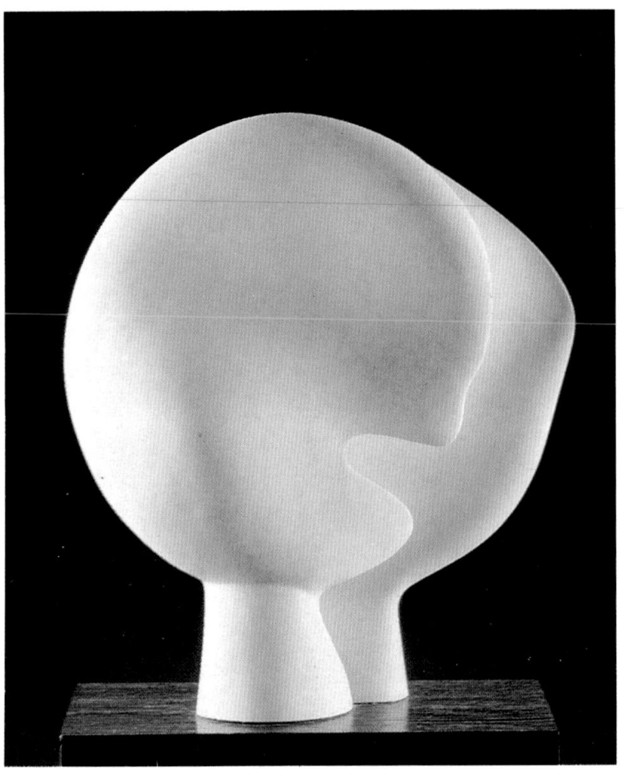

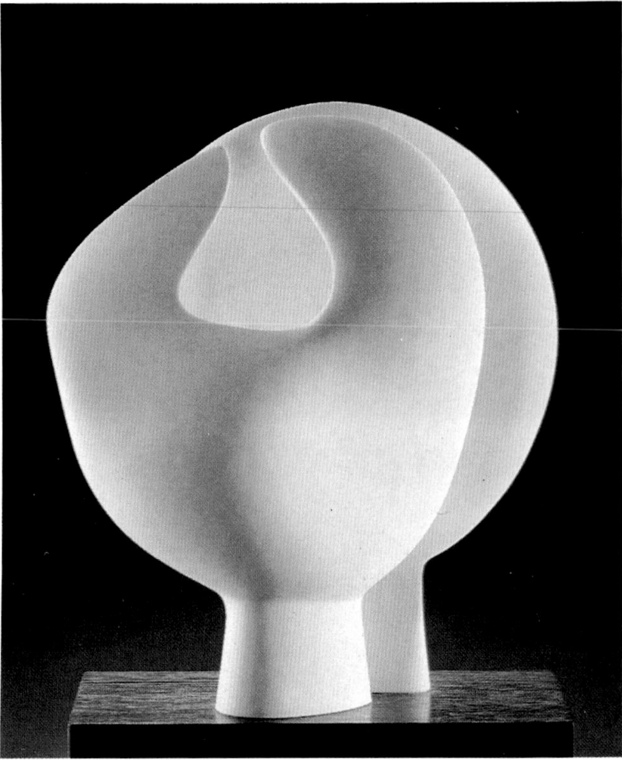

Moonhead
Design by Henry Moore, limited edition of six copies, Rosenthal Studio Line Relief Series, first made 1968
Ht. 40 cm with base/30 cm. Rosenthal Archives, Selb

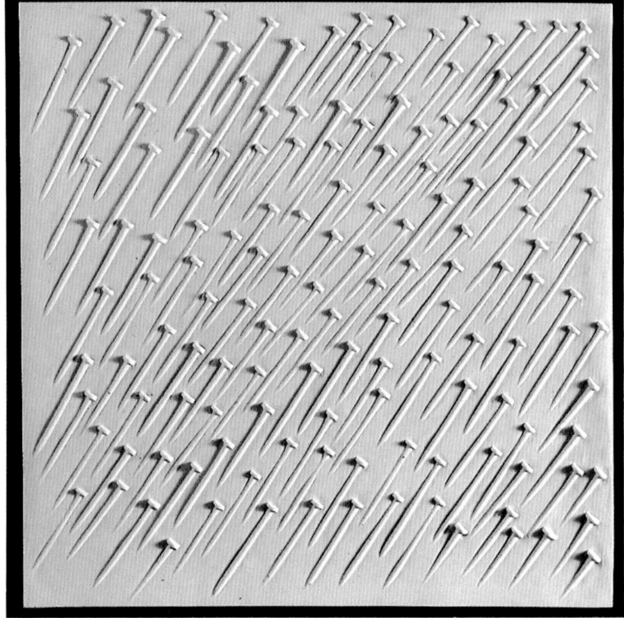

White Rain
Designed by Günther Uecker, limited edition of 100 copies, Rosenthal Studio Line, Relief Series, first made 1968
Lg. x width 45 x 45 cm. Rosenthal Archives, Selb

Relief
Designed by Günther Ferdinand Ris, limited edition of 50 copies, Rosenthal Studio Line, Relief Series, first made 1968
Wooden plate diam. 115/80 cm, depth 12 cm.
Rosenthal Archives, Selb

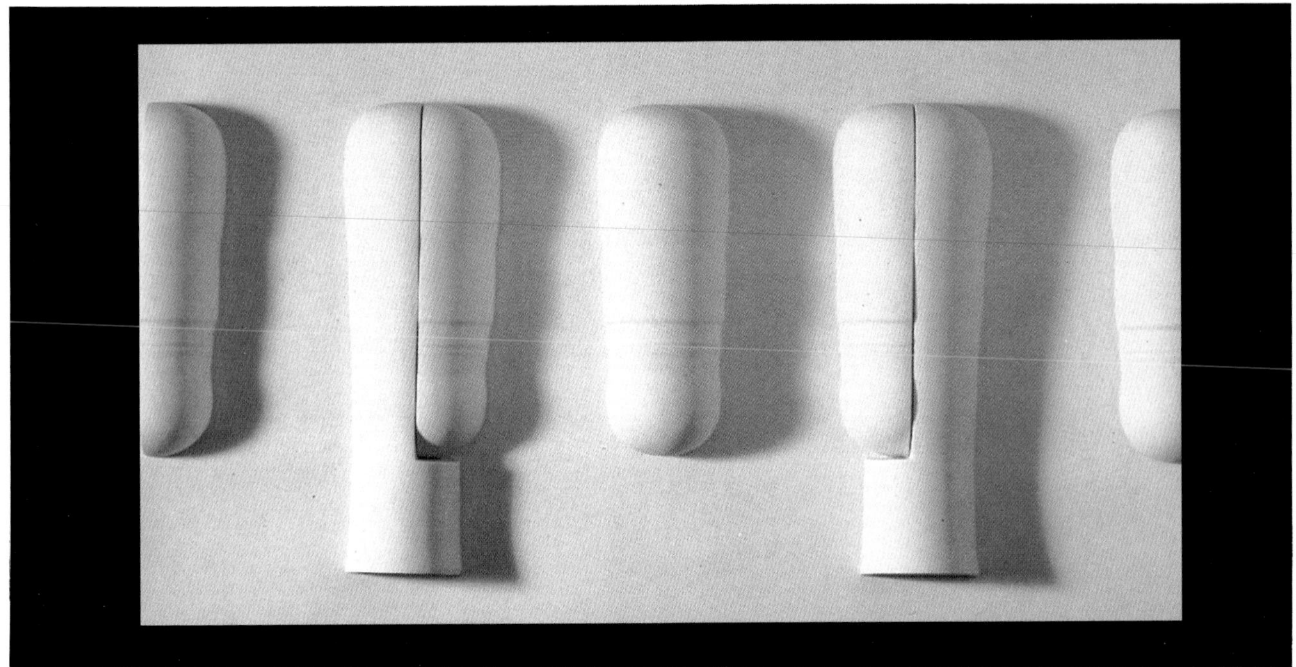

Relief 1967
Designed by Joannes Avramidis, limited edition of 50 copies, Rosenthal Studio Line, Relief Series, first made 1968
Ht. 39 cm, lg. 70 cm. Rosenthal Archives, Selb

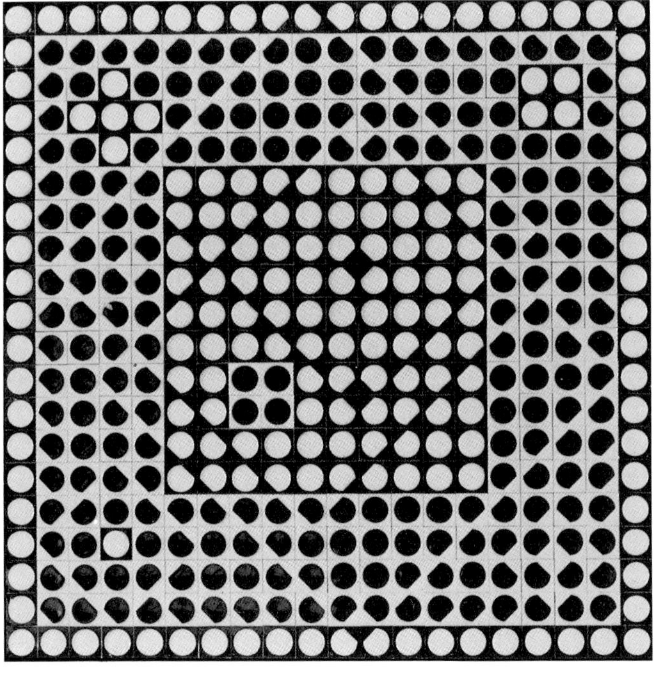

NB 22 Caope
Designed by Victor Vasarely, limited edition of 50 copies, Rosenthal Studio Line, Relief Series, first made 1968
Lg. 200 cm, width 200 cm. Rosenthal Archives, Selb

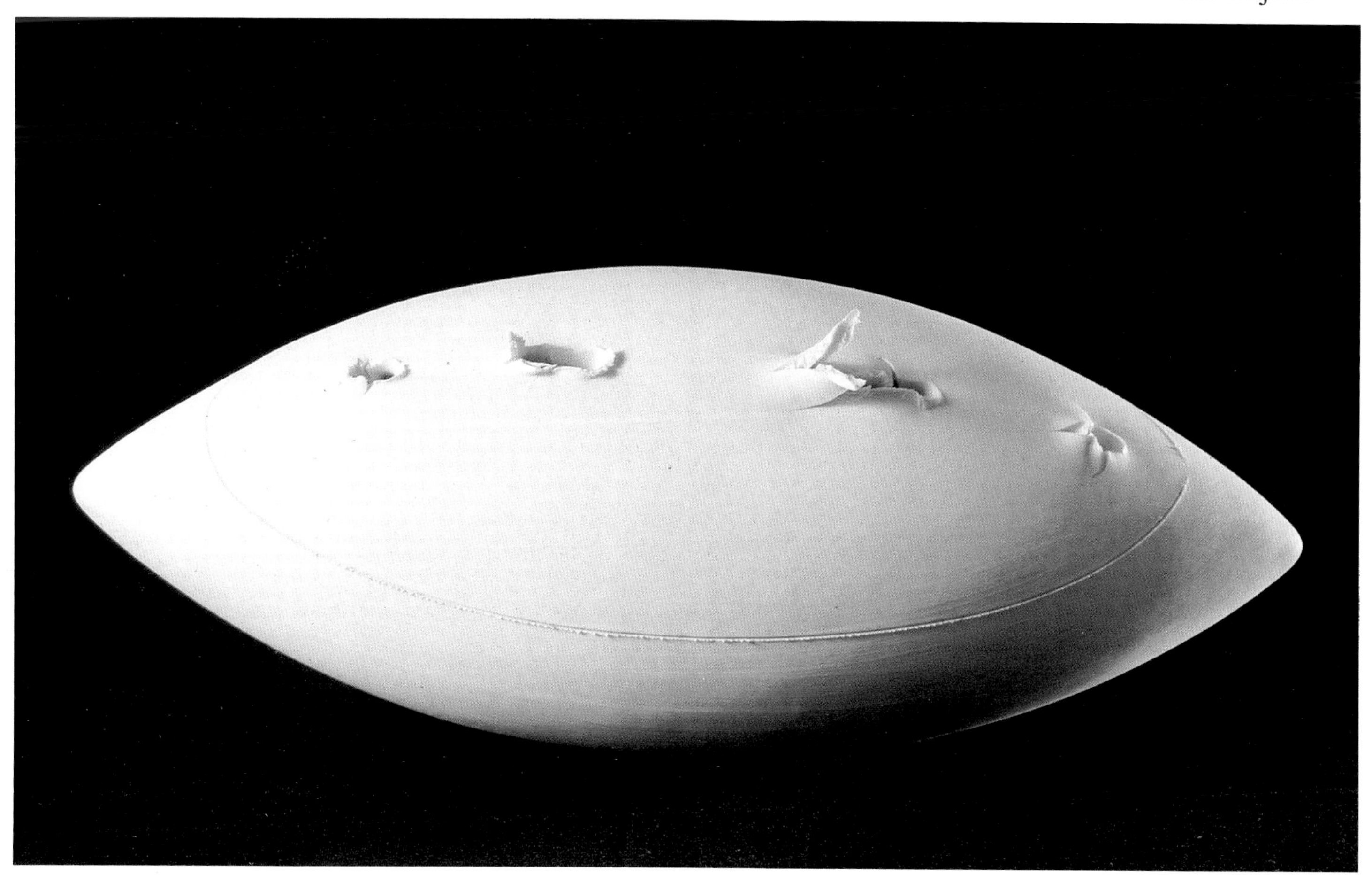

Concetto spaziale ovale
Designed by Lucio Fontana, limited edition of white and black together, 75 copies, Rosenthal Studio Line, Relief Series, first made 1968
Ht. 17 cm, lg. 44.8 cm, width 18.2 cm.
Rosenthal Archives, Selb

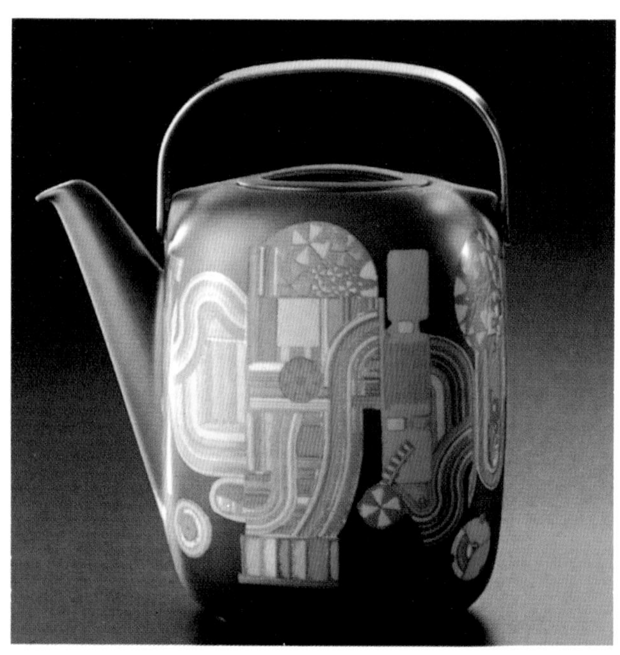

"Suomi" Objects:
1 = Bowl with Lid (upper right)
2 = Bowl (lower left)
3 = Coffeepot (lower right)
4 = Teapot (upper left)

Form designed by Timo Sarpaneva, decoration by Eduardo Paolozzi, 1977, limited edition of 500 copies, Rosenthal Studio Line, first made 1976
Teapot ht. 16.4/11.7 cm. Rosenthal Archives, Selb

"Suomi" Object 1 (Bowl with lid)
Form designed by Timo Sarpaneva, decoration by HAP Grieshaber 1976, limited edition of 500 copies, Rosenthal studio Line, first made 1976
Ht, 21.1/18.2/13.6 cm. Rosenthal Archives, Selb

"Suomi" Object 4 (Teapot)
Form designed by Timo Sarpaneva, relief by Otto Piene 1977, limited edition of 500 copies, Rosenthal Studio Line, first made 1976
Ht. 16/12/11.3 cm. Rosenthal Archives, Selb

"Suomi" Object 1 (Covered Bowl)
Form designed by Timo Sarpaneva, decoration by Ernst Fuchs 1979, limited edition of 500 copies, Rosenthal Studio Line
Ht. 21.4/18.8/13.8 cm. Rosenthal Archives, Selb

"Suomi" Object 3 (Coffeepot)
Form designed by Timo Sarpaneva, delief decoration by Salvador Dali, limited edition of 500 copies, Rosenthal Studio Line, first made 1976
Ht. 20.4/16.5 cm. Rosenthal Archives, Selb
At Dali's request, the same pot was decorated with the watch motif for his wife (below).

Coffee Service "Century"
Model no. 8000, Rosenthal Studio Line, first made 1979, designed by Tapio Wirkkala
Coffeepot ht. 22.5/16.3/15 cm, sugarbowl ht. 8/7 cm, cream pitcher ht. 7 cm, cup ht. 6 cm, saucer diam. 14.5 cm.
Rosenthal Archives, Selb

Tea Service "Drop"
Model no. 1282, Rosenthal Studio Line, first made 1971, designed by Luigi Colani
Teapot ht. 10.7 cm, lg. 24.9 cm, sugarbowl ht. 6.2 cm, lg. 13.2 cm, cream pitcher ht. 5 cm, lg. 9.9 cm, cup ht. 4.5 cm, saucer diam. 16.7 cm. Rosenthal Archives, Selb

Coffee and Dining Service "Suomi"
Model no. 7000, Rosenthal Studio Line, first made 1976, designed by Timo Sarpaneva
Coffeepot ht. 20.3/16.5 cm, (sugarbowl ht. 8.9/6.1 cm), cream pitcher ht. 9.3/6.8 cm, cup ht. 5.8 cm, saucer diam. 15.4 cm, ragout tureen ht. 21.5/18.7/13.7 cm, salt and pepper shakers ht. 7.5 cm.
Rosenthal Archives, Selb

Artist Service "Polygon" in four decorations
Model no. 6000, Rosenthal Studio Line, first made 1973, form designed by Tapio Wirkkala, Palladio decoration by Eduardo Paolozzi, 1978 (lower right)
Coffeepot ht. 21.7/20.1 cm, (sugarbowl ht. 7.4/5.6 cm), cream pitcher ht. 8.2 cm, cup ht. 6.7 cm, saucer diam. 13 cm, (cake plate diam. 19.4 cm)

Art Vase
Form designed by Elsa Fischer-Treyden, decoration by Victor Vasarely, 1979, limited edition of 100 copies, Rosenthal Studio Line, first made 1971
Ht. 32.7 cm, diam. 29.5 cm, dp. 13.4 cm. Rosenthal Archives, Selb

Art Vase
Form designed by Elsa Fischer-Treyden, decoration by Victor Vasarely 1979, limited edition of 300 copies, Rosenthal Studio Line, first made 1971
Ht. 28 cm, diam. 25.6 cm, dp. 11.6 cm. Rosenthal Archives, Selb

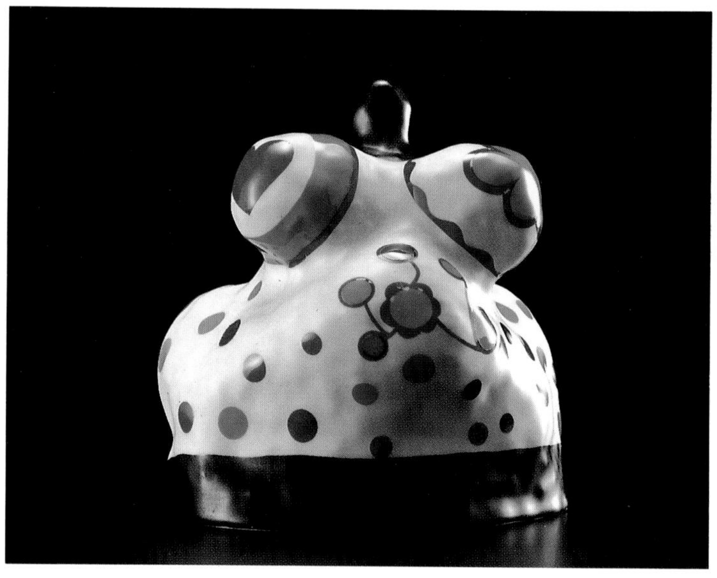

Nana
Form and decoration designed by Niki de Saint Phalle, limited edition of 200 copies, Rosenthal Studio Line, first made 1973
Ht. 12.4 cm. Rosenthal Archives, Selb

Art Vase No. 5
Form designed by Timo Sarpaneva, decoration by Otmar Alt, limited edition of 500 copies, Rosenthal Studio Line, first made 1978
Ht. 27.2 cm. Rosenthal Archives, Selb

Rainbow Object
Form and decoration designed by Otto Piene, limited edition of 200 copies, Rosenthal Studio Line, Rosenthal Gallery, first made 1974
Ht. 18.4 cm, lg. 46 cm, dp. 13.3 cm.
Rosenthal Archives, Selb

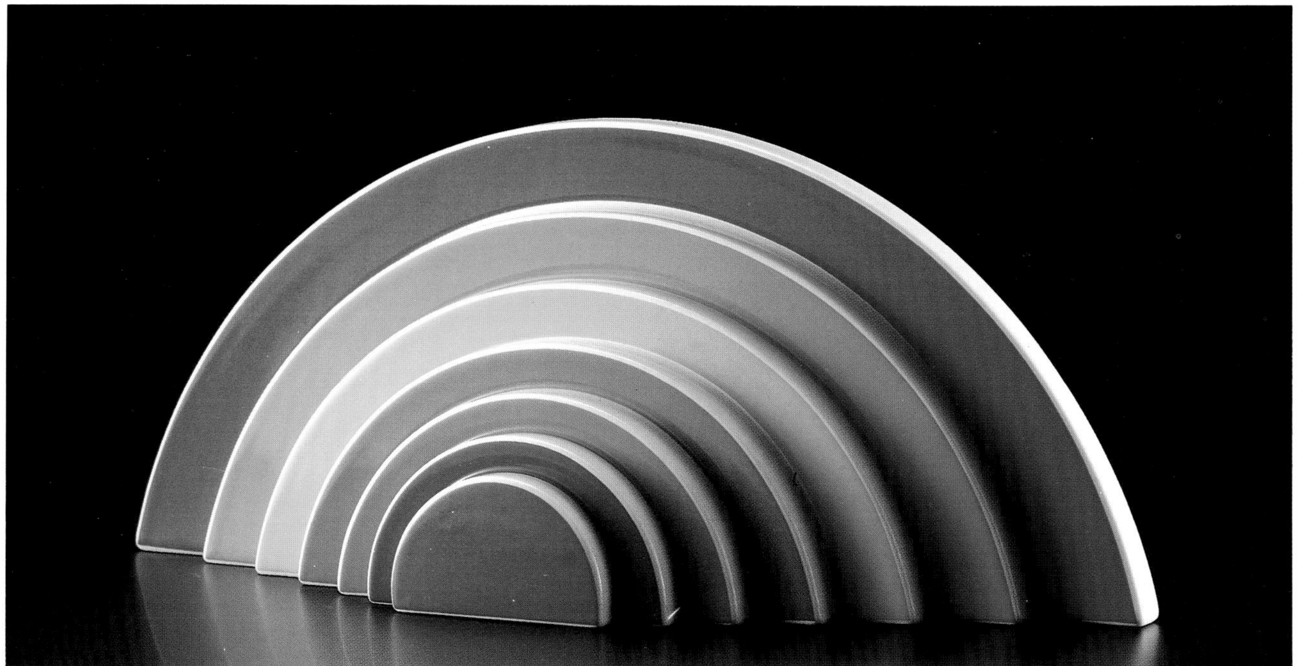

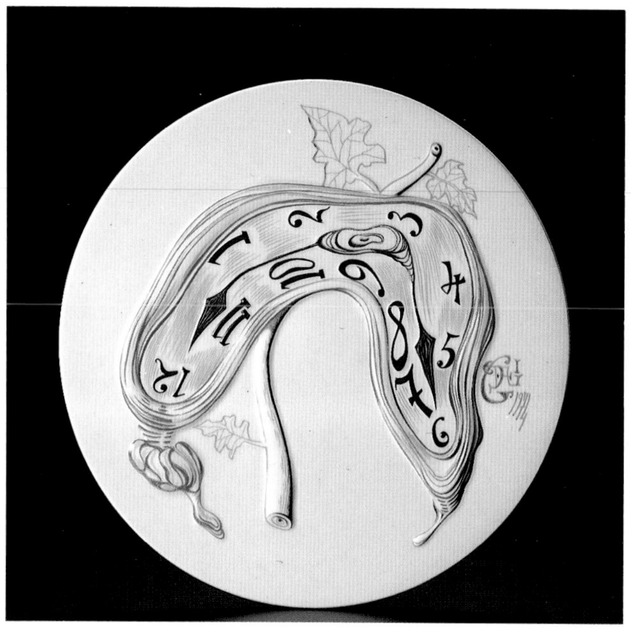

Year Plate 1976
Decoration designed by Salvador Dali 1974, limited edition of 3000 copies, Rosenthal Studio Line, first made 1976
Diam. 34.4 cm. Rosenthal Archives, Selb

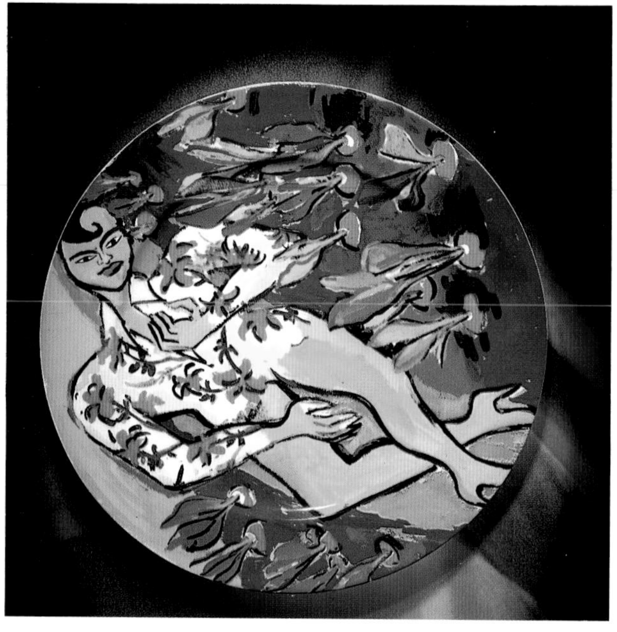

Artist Plate
Designed by Elvira Bach, limited edition of 2000 copies, Rosenthal Studio Line-Gallery Collection, first made 1993
Diam. 30 cm. Rosenthal Archives, Selb

Year Plate 1971
Designed by Tapio Wirkkala 1971, limited edition of 3000 copies, Rosenthal Studio Line, first made 1971
Diam. 34.4 cm. Rosenthal Archives, Selb

Artist Plate
Designed by Roy Lichtenstein, limited edition of 3000 copies, Rosenthal Studio Line-Gallery Collection, first made 1990.
Diam. 30 cm. Rosenthal Archives, Selb

"Cupola" Artist Espresso Year Cup 1994
Model no. 8600, Rotbühl Works, Selb
Form designed by Mario Bellini 1985,
decoration by Paul Giovanopoulos
Ht. 6.1 cm. Rosenthal Archives, Selb

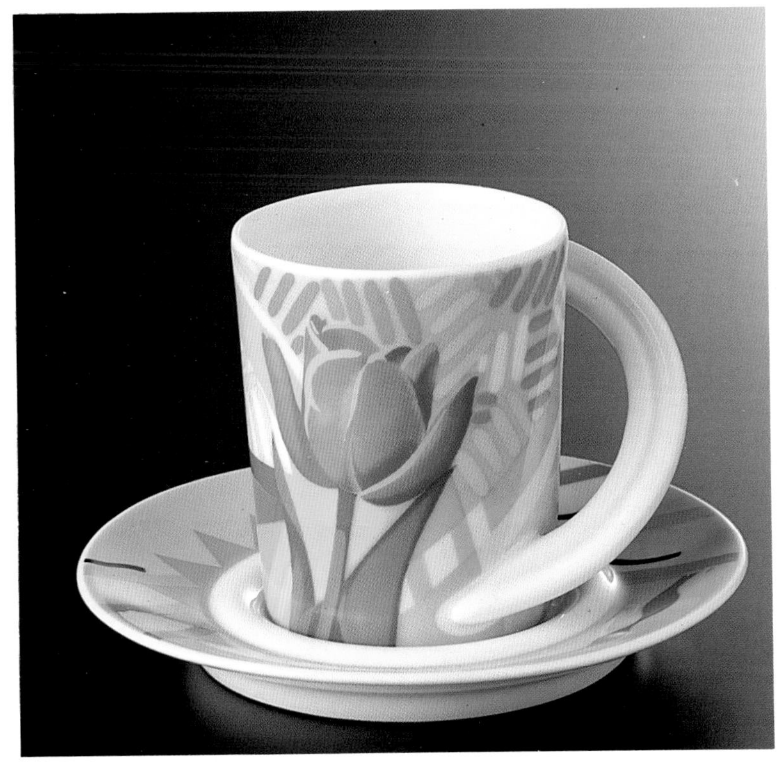

"Cupola" Espresso Collector Cups
Model no. 8600, Rotbühl works, Selb
Form designed by Mario Bellini 1985,
decoration: no. 1-12, 1990; no. 13-16, 1991.
Decoration no. 1 J.-C. de Crousaz; no. 2,
Barbara Brenner; no. 4, Brigitte Doege; no.
5 U. & K. Scheid; no. 17, Salomé; no. 18
Nuriye Akeren
Ht. 6.1 cm. Rosenthal Archives, Selb

Artist Collector Cups
Design of no. 1 Otmar Alt, no. 3 Barbara Brenner, no. 10 Johan van Loon, no. 15 Gilbert Portanier, no. 20 Paul Winderlich, no. 23 Otto Piene, no. 28 Ernst Fuchs *
Rosenthal Studio Line
Rosenthal Archives, Selb.

top row: **No. 1** = Cup ht. 8.1, wd. 12.7, dp. 8.8 cm; Saucer ht. 4.7, wd. 18.6, dp. 10.3 cm.
No. 3 = Cup ht. 9.8, wd. 10.2, dp. 7 cm; Saucer ht. 1.6, wd. 15, dp. 12.5 cm.
No. 10 = Cup ht. 10.2, wd. 7.8, dp. 11.6 cm; Saucer ht. 2.2, diam. 14.8, dp. 17.7 cm
bottom row: **No. 15** = Cup ht. 10.5, wd. 12.1, dp. 21.7 cm.
No. 20 = Cup ht. 11.5, wd. 6, dp. 10.1 cm; Saucer ht. 2.3, diam 15.6 cm.
No. 23 = Cup ht. 10.6, wd. 11.5 cm; Saucer diam. 14.1 cm.

"Mythos" Artist Espresso Year Cup 1994
Model no. 9000, Rotbühl works, Selb
Form designed by Mario Bellini, decoration by Daniel Groen
Cup ht. 7.7 cm, saucer diam. 12.1 cm
Rosenthal Archives, Selb

"Avenue"
Model no. 9200, Rotbühl works, Selb
First made 1992, designed by frogdesign
Rosenthal Archives, Selb

Coffee and Dining Service "Cupola"
Model no. 8600, Rotbühl works, Selb
First made 1985, designed by Mario Bellini
Coffeepot ht. 26.6/22.5 cm, cream pitcher ht. 10.3/7.4 cm, sugarbowl ht. 9.5/6.1 cm, cup ht. 7.9 cm, saucer diam. 16 cm.
Rosenthal Archives, Selb

"Mythos"
Model no. 9000, Rotbühl works, Selb, first made 1991, designed by Paul Wunderlich, Rosenthal Archives, Selb

Dining Service "Il Faro"
Model no. 9400, Rotbühl works, Selb, first made 1994, form designed by Aldo Rossi, decoration by Yang
Coffeepot ht. 24.5/16.5 cm, pitcher square ht. 11.6 cm/round 10.5 cm, sugarbowl ht. 15/7 cm, cup ht. 5.5 cm, saucer diam. 15.5 cm. Rosenthal Archives, Selb

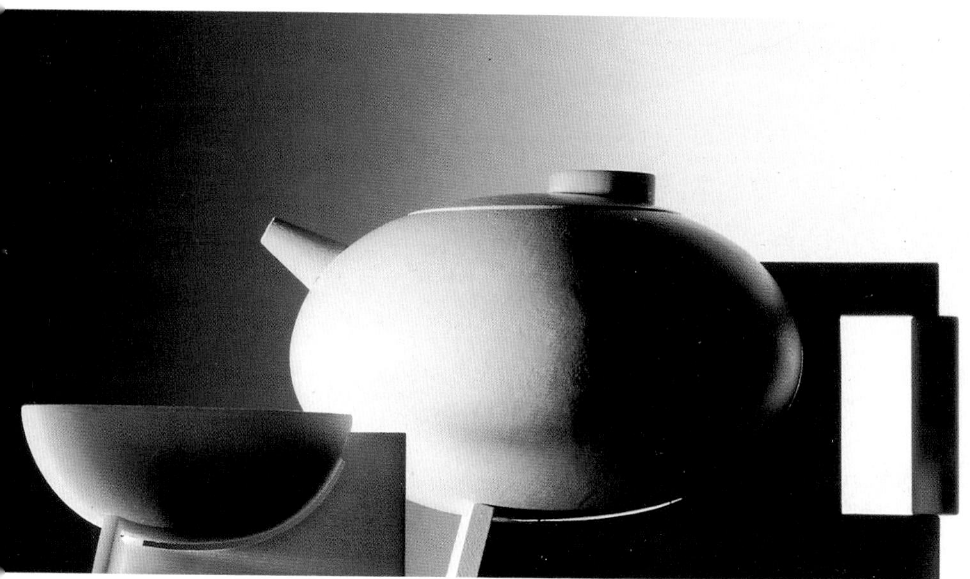

Tea Service "Naomi"
Model no, 1289, Rotbühl works, Selb
First made 1994, designed by Bernhard Gutter
Rosenthal Archives, Selb

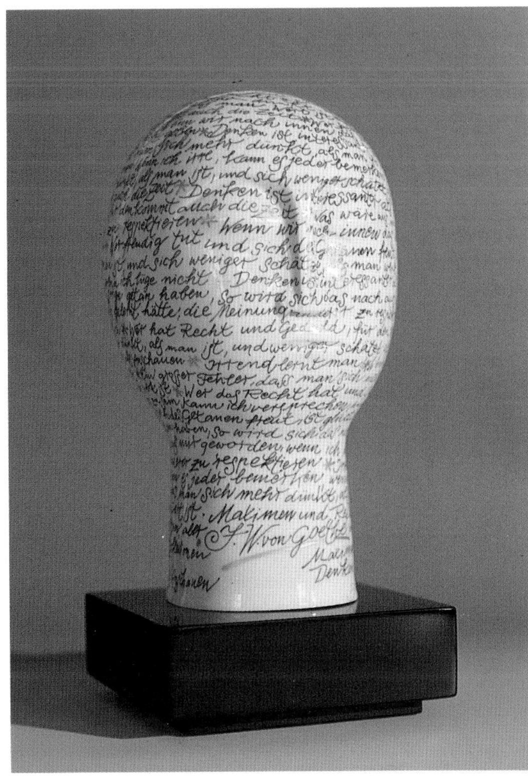

Head, Porcelain Object
Designed by Janos Kass, limited edition of 100 copies, Rosenthal Studio Line, first made 1987
Rosenthal Archives, Selb, photo by Rudolf Majonica, Munich

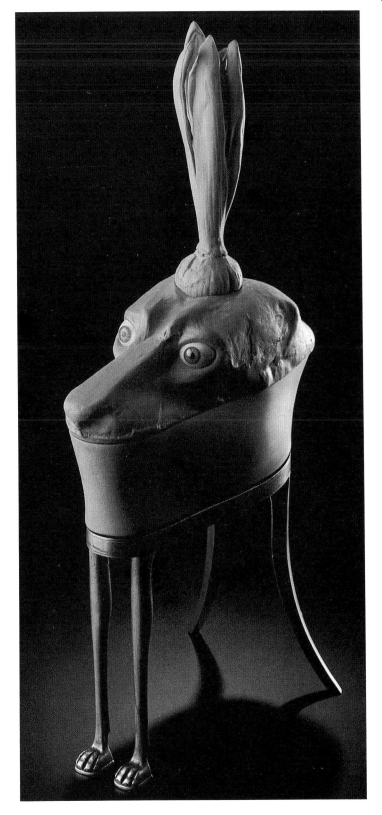

Anubis
Designed by Paul Wunderlich, limited edition of 100 copies, Rosenthal Studio Line-Gallery Collection, first made 1980
Ht. 49 cm. Rosenthal Archives, Selb

Onda construtta
Design by Marcello Morandidi, limited edition of 100 copies, Rosenthal Studio Line-Gallery Collection, first made 1980
Ht. 24 cm. Rosenthal Archives, Selb

Flowering Tree
Designed by Brigitte and Martin Matschinsky-Denninghoff, limited edition of 50 copies, Rosenthal Studio Line-Gallery Collection, first made 1980
Ht. 36 cm. Rosenthal Archives, Selb

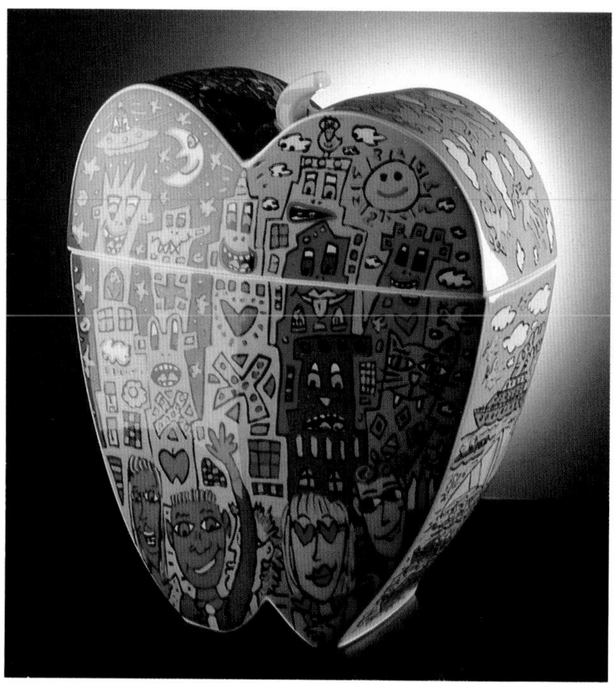

Big Apple Box
Designed by James Rissi, limited edition of 500 copies, Rosenthal Studio Line-Gallery Collection, first made 1995
Ht. 21.7/15 cm, wd. 20.2 cm.
Rosenthal Archives, Selb

Bowl Tissu
Designed by Alan Whittaker, limited edition of 500 copies, model no. 3512, Rosenthal Studio Line, first made 1980
Ht. 16 cm with base/14 cm. Rosenthal Archives, Selb

Man's Head on Pedestal, Portrait of a Young Man
Designed by Paul Wunderlich, limited edition of 99 copies, Rosenthal Studio Line, first made 1993
Rosenthal Archives, Selb, photo by Rudolf Majonica, Munich

Tigerman, Porcelain Object
Designed by Salomé, limited edition of 75 copies, Rosenthal Studio Line, first made 1992
Rosenthal Archives, Selb, photo by Rudolf Majonica, Munich

Ars Poetica
(far left) Designed by Jiri Kolar, limited edition of 1000 copies, Rosenthal Studio Line, first made 1986
Rosenthal Archives, Selb, photo by Rudolf Majonica, Munich

Palio black, Porcelain Object
(near left) Designed by Sandro Chia, limited edition of 125 copies, Rosenthal Studio Line, first made 1989
Rosenthal Archives, Selb, photo by Rudolf Majonica, Munich

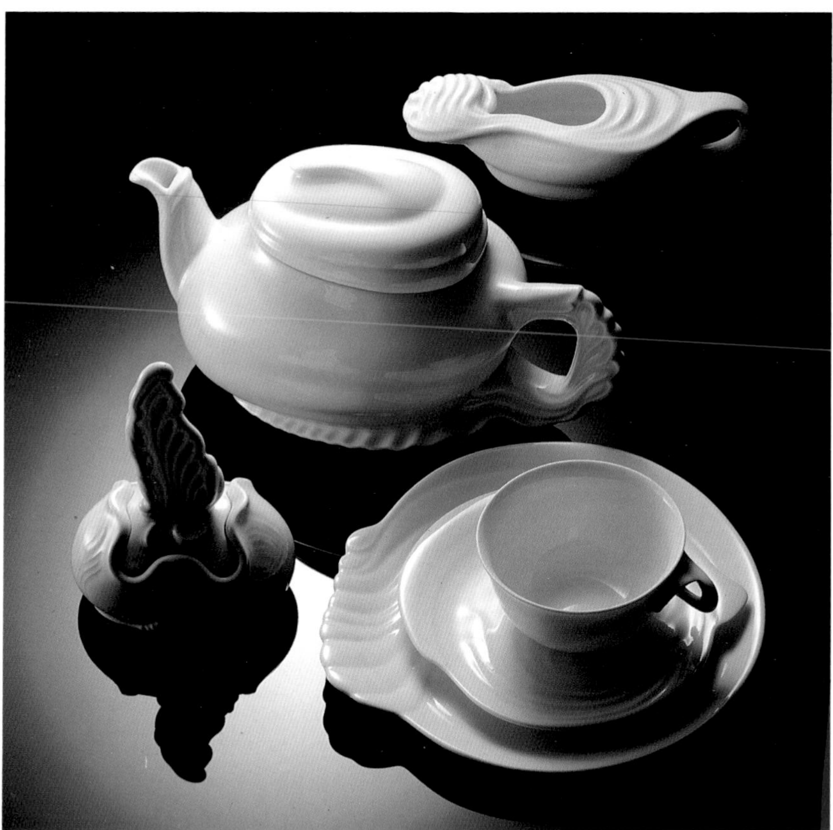

Tea Service "Magic Sea"
Designed by Ernst Fuchs, limited edition of 500 copies (white and underglaze blue), model no. 7500
Rosenthal Studio Line-Gallery Collection, first made 1980
Teapot ht. 14/10.4 cm, wd. 27.5 cm, sugarbowl ht. 14.9/6.8 cm, cream pitcher ht. 6.4 cm, wd. 19.2 cm, cup ht. 5.3 cm, saucer diam. 17.5 cm.
Rosenthal Archives, Selb

Tea Service
Designed by Roy Lichtenstein, limited edition of 100 copies, Rosenthal Studio Line-Gallery Collection, first made 1984
Teapot ht. 17.2/14.3 cm, pitcher ht. 8 cm, sugarbowl 12/9 cm, cup ht. 5.8 cm, saucer diam. 15.5 cm.
Rosenthal Archives, Selb

Collectors Tips

For everyone who would like to collect porcelain, this rule is valid:

First inform yourself, then buy. You can inform yourself from reliable literature on the subject, such as is listed in the bibliography of this book. If the books you seek are out of print, you can withdraw them from the nearest large library.

Unfortunately, there is no periodical solely devoted to porcelain. Thus the interested person must turn to art and antiques publications (like *Antiquitätenzeitung* or *Weltkunst*) which dealers also read. In them you will find information on many other antiques, but also reports and advertisements that will be of use to you.

In general, it is worthwhile to talk with dealers. Note: *with the serious dealer*. But how does one recognize him? Surely not by the fact that his shop is stuffed to the ceiling with "antiques." Whoever talks with several dealers will slowly develop a feel for who gives him sensible answers and who does not. One can, for example, visit several dealers and ask what one can expect with a reasonable budget if one, for example, likes to collect dancer figurines.

Many collectors specialize from the beginning, according to personal interests and ready cash, on a certain type, such as Art Nouveau, Art Deco, the fifties, animals, women, Moors, colors, or vases. There is not much point in judging by the current prices and fashions alone, since fashions are known to change quickly.

Whoever wants to buy at auctions should gain experience. It is best to make a "dry run" at first and visit auctions just to learn. At first dealers often bid too; they like to go to auctions because they know values and have the chance to buy at low prices. When one bids along with dealers, it can happen that the dealers suddenly stop bidding before one notices it--that can happen very fast--, and one then has possession of a piece that, on reflection, was too expensive.

For that reason, here is a rule for auctions:

Always look at the items before the auction, and then set oneself a limit.

Those who know auctions well, though, often buy for less there than from a dealer.

The collector should try to find out, when possible, when an object was first made (see the lists in this book), but also how long it was in production, or if it was put back into production later. Even the Rosenthal archives do not always have complete information on this. The trademarks can give you your first clue (see the trademark table on page 133).

Details of shape and decoration can change over the course of time, including from one piece to another. Changes in shape are due to technical modification. It can be especially important to know whether an object was included in the "Classic Rose Collection" in the last few decades (see also the trademarks table on page 133). Such reissues surely indicate the popularity of an object, but are obviously worth less than objects from the old original production. Sometimes reissues also show changes in relief and decoration which even the layman can recognize.

Many models appeared in various sizes. Here too, more precise information is not easy to obtain.

The collector of Rosenthal porcelain still has the advantage of knowing that no counterfeits are known to date. But one should look for signs of damage. Even first-class porcelain can be repaired so well today that even a specialist cannot detect the fault with the naked eye. For that he needs an ultra-violet light, which may be too expensive for the collector. A serious dealer also guarantees his wares after they are sold.

But there are other faults besides repaired breakage, such as fire damage, color loss, small bubbles, etc. These faults can be recognized if one takes the trouble.

One should not buy damaged objects; or, if one does, a price reduction of about 50% is called for. One does not find such goods at a serious dealer's shop anyway, but more probably at a flea market or a smaller, regional auction house.

A particular problem involves undecorated whiteware. There are undecorated whiteware pieces, such as the Rosenthal figures by Klimsch, Schliepstein, Steeger and Wenck, that were never painted and that have a particular value precisely as whiteware. For all other objects, such as all Art Deco porcelain, whiteware is worth about 50% less than the decorationated object.

Anyone who has assembled a large collection should always keep thorough information about his items on file, photograph them in color, and insure them above the household insurance or through special art insurance.

Tips for Dining Services

The following information is based on discussions and letters between Mrs. Elisabeth Hoffmann and the author. Mrs. Hoffmann is the proprietress of the Geschirrbörse Hoffmann shop at Lerchenstrasse 11, 53560 Vettelschoss, Germany, and has in her computer, along with many other porcelain firms, 1300 different Rosenthal services and decorations listed. She has read and authorized this text.

Dining services are bought by two very different groups of customers. The larger group buys them to use them. A second, smaller group, buys services in order to display them in showcases.

The first group generally wants services that, if they are not new, at least show as few signs of wear as possible. For cups with chipped rims or plates with discolorations or glaze cracks do not exactly invite one to enjoy an appetizing meal.

The second group, on the other hand, consists of admirers who are satisfied with services or pieces that show that they have been used. There is always the feeling that one can replace them later with better examples.

These different interests must be kept in mind when dealing with Rosenthal services, because many of their possessors take the attitude that they automatically possess works of art. But the answer to the question of what a service is worth is also strongly influenced by what one has in mind.

What price one should pay for a service depends on a variety of factors. One influential factor is always its relative rarity. This is not just a matter of the model itself, but also of its decoration. A certain model can be produced in great quantities, but can be very rare when painted with a given decoration, and thus this model with this special decoration is more valuable than with any other decoration.

For "normally" widespread services from the period since World War II, and with a "normally" produced printed decoration, this rule of thumb applies: *half the price of a comparable new service*, and this applies without regard for whether the accessories (pots, bowls, tureens, etc.) are included or not.

These are services that generally only interest someone who wants a service to use or wants to expand what he has to serve a greater number of guests. But be careful with individual plates and cups! Whoever wants to expand his service can experience an unpleasant surprise, for individual components are almost always considerably more expensive, in relative terms.

Insurance cases point up this problem: *If a single piece of a complete, valuable service is broken and cannot be replaced, then in place of this piece, an entire new service of like value must be paid for.* On the other hand, though, there are individual pieces that already have their individual value. This is true, for example, of Sarpaneva's "Suomi" service.

A difficulty comes up in learning original production numbers. This turns out to be very difficult or impossible, because even the manufacturer often has no records of production numbers. Here only the experience of prominent collectors and perhaps a few serious dealers will help.

On the other hand, one needs little experience to determine the completeness of a service. Services are counted in terms of twelve, or at least six, cups and plates. This can be determined quickly. An incomplete service with, for example, only five cups, is naturally worth considerably less than a complete one.

Greater age, contrary to a widespread opinion, is not always an indication of high value. Many Rosenthal services were produced for decades, as were the decorations used on them. The year of production can be determined fairly well with the help of the trademarks, but in spite of that, the piece being examined may have been produced for years absolutely unchanged. Here too, only the experience of a collector or dealer, who clips old advertisements from every old magazine and collects old catalogs, will be able to comment by providing an overview.

Anyone who wants to start collecting should be advised to concentrate, for example, on a particular time or the signed pieces by a particular artist. Coffeepots make a good starting place, for they are often "left over" somewhere and thus can be reasonably priced. But please do not start to collect for reasons of speculation! One can take a big loss when one sells objects, especially if one needs money quickly.

What price is "reasonable" is hard to say, because the market for dining services is small. Anyone who has, for example, inherited a service that he does not care for or has no room for may be happy just to get rid of his unloved treasures. But he can just as well be of the opinion that he possesses valuable objects that are worth their weight in gold.

And there are fashion trends. Some very nice dining services gather dust in the shops despite their low prices until, quite unexpectedly, the fashion changes, and incredible prices are suddenly being asked and being paid for the same services. Likewise, events like the opening of Eastern Europe are also hard to predict, but bound to affect the market.

Price Guide for Figures, Ornaments, and Dining Services

These values were collected from various auction catalogs of the last few years, and are arranged alphabetically by artist. The interested person should expect to pay the higher price in the art and antiques trade. Prices are in US dollars.

Human Figures

Aigner, Eros, #73, 1913: $625-935
--, Liebesfrühling, #295, 1913: $935-1125
Antes, Dreaming Girl, no #, 1927: $2370
Bachem, Shepherd and Muse, #1860: $155-250
--, Boy with Dog, #1905: $190-315
Backmund, Man with folded arms, #5016: $190-315
--, Smoker, #5017: $250-375
--, Telephoning Man, #5023: $190-315
--, Lady with Umbrella, #5024: $240-375
--, Telephoning Woman, #5025: $190-315
Bessom, Girls Hand in Hand, no #: $470-625
Beyrer, Bagpiper, #194, 1935: $345
Boess, Ionic Dancer, #201, 1917: $316-810
--, Snake Dancer, #442: $500-935
Caasmann, Faun, #175: $315-625
--, Storming Bacchantes, #190, 1960: $1060
--, Teddy School, #253, 1917: $315-500
--, Magic of Love, #304, 1920: $405-470
--, Faun's Flight, #346: $375-935
--, Ariadne, #346, 1914: $155
--, Gliding Flight, #354: $315-530
--, Playmates, #355: $280
--, Musical Clown, #436, 1916: $315
--, Snail with Elf, #602: $315-500
Charol, Pierrot with Guitar, #78: $750-935
--, Pierrot Standing, #79: $935-1125
--, Dancer, #204 & 222: $935-1250
--, Yvonne, #206a: $315-470
--, Spring, #211a: $315-470
--, Pierrot Lying, #251: $1125-1250
--, Dancing Pair, #289/1: $935-1125
--, Musical Pierrette, #333, 1928: $935
Disney, Mickey Mouse, #493, 554: each $315
Engel, Girl Scholar, #5013: $125-175
Förster, Badajere, #71, 1921: $780
--, Oriental Girl Lying, #126, 1926: $435
--, Snake Dancer, #138, 1926: $780
Friedrich-Gronau, Lilian Harvey, #1667: $315-470
--, Emperor Waltz, #1683: $315-470
--, Deinert, #1714, 1939: $220-345
Fritz, Cherub, #1282, 1283: each $190-280
Grath, Amazon, #519, 1933: $590
Harth, Caruso, #299, 1920: $435
--, Durreiux, #343: $500-935
Himmelstoss, Spring's Awakening, #98: $315-375
--, Tyrolean Boy, #123, 1920: $155-220
--, Faun with Butterfly, #124, 1922: $190-315
--, Hunting Horn Player, #137: $315-375
--, Dutch Girl, #139, 1912: $175-240
--, Tyrolean Girl, #168, 1912: $155-190
--, Bass Violinist, #196: $375-500
--, Round Dance, #210: $625-2060
--, Turk with Bowl, #628, 1927: $935-1030
--, Silene, #682: $435-685
Höfer-Kelling, Accordion Player, #1656, 1937: $530
Holzer-Defanti, Indian Dancer, #53, 1927: $935
--, Harlequin with Drum, #61: $750-935
--, Pierrot and Columbine, #81: $935-1560
--, Harlequin, #471: $935-1560
--, Tschaokiun, #533: $1250-1870
--, Tschaokium, #534, 1919: $2560
--, Dying Swan, #545: $935-1560
--, Pierrot, #549, 1920: $1060
--, Rococo Dancer, no #, 1921: $435
--, Merry March, #551: $750-1060
--, Korean Dance, #566, 1919: $1560-2495
--, Pierrette, #579, 1920: $935-1250
--, Pierrot, #986: $625-750
Kaesbach, Torso Looking Out, #1603, 1941: $315-625
Kittler, Tennis Player, #843: $935-1250
Klimsch, Dancing Girl, #1550: $375-500
--, Crouching Girl, #1581: $315-435
--, Sitting Girl, #1623, 1938: $590-685
Koch, Sitting Woman Act, #1040, 1940: $280
--Meisel?, Moor with Platter, no #, 1900: $315-405
von Langenmantel-Reitzenstein, #206, 1920: $530
Lauermann, Sarotti Moor, #1977: $530-625
Liebermann, Dispute, #35, 1080, 1920: $750-1435
--, High School, #41: $625-750
--, Dancing Girl, #44, 1917: $625
--, Capriccio, #68: $3120-4370
--, Spanish Dancer, #70: $625-810
--, Latin, #72, 1911: $250-435
--, Fright, #74: $470-625
--, Jealousy, #84, 1910: $425
--, Congratulations, #234, 1912: $220-280
--, Faun with Grapes, #298, 1913: $220-280
--, Turtle Mail, #320: $315-435
--, Cellist, #342, 1914: $250-375
--, Faun, #349: $625-750
--, Teasing, #523, 1918: $300-435
--, Two Princesses, #537, 1929: $345
--, Caught, #538, 1927: $780
--, Harlequin with Inkwell, #592: $750-935
Marcuse, Bacchantes, #190: $315-935
--, On the Beach, #294: $315-435
--, Woman in Swimsuit, #294: $315-435
--, Duet, #311, 1913: $1370-1745
--, Cabaret, #328: $1250-1870
--, Grape Carrier, #477: $315-470
--, Snake Dancer, #497: $315-470
Meisel?, Serving Moors, #863-866: $280 each

--, Moor with Accordion, #1056: $405-435
--, Musical Moor, #1057, 1949: $405
--, Soccer Player, #1073: $375-500
Opel, Venus with Parrot, #288: $345-435
Oppel, Day and Night, #775: $625-750
--, The New Day, #778: $530-625
--, Kant Boy, #823: $560-685
--, China Boy, #851: $500-685
--, Newsboy, #1081: $625-750
--, First Aid, #1091, 1930: $315
--, Kathy, #1092: $530-625
--, Grace, #1119: $625-935
Otto, Cherub with Flute, #997, 1931: $280
Rhein, Boy with Book, #5131: $125-250
Röhrig, Newspaper Reader, no #: $810-935
Schelenz, Smoker, #1974: $250-375
--, Drinking Man, #5018: $250-315
Schliepstein, Beethoven, #401: $470-560
--, Swimming Girl, #783: $810-935
--, Prince, Princess, #826, 827: $8,110-9360 together
--, Maned Sheep, no #: $$2500-3745
--, Resting, #936: $500-935
--, Music, #945: $500-625
--, Autumn, #983: $810-935
--, Girl, #1001, 1932: $780
--, Madonna, #1052: $470-530
--, Masks of Man and woman, no #: $375-500 each
Schwartzkopff, Carmen, #425-1: $500-750
Stangl, Seated Woman, #1917: $190-315
--, Madonna, #1919: $235-375
Valentin, Ash Wednesday, #1040: $935-1125
Vierthaler, Lady with Muff, #426: $1125-1250
--, Lady with Dog, #427: $1125-1250
Weiss, Mother and Child, #47: $190-250
Weiss, Start, #835: $375-500
--, Seasons, #1149-52: each $500-625
--, Skier, #1170: $470-560
--, Soccer Player, #1189: $375-500
Wenck, Drinking, #752: $190-375
--, Sleeping Girl, #969: $500-625
Unknown, Clown with Accordion, no #: $315-470
--, Girl Gymnast, #724: $625-750
--, Soldiers and Nurse, between #311 & 400: $315-530
--, Harlequin with Rooster on Back (ornamental clock), ht. 2.75 cm, 1939: $405

Animal Figurines

For animals combined with people, see above. For animals, the following rule of thumb applies, with caution: between $75 and $500, depending on style, color and size.

Caasmann, Budgies, #257, 1916: $435-570
--, Grasshopper, #647: $190-375
Diller, Sneaking Fox, #278: $190-315
Eichwald, Runners, #446, 1930: $405-530
Fischer, Kingfisher, #867: $110-190
Fritz, Heron, #1212, 1950: $625
Geibel, Tiger, #942: $190-315
Heidenreich, Bird of Paradise, #1575: $220-315
--, Dove, #1589, 1943: $435
--, Pair of Doves, #1589, 1950: $1060
--, Greyhounds, #1599: $250-315
--, Scalare, large, #1636: $250-315
--, Bird, #1646: $190-315
--, Siskin, #1653, 1935: $125-155
--, Bird, #1654: $190-315
--, Wild Duck, #1671, 1937: $530
--, Kingfisher, #1678: $220-315
--, Pair of Terriers, #1688, 1941: $315
--, Bird, #1743: $190-315
Himmelstoss, Pair of Ducks, #153: $75-315
--, Duck, #172, 1912: $125-315
--, Pair of Chickens, #218, 1920: $125
--, Group of Sparrows, #1531, 1940: $155
Kärner, Lying Sheep, #196, 1930: $125
--, Lying Deer, #261: $190
--, Young Dachshund, #1247, 1940: $315
--, Sea Lion, #1289, 1934: $280
--, Sneaking Fox, #1538, 1940: $625
Küspert, Butterfly, #1835: $125-315
Küster, Birds, #574-578: $75-190
--, Severin Decoration, Grotesque Animals, #798-803: $125-250
--, Severin Decoration, Grotesque Animals, #913-918: $155-315
--, Polar Bear, #1009: $190-375
Moldenhauer, Parrot, no #, 1940: $250
--, African Yak, #22, 1935: $315
Obermeier, Hazel Mouse, #675: $75-155
--Group of Guinea Fowl, no #, 1950: $625
Röhrig, Sitting Rabbit, #801, 1939: $280
Scheibe, Severin Decoration, Fisch, #772: $125-250
Schliepstein, Deer Mouse, #765: $75-155
Schmitt, Mother Sow, #5083: $155-250
Stangl, Dog, #1953: $155-250
Valentin, Greyhound, #200/1, 1928: $125-155
Zschäbitz, Foh Dog, #912: $190-375
Zügel, Young Magpie, #127: $125-190
--, Pair of Ducks, #151: $250-375
--, Drake, #250: $250-500
--, Lying Cow, #270: $190-250
--, Duck, #352, 1920: $435
--, Lying Lamb, #672, 1929: $315

Unknown, Butterfly, #639: $75-250

Ornamental Objects

Clark, Decorative Vase, ht. 26.5 cm, ca. 1910: $530
Grüner, Decorative Plate (veiled lady), diam. 27.6 cm, ca. 1910: $435
Guldbrandsen, Covered Vase, #542, 1920: $935
Malec, Covered Bowl (Rococo skating scene), ht. 11 cm, ca. 1921: $315
Rosenthal, Ornamental Vase, ht. 14.5 cm, 1927: $65
Vogeler, Christmas Plate (3 Kings), diam. 20.3 cm, 1911: $435
Zumbusch, Wall Plate (cherub with Red Cross flag and two eagle emblems, diam. 21.4 cm., 1915: $250

Unknown, Covered Dish, Butterfly, ht. 6 cm., 1926: $125
--, Covered Vase, ht. 43.8 cm, 1910: $750
--, Punchbowl with foot, silver decoration (flowers, bird of paradise), ht. 17.5 cm, diam. 33 cm., ca. 1930: $500
--, Lamp Standard, ht. 38.2 cm., #849, 1927: $280
--, Writing Implements, 9 x 23 cm., ca. 1920: $280
--, Vase, ht. 14.5 cm., no. 61, ca. 1910: $155
--, Wall Plate, decoration #115/1115. diam. 23 cm., ca. 1910: $280
--, Wall Plate (Zeppelin), diam. 21,7 cm, ca. 1920: $810
--, Ornamental Vase, ht. 20.3 cm., ca. 1907: $220
--, Ornamental Vase, ht. 18.4 cm., ca. 1907: $190
--, Ornamental Vase, ht. 29.3 cm, 1907: $155
--, Ornamental Vase and Bowl, Maria pattern, #?, 1926, together $220
--, Ornamental Vase, ht. 13 cm., #276, 1928: $190
--, Ornamental Vase, ht. 28.8 cm., ca. 1930: $280
--, Ornamental Vase, ht. 28.4 cm, 1940: $155

Examples of Prices for Dining Services

These values derive from the most recent years, and were gathered from the most varying sources. They are alphabetized by the **name** of the service, followed in the parentheses by the **model number**, name of the Rosenthal **factory**, **designer**, and **year** of issue.
For the following services one can, with some caution, apply the following rule: *price when new or latest list price* (ask dealers), but perhaps less:
"Cupola" (8600, Rotbühl Selb, 1985)
"Drop" (1282, Selb, Colani, 1971)
"Lotus" (800, Plössberg, Wiinblad/Wirkkala, 1964-67)
"Mythos" (9000, Rotbühl Selb, 1991)
"Suomi" (7000, Rotbühl Selb, Sarpaneva, 1976)
"Magic Sea" (limited, Fuchs, 1980)

For the following services the prices in the trade and at auctions have varied in recent years between these ranges:
- For Single-color, painted and printed decorations:

Coffee service: 150-1000
Dining service: 200-1500
Per coffee or dining setting: 20-200
- For lavish hand-painted decorations or precious-metal designs:
Coffee sercice: 250-3000
Dining service: 400-5000
Per coffee or dining setting: 50-300
"Berlin" (3000, Kronach, Baumann, 1959)
"Composition" (1350, Plössberg, Wirkkala, 1963)
"Duo" (1270, Plössberg, Pozzi, 1968)
"Fortuna" (650, Plössberg, Fischer-Treyden, 1956)
"Helena" (660-670), Selb, von Wersin, 1936)
"Lotus" (800, Plössberg, Wiinblad/Wirkkala, 1964-67)
"Plus" (5000, Rotbühl Selb, Karnagel, 1970)
"Polygon" (6000, Rotbühl Selb, Wirkkala, 1973)
"Romanze" (1250, Rotbühl Selb, Wiinblad/Wohlrab. 1959-60)
"Variation" (2500, Selb, Wirkkala, 1962)
"2000" (2000, Selb, Latham/Loewy, 1954)

For the following services the prices in the trade and at auctions have varied in recent years between these ranges. The lowest range is for easily exchangeable decorations, which can be found almost identical among pieces from all the firms, such as the gold rim and a little printed decoration above it. The higher and highest ranges are for hand-painted decorations.

Coffee service: 600-10,000
Dining service: 800-15,000
Per coffee or dining setting: 100-500

"Aida old" (320 white, 360 ivory, Plössberg, Koch,1937)
"Donatello old" (250, Selb, Reinstein/Rosenthal, 1905)
"Madeleine" (240, Selb, 1903)
"Sanssouci old" (480 white, 490 ivory, Selb, Bayreuther, 1926)
"Tirana" and "Li" (520, Selb, Fleischmann, 1927)
"Versailles" (120, Selb, 1894)

A few more examples
"Berlin," Friedrichstrasse decoration, no demand at present, coffee service: $32 each
--, dining service: $64 each
--, Coffee or tea service: $593
Composition," olive decoration with second color gray, not popular now: $32-64 per setting

"Donatello old," coffee service: $2,400
--, tea service: $936-1123
--, Fruit dishes, 6 pieces, diam. 22 cm., ca. 1920: 700-850.
--, Cordial decoration, plentiful: $18-31 per setting.
"Tirana," coffee service, 27 pieces: $560
"2000," grazing decoration, plentiful, coffee service: $125-220

Trademarks and Signets since 1887

These tables were taken from the exposition catalog *Rosenthal, 100 Years of Porcelain*, Kestner Museum, Hanover, see Bibliography, as well as the following explanations:

The factory marks were completed with underglaze bottom stamps after 1957.

Unless otherwise indicated, the marks are always in green under the glaze. Not all pictures are to the same scale.

Indications of years were only made public until 1949. More precise data (such as when the individual marks were used before the introduction of year markings) is not possible.

At the same time throughout, slightly different trademarks were used; this also applies to the time after the introduction of year markings.

Signets are always printed over the glaze, usually in black and gold.

The artists' signatures are likewise not to scale. Only accurate, not written-out names in brush writing or blind stamping are involved.

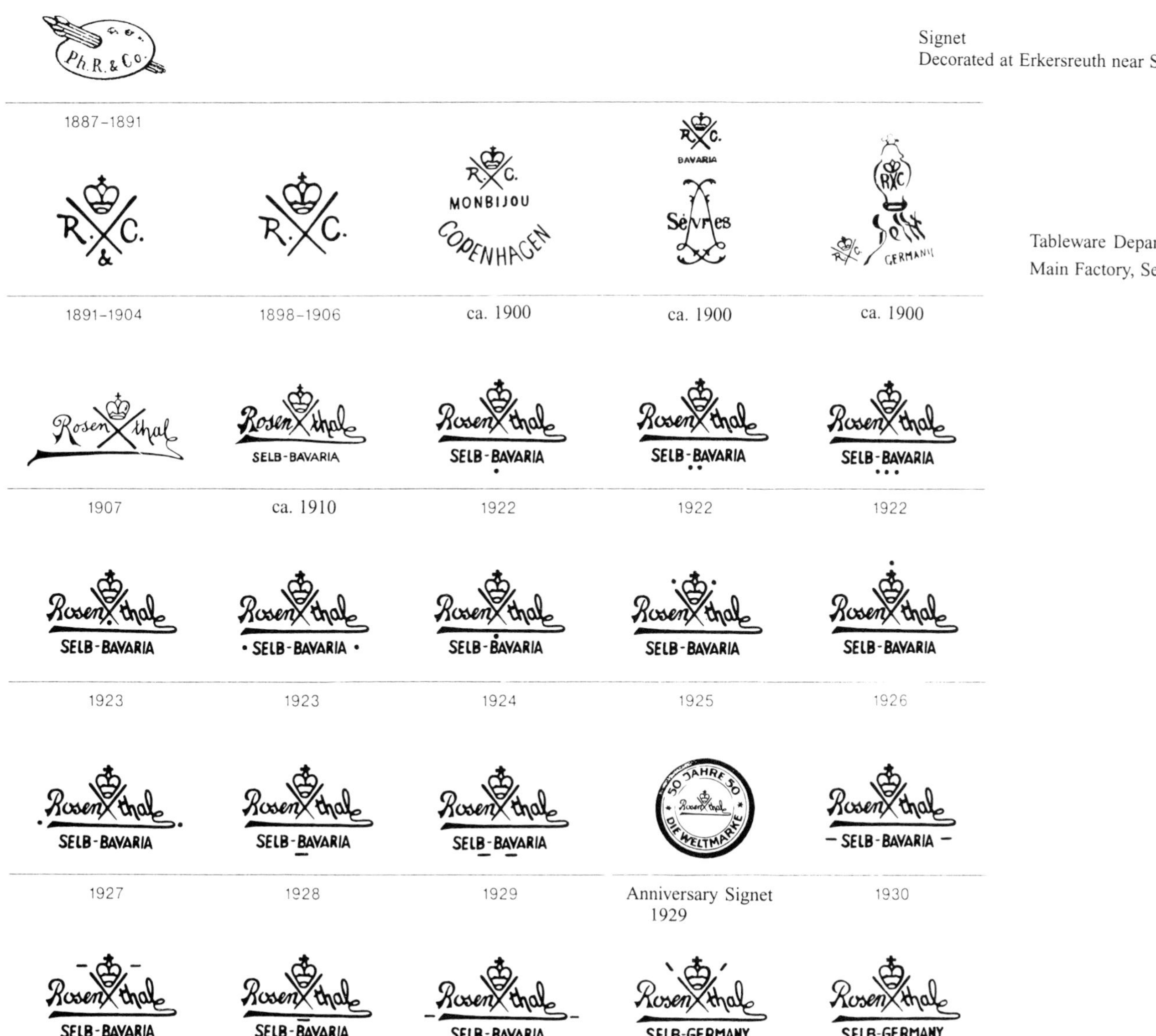

Signet
Decorated at Erkersreuth near Selb

Tableware Department
Main Factory, Selb

1931 1932 1933 1934 1935

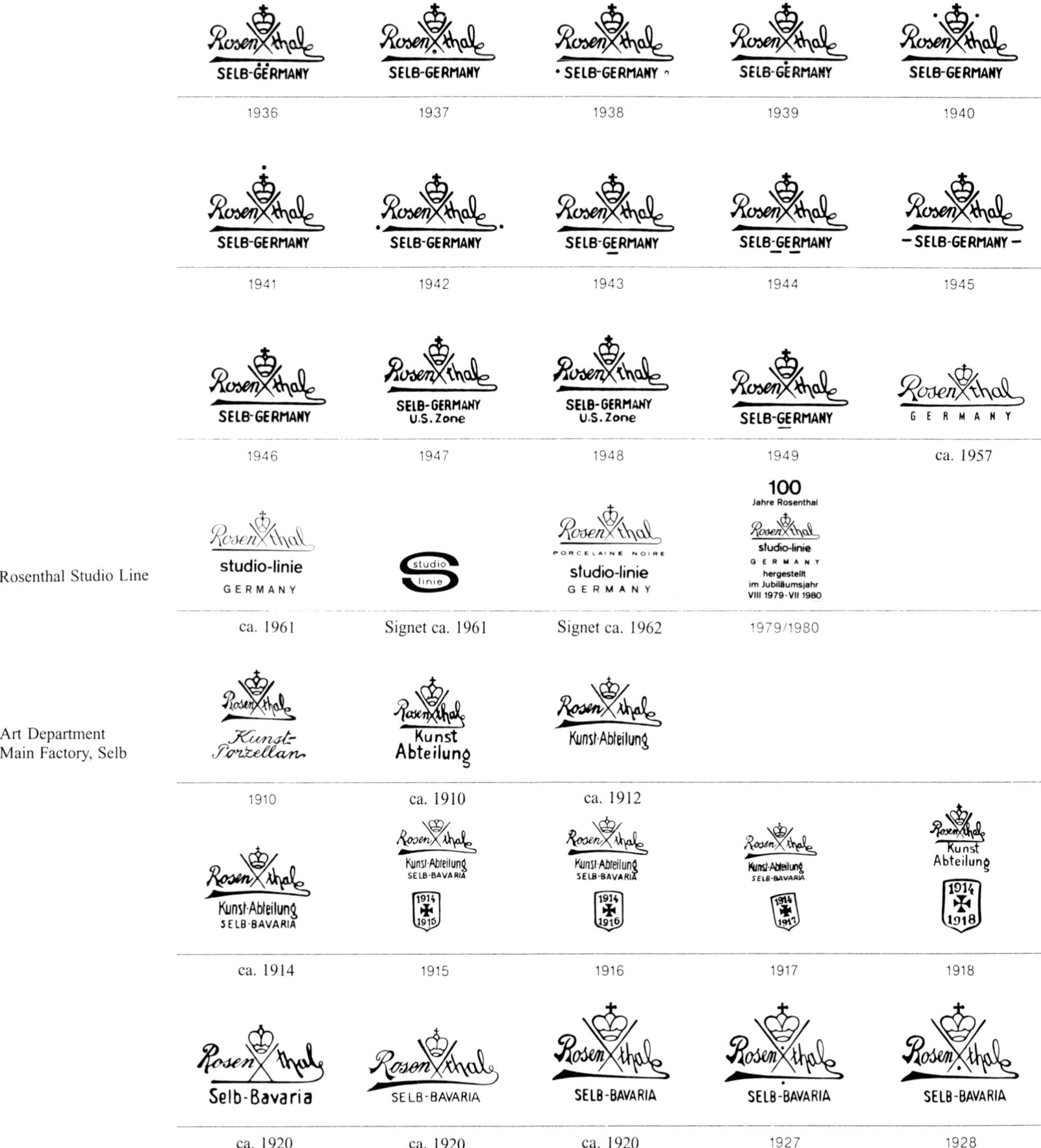
SELB-GERMANY
1936
1937
1938
1939
1940
1941
1942
1943
1944
1945
SELB-GERMANY U.S. Zone
1946
1947
1948
1949
GERMANY
ca. 1957
Rosenthal Studio Line
studio-linie GERMANY
ca. 1961
studio linie
Signet ca. 1961
PORCELAINE NOIRE studio-linie GERMANY
Signet ca. 1962
100 Jahre Rosenthal studio-linie GERMANY hergestellt im Jubiläumsjahr VIII 1979-VII 1980
1979/1980
Art Department
Main Factory, Selb
Kunst-Porzellan
1910
Kunst Abteilung
ca. 1910
Kunst-Abteilung
ca. 1912
Kunst-Abteilung SELB-BAVARIA
ca. 1914
1914 1915
1915
1914 1916
1916
1914 1917
1917
Kunst Abteilung 1914 1918
1918
Selb-Bavaria
ca. 1920
SELB-BAVARIA
ca. 1920
ca. 1920
1927
1928

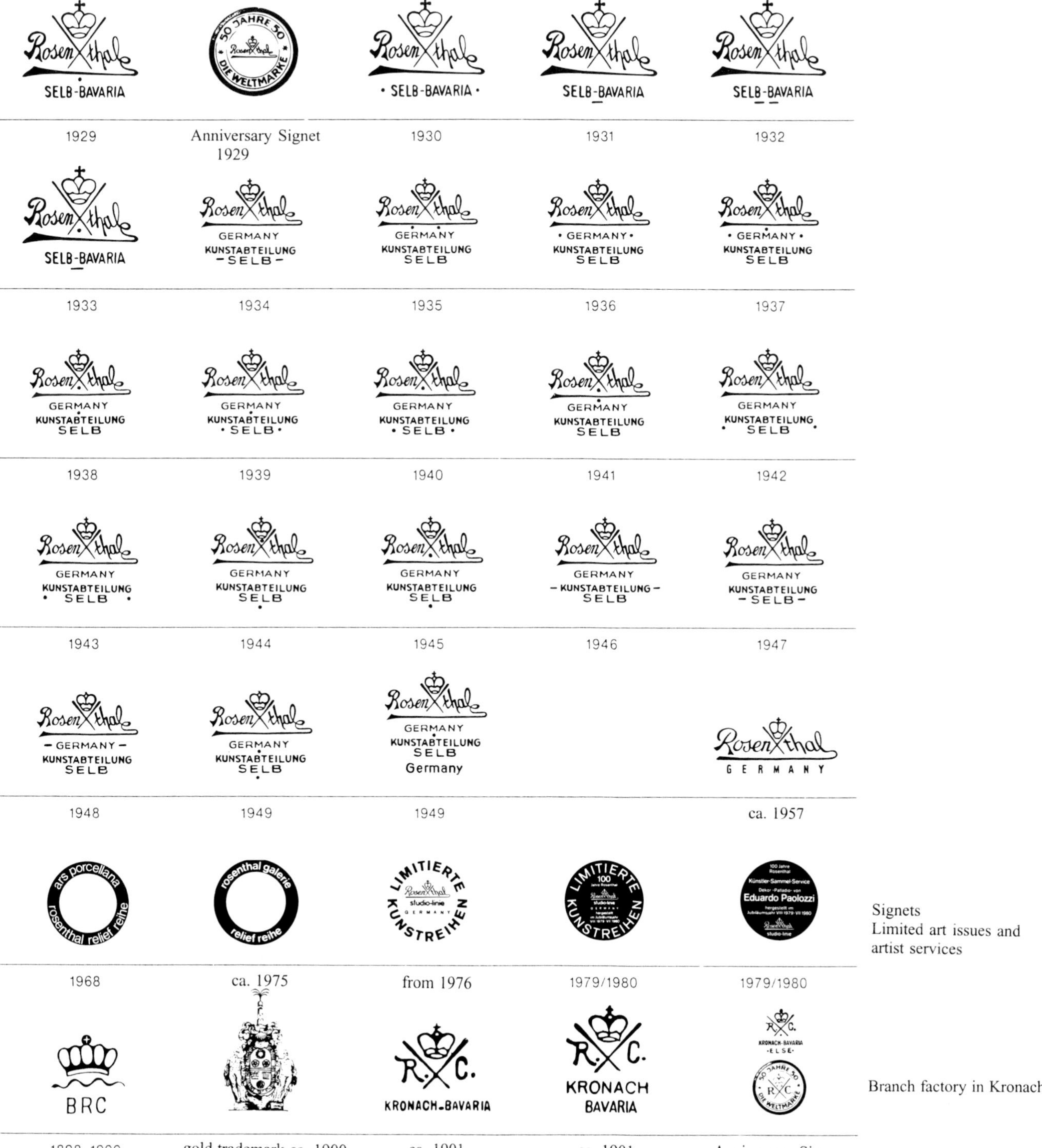

1929	Anniversary Signet 1929	1930	1931	1932
1933	1934	1935	1936	1937
1938	1939	1940	1941	1942
1943	1944	1945	1946	1947
1948	1949	1949		ca. 1957
1968	ca. 1975	from 1976	1979/1980	1979/1980
1898–1900	gold trademark ca. 1900	ca. 1901	ca. 1901	Anniversary Signet 1929

Signets
Limited art issues and artist services

Branch factory in Kronach

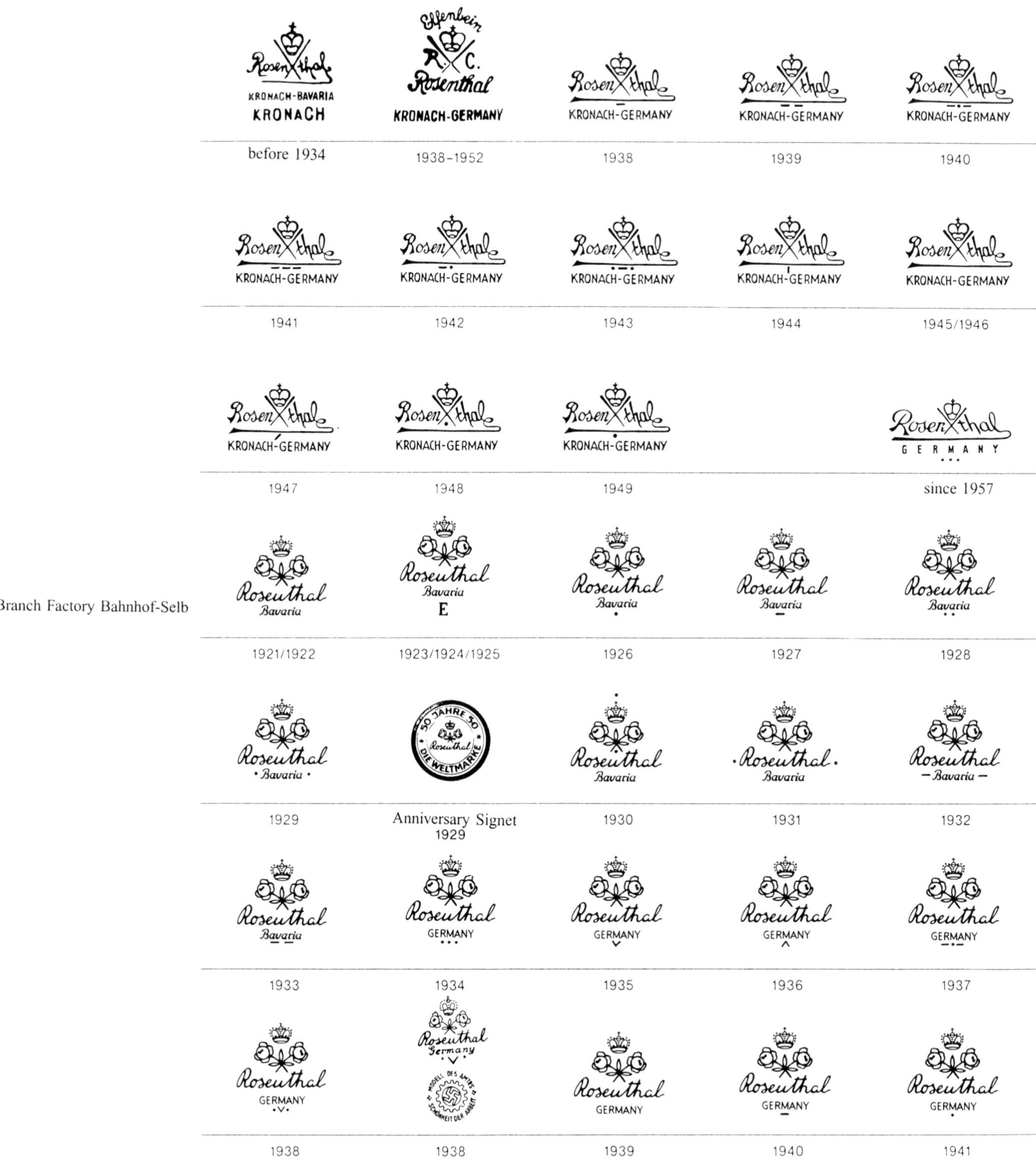
KRONACH-BAVARIA
KRONACH
Elfenbein
R. C.
Rosenthal
KRONACH-GERMANY
before 1934
1938–1952
1938
1939
1940
1941
1942
1943
1944
1945/1946
1947
1948
1949
GERMANY
since 1957
Branch Factory Bahnhof-Selb
Rosenthal
Bavaria
E
1921/1922
1923/1924/1925
1926
1927
1928
50 JAHRE 50
DIE WELTMARKE
1929
Anniversary Signet 1929
1930
1931
1932
1933
1934
1935
1936
1937
Germany
1938
1938
1939
1940
1941

1942 | 1943–1948 | 1949 | 1950 | 1951

SELB-PLÖSSBERG GERMANY | SELB-PLÖSSBERG GERMANY | SELB-PLÖSSBERG • GERMANY •

1952 | 1953 | 1954 | 1955 | 1956

1957 | since 1957

Relief mark since 1925 | Decoration Signet since 1930

1931 | 1932 | 1933 | 1934 | 1935

Branch Factory
Bahnhof-Selb, Ceramics

ROSENTHAL KERAMIK GERMANY

1936 | 1937 | 1938/1939/1940 | 1941

since 1975

Classic Rose Collection

Underglaze green design signets

1903

1904

Entwurf von
Ph. Rosenthal

ca. 1925

Painters' signatures

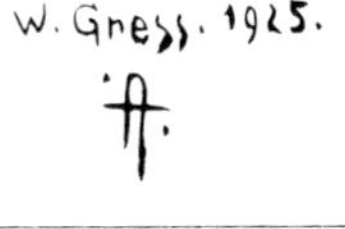

W. Gress

Otto Keitel

Julius-V. Guldbrandsen

Walter Mutze

Kurt Severin

Fritz v. Stockmayer

Tono Zoelch

Sculptors' signatures

Gustav Oppel

Richard Scheibe

Milly Steger

Ludwig Vierthaler

Factory Markings in underglaze bottom stamping, since 1957

Waldershof
no special
marking

Selb, tableware
department, one
dot under GERMANY

Plössberg
two dots under
GERMANY

Kronach
three dots
under GERMANY

Landstuhl
four dots under
GERMANY

Selb, Art Department
one horizontal line
under GERMANY

Thomas on Kulm
three horizontal lines
under GERMANY

Lists of Models

Dining Services with the Rosenthal Trademark to 1994

These dining services were made at the Rosenthal factories at Selb, Rotbühl-Selb, Kronach and Plössberg. This list was taken, to a great extent, from the book *Die Porzellangeschirre des Rosenthal Konzerns 1891-1979* by Bernd Fritz (see Bibliography), but extended to 1995.

The dining service types are abbreviated:
C: chocolate service
H: hotel service
K: coffee service
M: mocha service
S: dining service
T: tea service

No.	Name	Type Designer	Year
From the Rosenthal Selb Factory			
309	Rokoko	KT	1891
329	Stabhenkel	KT	1891
---	Rokoko/Louis XIV	KTCS	1892
93	Pompadour	KT	1893
94	Dolten/Louis Philippe	C	1894
100	Sanssouci	KTS	1894
110	Empire	KT	1894
120	Versailles	KTS	1894
130	Monbijou	KTS	1896
140	Meissen	KT	?
150	Tilly	KTS	1897
160	Empire	S	1898/1900
170	Carmen	KTS	1898
175	Flora	C	1899
176	Flora	C	?
180	Louis XVI	S	1899
181	Pâte sur Pâte	KT	1899
190	Iris	KTS	1900
195	Conical	K	1901
196	Conical with shell rim	K	1901
200	Secession	KTS	1901
201	Pensée	C	1901
207	Alice	KTC	1901
208	Montreux (bowls)		1902
209	Ellen/Malmaison	KTCS	1902
210	Claire	KC	1902
217	Hertha	S	1902 Friling
220	St. Cloud	KS	1902
230	Botticelli	KTS	1902 Reinstein
240	Madeleine	KTCS	1903
245	Miramare	C	1903
250	Donatello	KTS	1905 Reinstein/ Rosenthal
260	---	?	1906
270	Tizian	S	1906
280	Empire new	KTC	1906
290	Feston/Saarland	S	1907/27
300	Feston	KT	1907
310	Renaissance	K	1908
320	Isolde	KTS	1909 Rosenthal
330	---	K	?
340	Series issue, oval	KT	1909
350	Renaissance	S	1909
380	Kaffee Haag	H	1911
390	Canova	KTS	1913/19 Rosenthal
643	Graham Export Line	MTS	1911
400	Josephine	S	1913
410	Bruno Paul/Antik	T	1914 Paul
430	Maria	KTS	1914 Rosenthal
440	Balmoral	KTS	1916 1080 Kronach
450	Königsberg	T	1916
460	Rosalinde	KT/S	1916/23
470	Empire	K	1918
738	Pompadour white	KT/S	1926/30 Bayreuther
739	Pompadour ivory	KT/S	1926/30
480	Sanssouci white	KTS	1926 Bayreuther
490	Sanssouci ivory	KTS	1926
500	Corona white	KTS	1925 Bayreuther
510	Corona ivory	KTS	1925 Bayreuther
520	Li/Tirana	KTS	1927 Fleischmann
530	La/modern shape	TS	1927/31 Fleischmann
540	Lu	K	1927 Fleischmann
550	Cecil	KS	1923
560	Ideal	KT	1931 Fleischmann
600	Princess white	KTS	1932 Fleischmann
610	Princess ivory	KTS	1932
620	Winifred white	KTS	1933 Fleischmann
630	Winifred plate, smooth		?
645	Winifred-S	KTS	1953
650	Regina	KTS	1935 Bayreuther
660	Helena white	KTS	1936 von Wersin
670	Helena ivory	KTS	1936
690	Rheinsberg (1150 Kronach)	K	1937 Bayreuther
800	Perlrand/Vienna	KTS	1938 Bayreuther
880	Athene	KTS	1939/47 Bayreuther
2000	---	KTS	1954 Latham/Loewy
2500	Variation	KTS	1962 Wirkkala
7094	Tea for Two (black)	T	1964/67 Wirkkala
7253	Assam (black)	T	1968 Wirkkala
1282	Drop	T	1971 Colani
4001	1001 Nacht	T	1973 Björn Wiinblad
1286	Hommage á Darmstadt	T	1989 Lino Sabbatini
1287	Hommage	T	1992 Lino Sabbatini
1289	Naomi	T	1994 Bernhard Gutter
From the Rosenthal Rotbühl-Selb Factory			
3400	Modulation	KTS	1967 Wirkkala/ Scharrer
4000	Petite fleur	M	1971 Wiinblad
4400	Joy	KTS	1971 Karnagel

No.	Name	Type	Year Designer
5000	Plus	KTS	1970 Karnagel
6000	Vieleckform/Polygon	KTS	1973 Wirkkala
7000	Suomi	KTS	1976 Sarpaneva
8000	Century	KTS	1979 Wirkkala
8500	Asimmetria	KTS	1985 Björn Wiinblad
8600	Cupola	KTS	1985 Mario Bellini
9000	Mythos	KTS	1991 Paul Wunderlich
9200	Avenue	KTS	1992 frogdesign
9300	Ikarus	KTS	1995 Paul Wunderlich
9350	Idillio	KTS	1995 Paul Wunderlich
9400	Il Faro	KTS	1994 Aldo Rossi

From the Rosenthal Kronach Factory

No.	Name	Type	Year Designer
---	Chantilly	K?	1898
---	Bristol	K?	1898
---	Gladstone	KT	?
---	Alice	KT	?
300	Molière	KT	?
---	Voltaire	KTS	?
---	Racine	KTC	?
---	Viola	KT	1900?
---	Pensée	S	1900?
700	Dagmar	KT	1904
936	Crab tureen		1905?
1000	Chrysantheme	KT	1905
1020	---	?	---
1030	---	S	1908
1040	---	?	1909
1050	Sylvia	KT	1910
1060	Hortense	S	1911
1070	Wilhelmine	KT	1913
1075	Helene	S	1913
1080	Else	S	1913 Rosenthal
1085	Irmgard	KTS	1916
1086	Anita	S	1917
1090	Lucas Cranach	KT	1922
1095	Ruth/Hildegard	KT	1925
1100	Excelsior	C	1925
1105	Vera	KT	1926 Fleischmann?
---	Maja (1650 Thomas)	KTS	1927 Fleischmann
1115	Helga	KT	1928 Fleischmann
1120	Hella	KTS	1929 Fleischmann
1130	Dorit white	KTS	1932 Kohler
1140	Dorit ivory	KTS	1932
1150	Rheinsberg ivory	K	1934
1160	Fruit service		1935
1165	Markgräfin ivory	S	1935
1170	Viktoria white	KTS	1935 Kohler
1175	Viktoria ivory	KTS	1935
1185	Else new white	KTS	1938
1190	---	KT	1937
1195	Else new ivory	KTS	1938

No.	Name	Type	Year Designer
1200	Bettina ivory	KTS	1953 Scharrer
1210	Bettina white	KTS	1959 Baumann
3000	Berlin	KTS	1959 Baumann
3300	Forme carrée	KM	1965 Bernadotte/Scharrer

From the Rosenthal Plössberg Factory

No.	Name	Type	Year Designer
30	Pearl rim	SKT	1918/24 Rosenthal/ Modrack
48	---	KT	1918 Zeidler & Co.
49	Greque	KT	1918 Zeidler & Co.
50	Barock	SKT	1919 Rosenthal
60	Holland	KT	1920/24
70	Elite	SKT	1922
100	Empire white	S/KT	1925/26
110	Empire ivory	SKT	1926
120	Fatime	KT	1926
130	Pearl band	H	1931
140	Smooth	H	1930
150	Moderna/Madeleine	KTSH	Fleischmann
160	Empire smooth	S	1930
170	---	KT	1927 Fleischmann
180	Coburg	K	1932 Neustadt works
190	Empire new	S	1928
195	Dresden court form	KT	1932
200	Madeleine/Danube	SKT	1929
205	Jedermann	K	1930
220	Chippendale ivory	KTSH	1931 Koch
225	Chippendale USA	ST	1931
230	Caprice/Rosa	T	1931
240	Chippendale white	KTS	1931
250	Stepped form	H	1930
260	Diäta	H	1932
270	Maria/Doll service		1926
280	Chippendale	H	1933
290	Conical	H	1933? 195 Selb
300	Olympia white	KTS	1932 Münch-Khe
310	Olympia USA white	S	1933
320	Aida white	KTS	1937 Koch
330	Olympia ivory	KTS	1933
340	Olympia USA ivory	S	1933
350	Barberina	KT	1933
360	Aida ivory	KTS	1937
400	Pearl rim new	S	1933
410	RAD	H	1934
430	Army & Navy	H	1940? Löffelhardt
450	Barock/Imperial	KSH	1934 Modrack
500	Parzival ivory	KTS	1934/35
520	E (plates & platters)		1952 Thomas form 3140
550	Parzival white	KTS	1934/35
600	Daphne	KTS	1936 Wagenfeld
700	Schönheit der Arbeit II	KTSH	1937 Löffelhardt
800	20:1	K	1938 Koch
900	Rhapsodie		not produced

No.	Name	Type Designer	Year
1000	(Decorative Porcelain)		?
1100	Oval	M	1950 Lunghard
1200	Sinfonie	M	1951 Koch
650	Fortuna	KTS	1956 Fischer-Treyden
1250	Romanze	KT/S	1959/60 Wiinblad/ Wohlrab
1350	Composition	KTS	1963 Wirkkala
800	Lotus	KT/S	1964/67 Wiinblad/ Wirkkala
1260	Magic Flute	KTS	1968 Wiinblad
1270	Duo	KTS	1968 Pozzi
1280	TAC I	T	1969 Gropius/De Sousa
1290	TAC II	K	1969 Gropius/De Sousa

General Introduction to the following Model Lists

In the following lists, *only* the objects made by

1. the Selb works from circa 1898 to 1910 and
2. the Art Department of the Selb works from circa 1910 to 1960 are listed.

Many numbers were followed by letters such as a, b or c, or numerals such as I, II and III, or the word "new."

Note: Objects from the other Rosenthal factories can have the same numbers!

In particular, these lists do *not* include the products of the art department of the Bahnhof-Selb works in Selb-Plössberg, since no model book is available. Some of the same artists who worked in the Selb art department worked on similar products there from 1921-22 to 1969-70, producing an estimated 1250 pieces.

The author and publisher can offer no guarantee of completeness and correctness of the data in these lists, despite all their efforts.

Numeral-chronological lists of models made by the art department of the Selb works can be found in the Rosenthal catalog of the Kestner Museum, and lists of all services in the Rosenthal catalog by Bernd Fritz. This book essentially follows those lists. The two titles are marked in the bibliography with a *. The first catalog also notes the breaks in the numbering system (1315 to 1498 and 2000 to 4999).

The following numbers are not traceable:
from the Selb works before 1910: 175, 177.
from the art department of the Selb works: 50, 193, 236, 241, 248, 254, 277, 279, 291, 292, 348, 406, 418, 420, 429-434, 466, 1507, 1703, 1731, 1732, perhaps because they were not assigned to designs or the designs did not go into production.

Figures and animals that are combined with vases and other ornamental objects are in the lists of ornamental objects.

If no artist's name is given, the designer is not known. A question mark means that the ascribing is not definite. If the name is set in parentheses, then it was based on a classic model.

The years cited are the years of introduction. The objects may have been designed earlier, and were often finished over a long period of time.

Limited editions, such as Rosari decorations and Wendler objects, are not noted, since details are not known.

Since the author has not seen every object, mistaken attributions are possible.

Figures that are combined with ornamental objects are in the lists of ornamental objects.

Figurines from the Selb Works Art Department to 1960

Year, Model Number, Artist, Object

Famous Names (also listed individually):

1951, 1852, (Grupello), Elector Jan Wellem
1953, 1942, Bolivar bust
1958, 5139, Küspert, Jan Wellem small
1959, 5182, Obermaier, Röntgen bust

Christian Motifs:

1918, 525, Boess, Penitent
1922, 614 new, Liebermann, Madonna; 619, Limburg, Don Ugo (Priest)
1923, 700, Pantot, Madonna
1927, 933, Limburg, Pius XI bust
1929, 1052, Schliebstein, Madonna
1933, 1232, Küster, Praying Woman; 1251-1252, Moshage, seating and standing Madonna
1934, 1536-1537, Fehrle, Guardian Angels
1935, 1556-1562, Fehrle, Angel with drum, harp, flute, triangle, clarinet, violin, lyre; 1568-1570, Fehrle, Maria, Joseph, baby Jesus
1936, 1583, (Egell), head of Jesus
1947, 1769, Heidenreich, Madonna
1948, 1778, Janssen, Madonna with lamb; 1791, (Riemenschneider school), Madonna with child (wall plate)
1949, 1800, Burgundy Madonna; 1814-1815, Karl, Annunciation of Mary
1950, 1820, (Riemenschneider school), Crucifix; 1821, (Donatello), large Crucifix; 1822, Nürnberg Madonna; 1823, Benodetto-Jano, Madonna with

child, large; 1824, Limburg, Immaculate Madonna; 1825, 1828, 1829, 1831, Karl, Heart of Jesus
Madonna of Fatima with.without doves, small wall Madonna, child Jesus' 1939, Lang, Crucifix with four angels
1951, 1851, Hauenstein, Mary's children
1953, 1919, 1924, Stangl, Madonna, small Madonna; 1928-1929, Lang, Angel with flute/clarinet; 1945, Stangl, Jesus; 1946, Lang, Ascension
1954, 1958-1959, Fritsch, Lucifer I with raised hands, II hands down; 1969-1970, Lang, Angel with violin/lute
1956, 5035, Stangl, Evening Prayer; 5044, Hauenstein, Madonna large
1958, 5114, Friedrich-Gronau, Madonna large
1959, 5178, Friedrich-Gronau, Madonna with child (wall plate)

Exotic Motifs (see also Dance):
1914, 395 new, Liebermann, Pagoda I/II
1920, 567, Marcuse, Bedouin
1923, 696, Himmelstoss, Parvati
1925, 760, Zschäbitz, Small Moor
1927, 940, Oppel, God of Satisfaction (Miao Pudso?)
1928, 1019-1021, Metzger, Dalmatian Farmer with donkey, Donkey Rider, Negress with burden
1931, 1147, Katchamakoff, Indian Woman
1952, 1872, Bachem, Donkey Driver
1955, 5015, Moschak, Spanish Woman with fish
1956, 5065, Schelenz, Greek Woman with child
1959, 5176, Daudert, Greek Woman

Women (Acts, with child, etc., see also Genre):
1910, 53, Lady on Divan
1913, 202, Boess, After the Bath; 204, Langenmantel, Favorite
1923, 656, Limburg, Joy of Life; 697, Harth, Lady Seated
1924, 752, Wenck, Woman Drinking
1925, 810-812, Steger, Staggering, Alter Ego, Crouching
1926, 863, Schliepstein, Departure
1927, 936, Schliepstein, Sunning Herself (lying); 954, Zoelch, Mother and Child
1929, 1037, Wenck, Mother and Child
1934, 1268, Bredow, Woman Lying
1935, 1577, Oppel, Rocking the Cradle
1936, 1581, Klimsch, Crouching; 1603-1604, Kaesbach, Looking Out (Torso), Thinking (Torso)
1937, 1620, 1623, Klimsch, Lying, Crouching; 1643, Schievelbein, Sitting; 1655, Kaesbach, Looking Out large
1938, 1681, Kaesbach, Thinking large; 1702, Begas, Longing (Act)
1939, 1724, Kaesbach, Mother and Child
1940, 1734, Friedrich-Gronau, Kneeling (Edith)
1941, 1738, Philippsborn, Sisters; 1740, Lang, Woman Sitting
1947, 1777, Klimsch, Narcissus
1948, 1784, 1789, Friedrich-Gronau, Susanne, Woman's Head with kerchief
1952, 1884, Liebermann, Woman Lying
1953, 1917, 1937, Stangl, Woman Sitting large/small
1954, 1957, Stangl, Mother and Child; 1972, Bidlingmaier, Sabine; 1981, Stangl, Woman Lying
1955, 1989, 5003, Stangl, Lying, Dreaming
1956, 5034, Brock, Beatrice (wall relief); 5057, Fucik, Mother and Child; 5060, Friedrich-Gronau, Woman;s Head with Kerchief (wall plate)
1957, 5102, Moshage, Woman with Child; 5106, Klimsch, Looking
1958, 5123-5125, Heshmat, Woman with Bowl, standing half-plastic; 5126, Friedrich-Gronau, Bust of a Woman

Genre (see also Fashion):
1910, 45, Lady of Fashion; 75, 91, Liebermann, Jolly Ride (Straussenritt), Vanity; 76, Opel, Congratulations
1912, 162, Himmelstoss, Lady of Fashion
1913, 203, Himmelstoss, Rococo Lady (Finale); 244, Lady of Fashion 1913; 331, Harth, Lady of Fashion 1914
1915, 426-427, Vierthaler, Lady with Muff/Dog
1916, 435, Harth, Lady of Fashion 1916
1917, 446, 450, Himmelstoss, Pearl Seeker, Loose Bird; 452-453, Boess, Miniatures, masculine/feminine; 465, Boess (?)/Opel, Coat of Frost; 470, 476, Opel, A Question, Expectation; 471, Important Visit; 477, Marcuse, Grape Carrier
1918, 498, Opel, Wine, Women and Song; 506, Lady with Dog; 522, Deep in Thought
1919, 558-560, Opel, The Marquise's Bath, The Dunce, Congratulations
1921, 599-601, Holzer-Defanti, Piquant Question (Cavalier), Piqued (Lady), Off Like lightning (Lady with Moor); 605, Caasmann, Ashamed
1922, 617 new, Liebermann, Spring
1923, 661-662, Himmelstoss, Shepherd, Shepherdess
1924, 706, Himmelstoss, At the Fountain; 744, Oppel, Ballad (Crocodile); 746-747, Dasio, Shepherd Group, Shepherdess
1925, 777-778, Oppel, Marquis, Marquise
1928, 1018, Rame, Wisdom (Archivist); 1024, Oppel, Vanity (Woman on Antelope)
1929, 1034, Schliepstein, Shepherdess; 1039, Grath, Distant Sound; 1041, Garth, Prophetess
1930, 1081, Oppel, Newsboy
1934, 1310, Brock, Shepherdess; 1530, Tuaillon, Leading Horses
1935, 1553, Oppel, Lady with Whippet
1938, 1679, Kaesbach, Large Garden Figure; 1694, Feldtmann, Spring
1939, 1723, Tuaillon, Leading Horses; 1729, Bernhardt, Mower
1947, 1767, Kompatscher Hubertus; 1770, Heidenreich, Shoe Binder
1949, 1796, Oppel, La visite
1950, 1843, Krebs-Himmelstoss, Reverence (Lady with Fan)
1951, 1847, Lang, Postillion; 1848, Bamberg Knight, small head; 1858-1959, Bachem, Fountain Idyll, still life
1954, 1974, Schelenz, Smoker; 1976, Friedrich-Gronau, Lady with Mirror; 1978-1979, Seibold, Night (portrait, wall picture), Lilofee (portrait, wall picture)
1955, 1997, 5018, Schelenz, Woman with Umbrella, Drinking Man; 5013, Angel, Student; 5016-5017, 5023-5025, Backmund, Man with folded arms, Smoker, Man Telephoning, Woman with Basket, Woman Telephoning
1956, 5067, Schelenz, Woman with Basket (wall picture)
1957, 5091, Hemrich, Falconer on Horse (wall relief), 5108, Moshage, Woman with Pitcher
1958, 5113, Thorak, The Light; 5119, Peynet, Knitter
1960, 5225-5230, Wiinblad, Rose Grower, Disappointed, Oh This Aroma, My Dearest Flower, Sunk in the Aroma, The Observer (with other titles as #1225-1230, by the Plössberg art department)

Goethe Motifs:
1926, 832-838, Oppel, Host/Hostess, Hermann, Dorothea, Mignon, Philine, Harper, Wilhelm Meister
1949, 1794, Rogge, Bust of Goethe

Hitler, Typical Motifs of his time:
1933, 1240-1242, Boess, Youthful Strength, Toward the Sun, Frederick the Great; 1250, Moshage, Hitler as Drummer
1934, 1301, Oppel, Bamberg Knight; 1529, Tuaillon, Old Fritz; 1544-1545, 1548, Oppel, Grenadier, Officer (Hatschier), Drummer; 1549, Kärner, SS Rider
1935, 1563-1564, Oppel, General Seydlitz, Bamberg Knight bust
1936, 1584, Oppel, Old Fritz standing; 1596, Uta of Naumburg bust; 1605,

Oppel, Torchbearer
1937, 1635, Larlauf (?), Barbara of Strassburg
1938, 1696, Seger, Feeling of Strength

Seasons of the Year:
1928, 981-984, Schliepstein, Spring, Summer, Autumn, Winter
1932, 1149-1152, Weiss, Spring, Summer, Autumn, Winter

Children, Youth:
1910, 84, Liebermann, Jealousy
1913, 217, Child with Mouse; 253, 256, 303, Caasmann, Teddy School, Duck Maid, Roses (Girl)
1914, 359-361, Caasmann, Child with Cat/Dog/Flowers
1919, 544, Boese, Surprised
1923, 655, Limburg, Young Love; 692, Boess, Youth
1925, 807-809, Steger, Kneeling/Thinking/Crouching Girl
1927, 969, Wenck, Sleeping Girl
1928, 990, Otto-Eichwald, Kissing Children; 1002-1005, Oppel, Good Friendship, Curious Doll, Tancing Lesson, Frog Rider; 1017, Wenck, Dreaming Boy
1929, 1035, Schliepstein, Girl with Dove
1930, 1082, 1091, Oppel, Lily (Girl), First Aid; 1104, Meerling, Boy with Two Fish
1932, 1163, Zschäbitz, Boy with Horse; 1173, 1190, Weiss, Girl with Umbrella, Girl with Doll
1933, 1207, Zschäbitz, Resting Girl; 1233-1235, Weiss, Two Children, Girl with Dog/Bow; 1245, Boess, Sitting Girl; 1257-1259, Fritz, Child with Angora Cat/King Penguin/Dog (Secret)
1934, 1281, Oppel, Girl with Deer; 1305-1308, Weiss, Gänseliesl, Girl with Dove/Hen/Cat; 1503, Fritz, Child with Penguins (Model 1258 on new list); 1516, Zschäbitz, Boy with Horse; 1527, Obermaier, Walking Girl; 1532, Heidenreich, Sitting Girl
1935, 1576, Heidenreich, Girl with Greyhound
1936, 1587, Girl with Sheep Dog; 1592, 1597, Oppel, Girl with Bears/Whippet; 1616-1618, Specht-Büchting, Kneeling Girl
1937, 1630, Schliepstein, Girl with Deer; 1639-1640, Friedrich-Gronau, Child with Rabbit/Chicks; 1661, Schievelbein, Lying Girl small; 1663-1666, Friedrich-Gronau, Child with Squirrel/Bird/Deer/Lamb; 1668-1669, Kaesbach, Standing Girl, clothed; Sitting Girl surprised
1938, 1707, Schliepstein, Child's Head
1946, 1759, Philippsborn, Standing Girl
1947, 1771, Friedrich-Gronau, Sitting Girl (on the beach)
1950, 1844, Scheibe, Innocentia (girl with dove)
1951, 1850, Hauenstein, Sybil (girl with vase or candle); 1856, 1862, Bachem, Child with Ram, Girl with Basket
1952, 1873, 1905, Bachem, Girl with Flute and Chicken, Boy with Dog
1953, 1913-1914, 1934-1935, Friedrich-Gronau, Kneeling Child with Vase/Candle, Girl with Vase/Candle, Boy Kneeling.Sitting with small vase
1954, 1971, Lang, Child in Cradle
1955, 1988, 5000, Stangl, Sitting Girl/Child
1956, 5036, von Martin, Girl on Horse; 5076, Friedrich-Gronau, Little Girl Tying Shoe
1958, 5115, Friedrich-Gronau, Christl (sitting girl); 5130-5132, Rhein, Piggyback, Boy with Book, Round Dance; 5134, Rücker, Girl with Hat
1959, 5149, Schütt, Teenager; 5156-5157, 5190, Rücker, Girl Sitting on Chair/with Cat. Boy's Head

Comedy, Comedians, Circus:
1910, 92, Liebermann, Clown, 95, Liebermann, Mardi Gras
1912, 100, Gsell, Pierrot with Dog; 111. Finale; 169 new, Dear-man, Mardi Gras small; 176 Caasmann, Clown (with duck)
1913, 232, Rauth, Swearing Love, 311. 330, Marcuse, Duet large/small, Juggler
1916, 436, Caasmann, Pierrot with Harmonica (musical clown)
1917, 449, Himmelstoss, Bajazzo
1919, 549, Holzer-Defanti, Pierrette
1923, 690, Tauschek, two Strange Ones
1928, 994-995, Himmelstoss, Pierrot, Pierrette
1929, 1040, Valentin, Ash Wednesday
1932, 1153, Parzinger, Grock; 1154, Fratellini
1955, 1994, Thiersch, Colombella
1959, 5164-5165, Schmitt, Pony with Circus Child, Circus Rider

Love Motifs (see also Genre):
1913, 295, Aigner, Spring of Love; 304, Caasmann, Magic of Love (girl with elf)
1916, 439, Courtship
1917, 472, Opel (?), Boess, Talk for Two (courtship); 475, Boess, Shepherd's Hour
1918, 510, Opel, In the Arbor (explanation); 524, Jermann, Far from the World
1923, 691, Himmelstoss, Courtship; 695, Pellar, Shepherd's Hour
1927, 955, Zoelch, Man and Woman
1932, 1156, Kärner, White Horse
1934, 1515, Kärner, Love's Messenger (after model 1156)
1948, 1779-1780, Oppel, Hand-kiss, Courtship
1953, 1918, Stangl, Affection
1956, 5055, Schelenz, Loving Couple on a Bench; 5056, Gäbler, Innocence
1957, 5092-5094, 5096, Peynet, Spring Song, Girl/Cavalier with Heart in Hand, Little Loving Couple
1958, 5116, 5120-5121, Peynet, Gardener and Mamsell, Girl/Cavalier with Heart, small
1959, 5150-5151, Peynet, Romance with Book, Loving Couple with Heart as Mirror

Fairy-tale Motifs:
1913, 233, Rauth, Frog King
1919, 536-537, Liebermann, From Faraway Lands, Two Princesses
1923, 678, Tauschek, The Little Muck
1924, 707, Himmelstoss, Fairy Tale
1925, 790-795, Zacherl-Klee, Sheheran, Sheherezade, Kadi, Alladin, Robber, Fisherman
1926, 826-827, Schliepstein, Prince, Princess
1928, 1001, Schliepstein, Fairy Tale
1929, 1033, Norvil, Agnete and the Oceanman; 1043, Oppel, Sheherezade; 1060, Eulenspiegel
1930, 1083-1084, Oppel, Devil, Witch; 1106, Winterfeldt, Bride of the Wind (Fön)
1934, 1511, Liebermann, Two Princesses (model 537 on new list)
1936, 1588, Heidenreich, Flower Elf
1948, 1793, Friedrich-Gronau, Frog Queen
1951, 1868, Hauenstein, Hans in Luck
1954, 1967-68, von Bohr, Seahorse with Boy/Maiden
1955, 5014, Friedrich-Gronau, Cinderella
1956, 5075, Friedrich-Gronau, Princess with Swineherd
1958, 5145, Friedrich-Gronau, Snow White
1959, 5159, 5167, Schmitt, Bremen Musicians, Undine

Music and Musician Motifs:
1910, 96, Himmelstoss, Spring's Awakening
1912, 138, Himmelstoss, Carmen
1913, 194, Beyrer, Bagpiper; 196-197, Himmelstoss, Bass Violinist, Hunting Horn Player; 299, Harth, Caruso
1917, 487, Himmelstoss, Reverie (cellist)
1918, 501, Sonata (Mozart)
1919, 547, Boese, Flutist
1921, 593, Liebermann, Musika; 604, Himmelstoss, Musician
1926, 899, Zacherl-Klee, Papageno
1927, 945, Schliepstein, Music
1933, 1246, Schliepstein, Flutist

1935, 1552, Johannes Brahms
1936, 1595, Bust of Furtwängler
1937, 1631, Schott, Music; 1656-1657, Höfer-Kelling, Accordion and Harmonica Players
1938, 1684, Wenck, Head of Richard Wagner
1939, 1728, Mathias, Bust of Beethoven
1952, 1897-1898, Friedrich-Gronau, Melody, Downbeat
1953, 1911m Friedrich-Gronau, Accord; 1920, Stangl, Rhythm; 1930-1933, Friedrich-Gronau, Capriccio, Allegro, Andante, Adagio
1956, 5028-5030, Brock, Bust of Mozart, Richard Wagner and Albert Schweitzer reliefs; 5039-5042, Himmelstoss, Clarinet Player, Guitarist, Bass Player, Violinist; 5046, Lang, Flutist; 5048, Klingler, Bust of Mozart
1958, 5118, Peynet, The Mandolin Player; 5138, Seibel, Song to the Moon
1960, 5232, Obermaier, Bust of Verdi

Mythologies, Allegories (see also Cherubs):
1910, 35, 41-43, 68, 72, 74, Liebermann, Philosophical Dispute, High School, Io, Small Bacchante, Capriccio, Latin, Faun Bust: Terror; 73, Aigner, Eros
1912, 124, Himmelstoss, Faun with Butterfly, 126, 173, new Liebermann, Temple Dedication Without Dress, Capriccio small (model 68); 142, Leipold, Flora; 174-175, 190, Caasmann, Sleeping Faun, Faun with Pail, Storming Bacchantes
1913, 192, Temple Dedication; 195, 208, Caasmann, Small Faun on Pedestal, Faun Flight; 198, 296, Schott, Faun with Nymphs large/small; 246, 298, Liebermann, Symphony, Faun with Grapes; 288, Opel, Venus with Parrot
1914, 346, Caasmann, Ariadne; 394, Liebermann, Faun with Crocodile
1918, 519, Grath, Amazon
1921, 603, Opel (?), Europa
1923, 682, Himmelstoss, Silene (Faun with Pitchers), 694, Pellar/Caasmann, Faun Group
1924, 753, Wenck, Leda with Swan
1934, 1520, Liebermann, Philosophical Dispute small (model 35/1 on new pedestal)
1937, 1634, Moshage, Goddess of Luck (Fortuna)
1938, 1700, Maass, Bust of Flora
1939, 1722, Klimsch, Naiad; 1730, Hussmann, Amazon
1940, 1735, Wenck, Leda with Swan
1942-1943, 1748, Klimsch, Aglaia
1949, 1795, Klimsch, Aurora (Sunrise); 181201813, Bohr, Echo, Narcissus
1951, 1853, Fritsch, Europa; 1860-1861, Bachem, Shepherd and Muse, Daphne; 1869, Heidenreich, Pegasus
1953, 1912, Friedrich-Gronau, Blue Flower kneeling
1956, 5038, Bachem, Europa; 5059, Friedrich-Gronau, Blue Flower
1957, 5095, Peynet, The Magician
1960, 5224, Friedrich-Gronau, Sylphide

Patriotic Motifs:
1914, 381, 383-384, 386, 391-392, 395-400, 402, Fight for the Flag, Hussar, Uhlan, Trumpeter, Storming Infantrymen, Ensign, Infantry kneeling, Drummer, On Guard, Messenger of Love, Home Guard, Infantryman in Trench, Forward; 382, Boess, Nurse; 385, Himmelstoss, Infantryman; 390, 393, Caasmann, Comrades, Seaman
1915, 410, Gsell (?), Uncle Doctor; 421, 423, Austrian Soldier, Soldier on Skis

Cherubs:
1910, 31, Opel, Congratulations; 62, Liebermann, Lousy Story
1913, 205, Caasmann, Snail Mail; 234, 320-321, Liebermann, Congratulations, Turtle Mail, Two Friends
1914, 342, Liebermann, Cellist; 354-355, Caasmann, Gliding Flight, Playmates
1916, 440-441, Caasmann, Summer Ride, Singing School
1917, 467, Departure; 473, Opel, Gentleness with Amor (Visit)
1918, 523, Liebermann, Teasing; 529, Holzer-Defanti, Rooster with Cherub
1919, 535, Holzer-Defanti, Cherub with Grapes; 538, 541, Liebermann, Caught, Amor with Roses
1921, Caasmann, Snail with Elf
1923, 657, Caasmann, Herald of Spring; 680-681, Himmelstoss, Cherub with Bird/Tambourine
1924, 723, Limburg, Departure; 738, Obermaier, Amor with Arrow; 740-743, 745, Oppel, Amoroso, Cherub with Cat/Dog, Riding the Waves (Putto), Teasing (2 cherubs)
1925, 804, Oppel, Small Watchman
1928, 997, Otto, Cherub with Flute
1929, 1032, Oppel, Idyll (cherub on pelican)
1930, 1080, 1094-1096, Oppel, Cherub on Turtle, as Congratulator, Spring, Winter
1934, 1282-1283, Fritz, Cherub with Whippet/Kid; 1288, Himmelstoss, Cherub with Lamb; 1500-1502, 1514, Oppel, Cherub with Flute (form 740 on new pedestal), Cherub with Cat (form 741 on new pedestal), Riding the Waves, Idyll (model 32/1 on new pedestal); 1504, Himmelstoss, Cherub with Bird (form 680 on new pedestal); 1513, 1519, Obermaier, Cherub without/with Arrow (form 738 on new pedestal)
1949, 1798-1799, Lang, Cherub with Lute/Flute; 1803-1806, Stefani, Cherub with Violin/same/Cello/Viola
1950, 1838, Oppel, Amor with Ball
1956, 5045, 5047, Lang, Singing School (two cherubs), Cherub with Mandolin

Show Business Motifs:
1913, 271-272, Harth, Johanna Terwin, Alexander Moissi; 328, Marcuse, Cabaret
1914, 343, Harth, Tilla Durieux
1918, 520, Himmelstoss, Fritz Massari
1926, 859, Oppel, Jackie Coogan
1937, 1667, Friedrich-Gronau, Lilian Harvey
1938, 1699, Maass, Bust of Gründgens (Hamlet)

Sporting Motifs:
1910, 85, Liebermann, Tennis Player
1913, 293-294, 316, Marcuse, In the Wind (swimmer), On the Beach (swimmer), Before the Bath
1919, 546, Holzer-Defanti, Riding Lady (Favorite); 552, Maison, Escaped (rider)
1925, 756, 758, 780-782, Kitler, Shotputter, Javelin Thrower, Runner, Boxer, Tennis Player
1926, 839, 843, 852, Kittler, Soccer Player, Tennis Player, Discus Thrower, 840, Oppel, Two Skiers
1927, 951, Kraus, Victor
1930, 1092, Oppel, Kathy
1932, 1170-1172, 1189, Weiss, Skier, Tennis Player, Boy on Beach, Soccer Player
1934, 1535, Obermaier, Discus Thrower
1935, 1578, Obermaier, Victor; 1580, Heidenreich, May Ride
1936, 1586, Klimsch, Tennis player large; 1607-1608, Oppel, Runner with Saluki/Deer; 1615, Daumiller, Swimmer
1937, 1658, Döbrich, Mounted Hunter
1938, 1685, Döbrich, Equestrienne
1939, 1715-1717, Kaesbach, Beach Runner Group (girls), Beach Runner lifting left/right leg
1946, 1760, Richter, Rider large
1951, 1854, Fritsch, Swimmers (wall relief); 1865-1866, Belloni, Domador Rider I: Lorvoveando/II: Prendido como abrojo
1953, 1947, Thiersch, Bullfighter (Matador)
1954, 1973, Fritsch, Two Skaters Faber

Dance Motifs (Dancers by name, see below):
1910, 44 new, Liebermann, Dancer large; 70 Spanish Dancer
1912, 116, 143, Liebermann, Dancer,

Greek Dancer
1913, 201, Boess, Ionic Dancer; 210, Himmelstoss, Round Dance; 206-207, Langenmantel, Empire-Rococo Dancer large/small; 324, Marcuse, Egyptian Dancer; 339, Liebermann, Tarantella
1914, 358, Boess, Nubian Dancer
1916, 437, 442, Boess, Indian Dancer, Snake Dancer
1917, 486, Krebs-Himmelstoss, Dancer; 497, Marcuse, Serpentine Dancer
1918. 521. Boess, Intermission
1919, 566, Holzer-Defanti, Korean Dance
1920, 573, Holzer-Defanti, Unmasked
1921, 598, Holzer-Defanti, Javan Dancer
1923, 688, Pellar/Caasmann, Round Dance; 698, Boess, Moon Dance
1924, 705, Himmelstoss, Indian Dancer
1925, 757, Marcuse, Egyptian Dancer
1926, 877, Oppel, Tarantella
1927, 952, 956-957, 961-963, Oppel, Charm, Salambo, Rhythm, Prayer Dancer, Scherzo, Charleston
1930, 1114-1119, Oppel, Animosa (dancer), Largo (dancer), Dream Dancer, Suite (dancer), Libelle (dancer), Grace (dancer)
1932, 1165, 1174-1176, Weiss, Toe Dance, Oriental Dancer, Fan/Dragonfly Dance
1933, 1231, 1236, Weiss, Dancer, Dancer
1934, 1261, Boess, Snake Dance, 1505, 1508-1509, 1517-1518, Oppel, Prayer Dancer (model 961/1 on new base), Salambo (model 956/1 on new base), Scherzo (model 962/1 on new base), Rococo Dancer/same; 1512, Himmelstoss, Rococo Dancer (model 203 on new base)
1935, 1550, Klimsch, Dancer; 1571, Oppel, Rondo (dancer)
1936, 1600, Moshage, Dancer; 1606, Oppel, Dancer (ex-model 1605)
1937, 1641, Oppel, Dancer (model 1608 minus deer)
1938, 1680, Kaesbach, Dancer
1941, 1744, Friedrich-Gronau, Largo
1947, 1772, Friedrich-Gronau, Tango I (kneeling dancer)
1948, 1785, Friedrich-Gronau, Graziosa
1950, 1840, Karl, Finale (dancing pair)
1953, 1921-1923, Stangl, Dance I-III; 1949, 1950, Thiersch, Spanish Dancer man/woman
1951, Oppel, Dancer (model 1606 in low base)
1956, 5062, 5077, Friedrich-Gronau, Ballet, Two Ballerinas with Mirror
1957, 5082, Ott, Ballerina
1959, 5158, Rücker, Dancer (standing girl), 5160, Schmitt, Dancing Pair; 5177, Friedrich-Gronau, Dancer
1960, 5223, Friedrich-Gronau, Dancer (wall plastic)

Dancers by Name:
1917, 451, Himmelstoss, Pavlova
1918, 531, Holzer-Defanti, Lady with Muff (Lo Hesse)
1919, 533-534, 545, 551, Holzer-Defanti, Chinese (Saber Dancer Chaokiun), Chinese (Dancer Chaokium), Dying Swan (Pavlova), Merry March (Lena Amsell)
1926, 876, Oppel, Toni Impekoven
1934, 1510, Oppel, Toni Impekoven (model 876/1 on new base)
1938, 1683, Friedrich-Gronau, Emperor Waltz (Höpfner brother and sister); 1701, Begas, Dancer (Baranova)
1939, 1714, Friedrich-Gronau, Dancer (Deinert)
1941, 1737, 1745-1746, Friedrich-Gronau, Tango II (Dancer L. Spalinger)
1951, 1864, 1867, Fritsch, Night Song (Harald Kreutzberg), Till Eulenspiegel (same)
1956, 5069, Friedrich-Gronau, Joy Kim

Peasant Costume Motifs:
1912, 115, 123, 129, 139, 168 new, Himmelstoss, Munich Child, Tyrolean Boy, Schmalzler, Dutch Girl, Tyrolean Girl
1917, 445, Boess, Black Forest Girl
1923, 699, Harth, Dirndl
1937, 1642, Oppel, Spreewald Girl
1949, 1817, Himmelstoss, Munich Child

Advertising Figures:

1926, 823, Oppel, Kant Boy, China Boy (Riquet)
1954, 1977, Lauermann, Sarotti Moor

Animal Figurines from the Selb Art Department

See the general introduction to the model lists.
Combinations of animals with vases, bowls, writing implements, lamps, etc., see model list for ornamental porcelain.

Many objects have fanciful names, such as "Homesickness" for an ape or "High Spirits" for a horse. Since the author has not seen all objects, faulty listings are possible.

The year is followed by the model number, then the artist, if known, then the title of the object.

Apes:
1923, 626, 659, Himmelstoss, Ape, Homesickness (bust of ape)
1925, 766, Sachäbitz, Ape
1927, 966-968, Otto, Ape sitting/on stump/pair
1930, 1133, Schliepstein, Baboon
1936, 1602, Bernuth, Young Ape (baboon)
1939, 1710, Heidenreich, Baboon

Bears:
1913, 332, Diller, Polar Bear
1914, 347, Diller, Polar Bear
1923, 683, Schliepstein, Little Bear
1924, 721, Scheibe, Bear; 737, Manz, Bear Group
1926, 831, Zügel, Young Bear
1928, 992, Simonis (?), Bear; 1009, Küster, Polar Bear
1931, 1148, Schliepstein, Young Bear
1934, 1269, Schliepstein, Teddy Bear
1936, 1593-1594, Oppel, Bear Group, Lone Bear
1947, 1763-1765, Heidenreich, Bear Group, Bear with Ball/Alone
1952, 1899, Klingler, Bear
1956, 5066, 5074, Heidenreich, Bear with Cubs, Standing Bear large

Kangaroos and Koalas:
1923, 689, Schliepstein, Kangaroo
1935, 1567, Kerzinger, Koala Group

Elephants:
1913, 335, Diller, Elephant; 338, Norvil, Mammoth
1923, 627, Krebs-Himmelstoss, Small Elephant
1924, 726, Himmelstoss, Dancing Elephant; 736, Manz, Elephant large
1927, 909, Zschäbitz, Elephant
1929, 1079, Schliepstein, Elephant
1932, 1195, Kärner, Elephant (Wastl)
1948, 1792, Heidenreich, African Elephant
1952, 1904, Küspert, Small Elephant
1954, 1963, Heidenreich, African Elephant (Jumbo)

Grotesque Animals:
1925, 798-803, Gravenitz, Miniature Grotesques: Tarzan (ape), Bucephalus (horse), Heidigeigei (cat), Axolotl (crocodile), Cerberus (unicorn), Dog (dachshund)
1927, 913-918, Küster, Ape, Weasel, Heron, Elephant, Duck, Marabu
1930, 1085-1090, Oppel, Bonzo as Cavalier, Fashion Show, Ape, Duck, Elephant, Sea Lion, Fox

Domestic Animals, see also Dogs, Horses:

1912,137, 144, 151, Zügel, Dalmatian, Grazing Donkey, Pair of Ducks with/without base; 153, 171-172, Himmelstoss, Pair of Ducks small, Duck alone, Duck alone

1913, 218, 247, Himmelstoss, Pair of Chickens, Rabbit; 249-250, 270, 341, ZÜgel, Duck, Drake, Lying Cow, Pair of Ducks

1914, 351-352, Zügel, Drake, Duck; 362, Rabbit; 404, Caasmann, Pair of Pigs

1917, 447, 489, Young Duck, Duck without base; 478, Himmelstoss, Pair of Chicks

1918, 527, Krebs-Himmelstoss, Pair of Turkeys

1919, 555, Kärner, Goat with Kid; 557, Himmelstoss, Goat

1922, 612, Ratleff, Pair of Rabbits

1923, 634, 670-672, Zügel, Kid, Group of Lambs, Standing Lamb, Lying Lamb; 673-674, Ratleff (?)/Himmelstoss, Rabbit lying/sitting; 684-685, Himmelstoss, Goose standing/sitting

1924, 728, Himmelstoss, Small Duck; 739, Obermaier, Pair of Cats; 750, Gravenitz, Kitten

1925, 783, Gravenitz, Bucking Goat

1926, 900-901, Kraus, Standing Goat/Licking Goat

1927, 935, 973, Kraus, Jumping Goat, Cat; 938-939, Himmelstoss, Hen/Rooster of Pair of Chickens, model 218; 950, Otto, Carrier Pigeon; 958-959, Zügel, Cow, Bull

1928, 976, Graevenitz, Walking Tomcat; 978, 1013, Oppel, Peacock, Hatching Duck; 1006-08, Küster, Sheep, Goat, Rooster

1929, 1046, Gaul, Group of Sheep

1934, 1302-04, Himmelstoss, Duck (Protest), Cat sitting/lying; 1547, Kärner, Pair of Ducks

1935, 1554, Rottmann, Calf Licking

1936, 1589-91, 1611,14, Heidenreich, Doves, Dove, Pair of Doves, Peacock, Rooster, Hen standind/hunting for food; 1619, Specht-Büchting, Jumping Calf

1937, 1621-22, Heidenreich, Lamb lying/standing; 1644, Krebs-Himmelstoss, Sheep Nursing

1938, 1698, Hussmann, Lying Cat

1949, 1811, Esser, Billy Goat

1951, 1857, Bachem, Ram with Bush

1952, 1883, 1885, 1888, Küspert, Baby Ducks, Young/Sitting Kitten; 1894-96, Schmitt, Boar, Goat I with head down/II

1953, 1907, 1941, Heidenreich, Lying/Black Cat; 1916, Oppel, Rooster alone; 1943, Himmelstoss, Chicks; 1948, Thiersch, Bull

1955, 1983, 1998, 5009, Heidenreich, Turkey, Young Donkey, Pair of Budgies; 1985, Gessner, Budgie on high pedestal; 1986, 1996, 5006-07, Schmitt, Fighting Cocks, Goat, Rooster, Pair of Cats

1956, 5037, Klingler, Rooster

1957, 5079, Küspert, Pair of Baby Ducks; 5083-89, Schmitt, Sow with Young, Sitting/Lying/Jumping/Eating/Small/Standing Piglet

1958, 5133, Rücker, Cat Sitting; 5137, Heidenreich, Persian Lamb

1959, 5166, Schmitt, Dove with Rose; 5183, Seemann, Chicken; 5193-94, Rücker, Cat Standing/Sitting

1960, 5211, Seemann, Group of Chickens; 5236-37, 5246, Rücker, Small Lying/Sitting Cat, Rooster; 5239, Heidenreich, Small Sitting Siamese Cat

Dogs:

1910, 77, Gsell, Playing Dachshund

1912, 104, Meyer (?), Playing Dachshund; 120, Dachshund; 191, Poodle

1913, 200, Valentin, Greyhound; 209, Greyhound with Rabbit; 243, Meyer-Pyritz, Sitting Dachshund large; 258, 260, 262, 275-276, 286-287, 289, 306-308, 325, 336, Diller, Pointer, German Shepherd, St. Bernard, Sitting Dachshund, Cocker Spaniel, Young French Bulldog, King Charles (dog), Whippet, Bulldog Pair, Bulldog standing/lying, Pinscher, Young Setter; 266, Zügel, Pointer; 273-274, Liebermann, Dachshund with/without basket; 297, Harth, French Bulldog; 333, Moldenhauer, Fox Terrier

1914, 345, Diller, English Bulldog

1916, 438, Moldenhauer, Fox Terrier

1917, 448, Himmelstoss, Dachshund; 479, Poodle

1918, 511, Himmelstoss, Whippet

1919, 540, Moldenhauer, King Charles (dog)

1920, 568, Kärner, Fox Terrier

1923, 649-650, Kompatscher, Longhaired/Shorthaired Dog; 651-652, Moldenhauer, Fox Terrier, Greyhound

1924, 727, Himmelstoss, Bulldog

1925, 773, Oppel, Poodle with Basket (Congratulations); 788-789, Otto-Eichwald, Dobermann Pinscher, Pointer

1926, 829, 872, Diller, German Shepherd, Wire-haired Terrier; 830, Otto-Eichwald, Wire-haired Terrier, 888, Otto, German Longhair

1927, 905, 960, 964, Diller, Dwarf Spitz, German Dog, Russelhund; 923, Norvill, Pekingese; 970, Otto-Eichwaldm Greyhound

1928, 974, Kraus, Whippet; 993, Otto-Eichwald, Tyrant

1930, 1110, 1132, Schliepstein, Greyhound Group, German Shepherd; 1120-23, 1134, Kärner, Wire-haired Terrier, Sitting Terrier small, Lying Terrier small/large, German Boxer

1931, 1135, Fritz, Russian Greyhound

1933, 1243-44, Fritz, Wire-haired Terrier, English Fox Terrier; 1247, 1249, Kärner, Young Dachshund, Waiting Terrier

1934, 1299, Fritz, Greyhound Group; 1533, Kärner, Young Sitting Shepherd; 1534, Obermaier, King Charles (dog)

1936, 1598-99, Heidenreich, Whippet Alone, Greyhound Group

1937, 1624-29, 1645, 1659, 1677, Heidenreich, Dachshund, Whistle, Batzel II, Hexel, Group of 3/2 Dachshunds, Waiting Terrier, English Bulldog, Irish Setter (Daphne); 1632, Küster, Greyhounds; 1633, Specht-Büchting, Dachshund; 1672-75, Rendlen-Schneider, Small Fox Terrier on 3/4 legs standing/sitting/playing

1938, 1686-88, Heidenreich, Terrier Head (Wire-haired)

1942-43, 1747, Heidenreich, Bobby (Scottish Terrier head)

1947, 1762, Heidenreich, Scottish Terrier

1949. 1797, 1808, 1818, Heidenreich, Dachshund Head, Lying Dachshund, Greyhound Group

1950, 1842, Heidenreich, Setter

1951, 1849, Heidenreich, Italian Whippet

1952, 1892, Eichler, Sealyham Terrier

1953, 1909, Küspert, Dachshund small; 1925-27, 1936, 1944, 1952, Heidenreich, Poodle standing with Caracul cut/sitting/sitting/lying, Boston Terrier, German Boxer standing

1953, 1953-55, Stangl, Sitting Dachshund, German Boxer, Standing Dachshund; 1960-61, Heidenreich, Lying Boston Terrier, German Boxer lying; 1964, Küspert, Lying Dachshund (Axel)

1955, 5012, Heidenreich, Poodle lying (Bianka); [p 147] 5020, Küspert, Astor Sheepdog

1956, 5049-53, 5058, 5063, Heidenreich, Pointer I-III, Pointer Group, English Setter, Dalmatian, Poodle; 5064, Küspert, Longhair Dachshund

1957, 5101, Heidenreich, English Bulldog; 5105, Küspert, Dachshund Standing

1958, 5140-41, 5143-44, Heidenreich, Chow-Chow Standing, Lying Shepherd, English Setter, Setter Group

1959, 5153-55, Heidenreich, Chow-Chow Sitting, Waiting Poodle/same (Rüde)

1960, 5233, Heidenreich, Lying Dalmatian; 5234, Rendlen-Schneider, Rottweiler

Insects:
1914, 381 new, 384 new, 385 new, 388 new, Himmelstoss, May Beetle, Butterfly, same, Cicada; 387 new, Küster, Stag Beetle; 390 new-393 new, Mourning Cloak, Buckeye, Swallowtail, Sulphur.
1923, 637-638, 642, 644-645, Himmelstoss, Azure, Buckeye, Dragonfly, May Beetle, Cicada; 387 new, Kaiser, Butterfly with wings up; 643, Küster, Stag Beetle; 647, Caasmann, Grasshopper
1924, 722, 732, Butterfly, Swallowtail; 733-734, Moldenhauer, Butterfly, same
1925, 762-764, Zschäbitz, Scarab, Hercules and Rhinoceros Beetles
1927, 924, Otto, Swarm of Bees
1950, 1835, Küspert, Swallowtail; 1836-37, Butterflies
1953, 1940, Klingler, Admiral
1956, 5033, Küspert, Butterfly large

Reptiles:
1914, 386 new, Himmelstoss, Lizard
1923, 640, Himmelstoss, Lizard; 641, Küster, Turtle; 646, Caasmann, Snail
1925, 761, Zschäbitz, Chameleon
1934, 1526, Lizard on new base

Lions:
1918, 526, Krebs-Himmelstoss, Small Lion
1919, 556, Kärner, Victorious Homecoming (Lioness with kill)
1929, 1049, Gaul, Lying Lion
1934, 1293, Fritz, Lion Group
1937, 1676, Rendlen-Schneider, Young Lion with Ball
1942-43, 1752, Heidenreich, Lion Group
1952, 1887, Heidenreich, Small Lion Group

Mythological Animals (see also Grotesque Animals):
1913, 301, Diller, Lucky Pig
1924, 708, Himmelstoss, Wonder Bird
1926, 880, Zschäbitz, Imaginary Bird
1927, 912, Zschäbitz, Fo-Dog
1928, 996, Oppel, Trojan Horse; 1016, Boess, The Little Bird
1931, 1140, Heidenreich, Small Swan for America
1949, 1810, Esser, Pegasus
1951, 1869, Heidenreich, Lucky Pig, same running
1954, 1966, Heidenreich, Hubertus Stag sitting
1960, Heidenreich, Stork

Rodents:
1912, 188, Himmelstoss, Pair of Mice
1913, 199, 259, 269, Himmelstoss, Mouse alone, Rabbit, same
1923, 675, Obermaier, Hazel Mouse
1924, 724, Himmelstoss, Small Rabbit
1925, 759, Zacherl-Klee, Squirrel
1934, 1290, Kärner, Squirrel
1951, 1863, Bachem, Squirrel with Woodpecker
1952, 1875-80, Heidenreich, Hedgehog sitting/running, Rabbit jumping, Mouse, Sitting/Standing Rabbit; 1893, Fritsch, Sitting Rabbit
1959, 5181, Seemann, Weasel

Horses:
1916, 443, Moldenhauer, Horse
1923, 626 new, Maison, Horse; 658, Moldenhauer, Small Horse
1925, 754, Schliepstein, Horse; 787, Graevenitz, Foal
1926, 861, Graevenitz, Jumping Foal
1927, 922, Graevenitz, Group of Foals
1934, 1524, 1528, Kärner, High Spirits, Foal; 1543, Graevenitz, Foal
1936, 1601, Rottmann, Farm Horse; 1609-10, Hussmann, Hannibal (horse's head), Trotter (Hannibal)
1938, 1689, 1697, Hussmann, Horse (Oleander), Lippizaner Head
1939, 1718-19, Hussmann, Foal Standing/Lying
1946, 1757-58, Hussmann, Jumping/Feeding Foal
1947, 1776, Heidenreich, Foal
1948, 1787, Heidenreich, Horse's Head (Arabian)
1950, 1830, Tuaillon, Horse from model 1723; 1832-33 Hussmann, Grazing Horse, Galloping Foal; 1834, Heidenreich, School Gallop
1951, 1855, Heidenreich, Climbing Horse
1952, 1886, Klingler, Lying Foal
1953, 1908, Schmitt, Lying Horse; 1939, Klingler, Climbing Horse
1954, 1956, Stangl, Horse
1956, 5043, von Martin, Horse (Chasala)
1959, 5161-62, Schmitt, Foal, Foal on Three Legs; 5195-96, Falchi, Climbing/Pacing Horse
1960, 5222, Falchi, Baroque Horse

Other Mammals:
1925, 755, Graevenitz, Young Antelope
1926, 822, Moldenhauer, Zebra; 862, Fritz, Lying Giraffe
1927, 906, 971-972, Fritz, Giraffe, Waterbuck, Kudu Antelope; 942, Geibel, Tiger Drinking
1930, 1097, Winterfeldt, Panther
1931, 1146, Perry, African Stag
1933, 1260, Schliepstein, Panther with Ball
1934, 1300, Schliepstein, Large Panther
1950, 1845, Heidenreich, Somalian Wild Ass Foal
1953, 1938, Klingler, Rhinoceros
1954, 1965, Heidenreich, Somalian Wild Ass Foal lying
1955, 5019, Heidenreich, Okapi
1956, 5026-27, Engel, Zebu, Guanaco
1958, 5136, Christmann, Giraffe; 5147, Heidenreich, Young Camel
1960, 5215, Falchi, Leopard

Birds:
1910, 56, Fischer, Kingfisher
1912, 97, 102, 102a, 106-108, 128, 132, Himmelstoss, Sparrow on large base, Robin on high/low base, Falcon, Owlet, Woodpecker, Wild Duck, Cockatoo; 97a, 108a, Sparrow/Woodpecker on small base; 127, Zügel, Young Magpie; 163, Veit, Owl on Base
1913, 257, Caasmann, Budgie large; 290, Diller, Heathcock; 322, Titmouse; 323, 329, Wunderlich, Robin Pair, Bullfinch; 340, Zügel, Buzzard
1914, 353, 356-357, Wunderlich, Sparrows, Budgie and Bullfinch pairs; 401, Eagle on Cross
1916, 444, Krebs-Himmelstoss, Parrot
1917, 485, Sparrow on Roof Tile
1919, 554, Moldenhauer, Parrot
1920, 574-578, Kärner, Bullfinch, Stilt, Bluebird, Goldfinch, Oriole
1921, 590, Two Budgies; 606, Himmelstoss, Falcon on high base
1922, 607, Wunderlich, Titmouse; 608, 610, Himmelstoss, Woodpecker, Robin; 609, Kärner, Bullfinch; 611, Fischer, Kingfisher [page 148]
1923, 632-633, 653-654, 679, 701, Kärner, Swallow, Canary, Cockatoo, same, Pheasant, Budgies; 676, Obermaier, Falcon; 677, 686, Schliepstein, Weaverbird, Magpie
1924, 725, Bastian, Bird; 729, Zügel, Lying Marabou; 749, Kärner, Parrot; 751, Zschäbitz, Young Jackdaw
1925, 767, Zschäbitz, Peacock
1926, 866, Wunderlich, Titmouse; 867, Fischer, Kingfisher; 868, Kärner, Bullfinch; 869-871, Himmelstoss, Woodpecker, Falcon, Robin; 874, 882, 885, 902, Otto, Woodpecker, Owl, Jay, Gull (Departing); (866-871 on new bases)
1927, 965, Otto, Grebe
1928, 988, 991, Otto-Eichwald, Titmouse, Bittern
1929, 1036, Metzger, Stilt; 1042, Küster, Ostrich Pair; 1048, Gaul, Hawk; 1074, Oppel, Marabou; 1076-78, Otto-Eichwald, Blackbird Group, Titmouse, Bluetail
1930, 1108, Zschäbitz, Owl

1934, 1291-92, 1531, Himmelstoss, Young Starling, Bird Group, Starling Group; 1521-23, 1539-41, 1546, Heidenreich, Flamingo, head down/on back-high, Stork, Heron, Gull, Pelican; 1525, Kingfisher on new base
1935, 1551, 1575, Heidenreich, Large Eagle, Bird of Paradise
1936, 1582, Feldtmann, Toucan
1937, 1646-54, 1660, 1662, 1670-71, Heidenreich, Titmouse/same/same, Starling, Yellowhammer, Finch, Cherrystone-biter, Siskin, Nuthatch, Wren, Jay, Ara, Wild Duck
1938, 1678, 1691, 1695, Heidenreich, Kingfisher, Woodpecker, Grouse
1939, 1709, 1725, Heidenreich, Falcon, Scissortail; 1727, Schmitt, Grebe
1940, 1736, Heidenreich, Lapwing
1941, 1741-43, Heidenreich, Titmouse, Kingfisher, Robin
1942-43, 1749-50, 1753-55, Heidenreich, Snipe male/female, Bird of Paradise, Shrike, Oriole
1946, 1756, Heidenreich, Small Eagle
1947, 1761, 1768, 1774, Heidenreich, Jay new, Silktail, Thistlefinch
1948, 1781-83, 1786, 1788, Heidenreich, Owl, Finch, Cuckoo, Paradise Widow, Crossbill Group
1949, 1801-02, 1807, 1809, 1816, 1819, Heidenreich, Shrike, Titmouse, Bullfinch, Crane, Sparrow Group, Roller
1951, 1846, Heidenreich, Ulm Sparrow
1952, 1901, Heidenreich, Kingfisher
1953, 1906, Heidenreich, Chickenhawk
1954, 1975, Friedrich-Gronau, Starling
1955, 1984, 1987, 1999, Heidenreich, Heron Group, Heathcock, Large Pelican; 1992, Fraas, Quetzal; 5005, 5021-22, Schmitt, Heron Group, Parrot Pair on low base, same on wall plastic; 5010, Küspert, Ringneck Pheasant
1956, 5031-32, 5054, 5070-71, 5073, Heidenreich, Playing Seals, Kingfisher (wall plastic), Turtledove, Large Pheasant/Hen Pheasant, Turtledoves, Pheasant Group
1957, 5080, 5100, Küspert, Seidenliest, Bird Nest with Adult Birds; 5090, Schmitt, Peacock Group; 5099, 5103-04, 5107, Heidenreich, Stilt, Starling Group, Titmouse, Bee-eater
1958, 5109, 5128-29, 5142, 5148, Heidenreich, Blackbird in Snow, Wallrunner, Finch Group, Bird (Irene), Kingfisher; 5110, Küspert, Bird Nest with Young; 5112, Gessner, Partridge in Snow
1959, 5191-5192, 5201-05, Heidenreich, Nightingale, Gold Wren, Crane watching/on one leg, Large Pheasant, Sparrow I-II; 5197-5200, Falchi, Redheaded Woodpecker, Gold Wren, Flycatcher, Bluebird
1960, 5206-07, 5212, 5221, 5231, 5235, 5238, 5244, Heidenreich, Heidenreich, Sparrow III, Crane Group, Titmouse, Gold Wren, Titmouse, Crane alone, Bunting, Gold Wren in Winter; 5208-09, 5213-14, 5216-17, 5220, 5240-43, Falchi, Sapsucker, Crane, Bird with Crest, Cuckoo, Redstart, Falcon, Bluejay, Peacock, Golden Pheasant, Flagsylph, Flamingo Group; 5210, Seemann, Bird Plastic

Water Animals:
1913, 302, Diller, Sealion
1914, 359 new-361 new, 389 new, 396 new, 400 new, Himmelstoss, three of Penguin on base, Tree Frog, four of Penguin
1923, 648, 693, Himmelstoss, Tree Frog, Penguin Pair
1925, 772, Scheibe, Fish
1927, 941, Oppel, Seahorse; 949, Otto, Lobster
1934, 1289, Kärner, Sealion; 1311, Himmelstoss, Sealion Group; 1506, Himmelstoss, Penguins (model 360 on new base)
1937, 1636-37, Heidenreich, Scalare Group/Alone
1939, 1711-12, 1720, Heidenreich, King Penguin standing, head up/down, Barn Owl Group
1947, 1766, Heidenreich, Scalare fleeing
1952, 1900, Heidenreich, Fighting Fish
1955, 5004, Heidenreich, Scalare Group small
1958, 5111, Küspert, Climbing Tree Frog
1959, 5169-75, Schmitt, Swan, Small Swan I-VI; 5179-80, Mahn, Lying/Sitting Sealion

Wild Animals:
1913, 261, 278, 334, Diller (?), Roebuck, Sneaking Fox, Fox with Goose
1925, 765, Schliepstein, Deer Group; 806, Graevenitz, Young Deer
1926, 824, Zügel, Resting Deer
1927, 919, 944, Graevnitz, Jumping Rabbit, Mountain Goat
1929, 1047, Gaul, Buffalo
1933, 1248, Kärner, Fox
1934, 1538, Kärner, Sneaking Fox; 1542, Sinkö, Small Fox
1935, 1555, 1565-66, 1579, Heidenreich, Stag large, Doe with Fawn, Fawn, Small Deer; 1572-74, Feldtmann, Weasel Group, Weasel standing/sneaking
1936, 1585, Heidenreich, Small Roebuck
1937, 1638, Rempel, Wild Goat with Kid
1938, 1682, 1690, 1704-06, Heidenreich, Grazing Young Deer, Large Elk, Elk Head, Young Fox, Playing Foxes, Three Playing Foxes; 1692, Himmelstoss, Chamois
1939, 1713, 1721, 1726, Heidenreich, Elk Head (wall plaque), Lying Deer, Small Elk
1942-43, 1751, Heidenreich, Standing Stag
1947, 1775, Heidenreich, Fawn large
1948, 1790, Heidenreich, Roebuck
1950, 1841, Heidenreich, Small Roebuck with arched back
1951, 1870, Heidenreich, Wild Goat
1952, 1871, 1881, 1903, Heidenreich, Deer Group small, Buffalo with base, Fawn seeking
1953, 1910, 1915, Heidenreich, Elk lying, Small Roebuck from model 1871
1954, 1962, Heidenreich, Small Fawn; 1980, Stangl, Lying Deer
1955, 1982, 1991, 5011, Heidenreich, Fawn Head looking backward, Wild Goat, Charging Roebuck; 1990, 5008, Küspert, Roebuck Head, Young Fox sitting; 1995, Schmitt, Wild Boar Group
1958, 5135, Christmann, Mountain Goat; 5146, Heidenreich, Fawn
1959, 5163, Schmitt, Young Stag

Ornaments from the Selb Art Department

See the general introduction to the model lists.

After 1934, the ornamental porcelain produced by the Art Department of the Selb factory, with one exception in 1959, was no longer included in the model lists. Ornamental porcelain from this factory was also produced in the tableware department of the Selb works. But there are no systematic accounts of this production available.

After the name of the object (such as "Vase," separated by a comma, are specific details of the object (such as Vase, engraved). Then comes the model number, then the artist's name, if known. If the artists designed the whole following series, then his name is right after the object, such as Vase, Oppel, ...

Object Details Model Number Artist

1898-1910 Selb factory numbers

Drinking Cup, with three feet, 204
Flowerpot, 180
Candy Dish, 157
Box, flat, pierced, 171, 195
Pitcher with handle, 104, 107
Jardiniere, +/- relief, 202, oval, 203, round, 209
Pot, 13
Box, large, 147a
 Flower box, 95
Lamp,
 Aromatic, with pierced shade, 22
 Light box, 154, 156
 Lamp foot with acanthus relief, 207
Platter, oval, 121, with three horses, 131
Rose bowl, 147
Bowl, 200
 Ashtray, 155, 158
Fruit bowl, with two handles, 31, on feet, 205
Bowl, with feet, 206, oval with cover, 208
Centerpiece, with pheasant, 86
Plate
 Plate, with dog, 130, with polar bear, 132, with horse head, 133
 Wall plate, 41, water sprite, 69, Loreley, 70, Rhine Maidens, 71, Mountain Fairy, 72, Wood Fairy, 73 (69-73 Diefenbach- Roth), Nürnberg, 120, Juleaften 1907, 140, 143
Urn, with goat's head, 194
Vase, 1-4, 6, 8-9, 11-12, 14-21, 23, 25-30, 32-40, 42, 45, 47- 54a, 56-60, 61b-68, Water Sprite, 74, Amor, 75, Mountain Fairy, 76, Loreley, 77 (75-77, Diefenbach-Roth), Owl, 78, Swans, 79, Wood Fairy, 80, Rhine Maidens, 81 (80-81, Diefenbach-Roth), 82, 84, Loreley, 88, Mountain Fairy, 89 (88-89, Diefenbach-Roth), Water Sprite, 90, Wood Fairy, 91, Rhine Maidens, 92 (91-92, Diefenbach-Roth), 96-100, 102-103, 105-106, 108-112, 114-119, 123, 125-129, 134-139, 141-142, 144, 149-153, 162-166, 178-179, 181-183, 185 Rosenthal, 186-187
 octagonal, 169, and pierced, 173
 with acanthus relief, 207
 bowed out, 44a
 with goats' heads, 198
 Covered vase, 7, 10, 24, with pierced top, 176, 191, hexagonal, 193, 196
 pierced, 148, 167, 168
 with four lizards, 83
 curved in, 5, 25a, 33a, 35a
 Empire vase, 199
 with angel, 87
 with fly, 43b
 curved, 43a, 46a, 47a, 48a, 51a, 55, 61a
 smooth, 43, 46, 61
 with smooth bottom, 44
 with three handles, 94
 with cherries, 124
 Crater vase, 190
 with crocodile, 85
 with lily shape, 101
 with mouse, 55a
 oval, smooth, 145-146, 174, 184 Rosenthal
 Ornate vase, 192
 round, pierced, 172
 with snails, 46b
 on base, 197
 with tiger, 93 large
 unpierced, 167a
 Trophy vase, +/- base, 188-189
 square, pierced, 170, not pierced, 170a
 cylindrical, 122

Unknown or not made objects: 113, 159-161, 175, 177

1910-1919 Selb Art Department numbering

Drinking Cup, with roses, 34
 Ashtray, 113 Training School
 Ice bowl, 530
Flowerpot, 165
Candy dish, 282-283
Brooch, 251, 252, Iron Cross, 403
Box, 285, 424, turning, 517, 528
 rectangular, 10
 Egg box, 117
 "He loves me," 409, Caasmann
 five-part, 496
 with three feet, pierced, 364
 with four oval feet, 413
 Jelly box, with apple, 66, with fruits, 419
 Cookie bix, with lid, 63, 65
 with chicks, 267-268
 Merry Ride, 305, Caasmann
 oval, 11, 284, on four feet, 312, 365, pierced, 491, four-part, 494, 503
 rectangular, 502
 Rococo, 344, 456, with four feet, 548
 round, with four feet, 17, 157, low, 219, high, 220, smooth, pierced, 227, on three feet, 313, 327, 366, 499
 hexagonal, high, 15
 four-part, arched lid, 495
 Cigarette box, 240, 512
Bell, with [Käuzchen], 101, Himmelstoss
Hatpin, 64, 78, 89, engraved, 90
 Hatpin holder, 71
Jardiniere,
 with kingfisher, 2, Liebermann
 on foot, 518, smooth, 518a
Lamp and Light, 351 new
 Ceiling light, 154, 156
 Faun light, 36
 smooth, 464
 engraved, 469
 lamp body with flower relief, 105, 110 (model 105)
 Lamp foot, 211-216, 367, 368 new-373 new, 457 (model 21), 458, 461 (Maria service) Rosenthal, 462-463, 468, 490, pierced, 492, 500, 504-505, 507-509, 513, 532 Markones, with grape cherub, 535a, with bowl on three feet, 539 Opel, in columnar form, 561, with cutout base, 562, with square shadem 563, with hexagonal shade, 564, with lion's head, 565
 with Greek dancer, 493 Liebermann (model 143)
Liqueur glass (?), 383 new
 Mocha cup, 20-25
Easter egg, with three feet, 474
Plaque, Munich Child, 114
Platter, 382 new
Platter,
 oval, 121 with advertising, 133, with mountain goat, 300
 Wall plate, round, 150

1920 to 1929

1930 to 1934

large, book shape 1128 Fleischmann
small, 1131 Fleischmann
Mirror frame, with two cherubs 1230 Kärner
Centerpiece, with figures, 1264 (model 1022), 1265 (model 1099), 1266 (model 1063), 1267 (model 1023)
Clock, with two cherubs 1237 Kärner
Saucer,
Hot plate, for Maria service 1298
Hot plate, smooth 1185, for Maria service 1187
Vase, 1113, 1161
large, with Mary relief 1112
Mary, 1155, low 1164 (model 1155)
two-part, with holes 1309
bowl vase (model 739), low 1144, high 1145
Vaporizer,
Bear, 1138 Küster
Elephant, 1101 Küster
Duck, 1102 Küster
Penguin, 1136 Küster
Sealion, 1137 Küster
Perfume atomizer 1100, 1105
Miracle ball (?), 1109
Cigarette holder, for Maria service, 1287

1950-1959
Ashtray and cigarette box in feminine form 5097 Peynet
Bell base, with peacock 1993 Fraas
Candlestick with horn of plenty right/left, 1826-1827 Lang
Light, two-armed water sprite 1874 Lang, as locomotive with loving couple 5098 Peynet
Table ornament Peynet, 5152 (model 5151), 5184-5185, Cloverleaf 5186, 5187-5190 Fisch I-III
Vase, as swan 5168 Schmitt
Wall relief I/II, 5001-5002 Stangl

Models since 1960

Pl.# indicates number of Plössberg issue of this model.

Number	Name	Artist
1960		
5244	Winter gold cockerel	Heidenreich
5245	Stork	Heidenreich
1961		
5246	Rooster	Rücker
5247	Scarlet Spint	Falchi
5248	Colored Lori Group	Falchi
5249	Butterfly group	Falchi
5250	Colored Lori alone, tail up	Falchi
5251	same, tail down, with berry	Falchi
5252	Flamingo group (3), large	Heidenreich
5253	Cavalier on carousel horse	Peynet
5254	Girl on carousel horse	Peynet
5255	Meteor (horse)	Kärner
1962		
5256	Butterfly (Pl.# 96)	Koch
5257	Pointer, lying (Pl.# 172)	
5258	Goose (Pl.# 223)	
5259	Deer jumping (Pl.# 249)	
5260	Cat on ball (Pl.# 250)	Nagy
5261	Carmen o.S. Klein (24)(Pl.# 425)	
5262	Sealion (Pl.# 533)	Fritz
5263	Pair of Ducks (Pl.# 575)	
5264	Group of Deer (Pl.# 576)	Fritz
5265	Seal with Ball (Pl.# 578)	Zügel
5266	Cat on Ball (Pl.# 590)	Nagy
5267	Emperor Pheasant (Pl.# 633)	
5268	Gazelle Group (Pl.# 641)	Fritz
5269	Cockatoo miniature (Pl.# 642)	Fritz
5270	Fox playing, miniature (Pl.# 644)	Fritz
5271	Bulldog miniature (Pl.# 646)	Fritz
5272	Lamb miniature (Pl.# 647)	Fritz
5273	Toucan miniature (Pl.# 673)	Fritz
5274	Fox, miniature (Pl.# 674)	Fritz
5275	Mary, small (50) (Pl.# 762)	
5276	Nefertiti, small (Pl.# 777)	Berlin State Museum
5277	Moor with Fish (Pl.# 866)	
5278	Cockatoo (Pl.# 867)	
5279	Heron (Pl.# 868)	Meisel
5280	Rhapsody (Pl.# 5280)[?]	
5281	Dachshund standing (Pl.# 960)	Fritz
5282	Silver Heron. large (Pl.# 964	Fritz
5283	Magpie (Pl.# 978)	
5284	Kitten playing (Pl.# 1120)	Kärner
5285	Young Fox sitting (Pl.# 1122)	Feldmann
5286	Rooster (Pl.# 1195)	
5287	Honey-eater (Pl.# 1243)	Legat
5288	Finch (Pl.# 1247)	Legat
5289	Kingfisher (Pl.# 1248)	Legat
5290	Teenager	Friedrich-Gronau
5291	Girl with Bowl	Friedrich-Gronau
5292	After the Bath	Friedrich-Gronau
5293	Galloping Horse	Falchi
5294	Sparrow	Falchi
1963		
5295	Wild Boar	Bohn
5296	Young Boar	Bohn
1965		
5297	Quetzal	Falchi
1973		
5299	Fox sitting	Röhring
1975		
5300	Bird-seller	Goebel
5301	Ice-diver, small	Wirkkala
5302	Ice-diver, large	Wirkkala

Number	Name	Artist
1976		
5305	Flower Girl	Goebel
1977		
5304	Poet and Muse	St. Phalle
5305	Candelabra woman, 3 arms, hat	Wiinblad
5306	Candelabra woman, two arms	Wiinblad
1978		
5307	Scholl Plate I	Scholl
5308	Scholl Plate II	Scholl
5309	Candelabra Rendezvous	Falchi
5310	Gazelle	Falchi
5311	Panther	Falchi
5312	Ostrich	Falchi
1979		
5313	Oath of Love (Plössberg)	Förster
5314	Buffoon (Plössberg)	Förster
5315	Comedian (Plössberg)	Förster
1982		
5316	Candelabra Griffin & Snake	Fuchs

Number	Name	Artist
1983		
5317	Phoenix	Fuchs
1984		
5318	Object	Paolozzi
1985		
5319	Candelabra Sculpture	Wiinblad
1986		
5321-5324	Horses of San Marco	Falchi
5360	Quadriga, left half	Falchi
5361	Quadriga, right half	Falchi
5325	Christmas Angel kneeling, one arm	
5326	Christmas Angel standing, one arm	
5327	Dolls' Head (for Neustadt)	
5328	Christmas Angel standing, two arms	
5329	Doll's Head, small	
1988		
5345	Pegasus	Fuchs

Limited Editions of Art and Other Items, 1968-1995

This list is complete as of December 1994. The limited-edition objects are alphabetized by the **artist's name**, then by the **year** of issue; then comes the **title** of the object, sometimes with notes on material or technique, then the **number issued**, and finally the **retail price** *in German Marks, including value-added tax, in the year in which it was first issued.* The word "Year" in the Issue column means that *as many were made as could be sold in that one year.*

The list has been compiled from records of the Rosenthal firm, which are unfortunately not complete, especially as regards the older objects.

The author and publisher cannot guarantee the correctness and completeness of the list.

Artist	Year	Title	Issue	Price-DM
Alt, Otmar	1978	Suomi-Vase, Object # 5	500	1480
"	1978	Suomi Mocha Service (15)	500	2700
"	1978	Ceramic Lantern Carrier	500	2878
"	1980	Circus Vase 18 cm	500	165
"	1980	" 22 cm	500	195
"	1980	Circus Box	500	125
"	1980	Ceramic Moonflower 20 cm	500	165
"	1980	" 27 cm	500	230
"	1980	Artist Plate	5000	135
"	1984	Ceramic Object Ulula	300	880
"	1986	Ceramic Clock Coq O'clock	99	3800
"	1987	Glass Object Hermes	500	1650
"	1989	" Girl in the Moon	99	2450
"	1989	" Merlin with red nose	99	2450
"	1990	Porcelain Girl Mask	500	1400
"	1900	Glass Object Bluebill	99	2850
"	1990	" Flower Singer	99	2850
"	1992	Ceramic Tempo Floralis	299	1350
"	1992	Glass Object Mister Max	99	3900
"	1992	" Miss Minie	99	3900
"	1993	" Turnip-nose	99	4900
"	1993	" Elephant Courting	99	4900
"	1994	" When the Rooster Crows	99	4900
"	1994	" Little Table Stag	99	4900
Arnulf, Rainer	1994	Gropius Pot Green Tree	99	1480
Attersee, Chr.	1991	15-pierce Service Tea Trout	99	5500
"	1994	Gropius pot Fox's Advice	99	1480
Avramadis, J.	1968	Porcelain Relief	50	6686
Bach, Elvira	1993	Vase on Wooden Platter	75	4900
"	1993	Artist Plate	2000	298

Artist	Year	Title	Issue	Price-DM
"	1994	Gropius Pot Poisonous Snake	99	1480
Bayer, Herbert	1982	Year Object Landscape	1500	1390
"	1982	Glass Scul. Winding Stairs	150	2200
Bill, Max	1975	Artist Plate no. 5	5000	
Boehm, Michael	1980	Filigree Glass "Reticelli":		
		White Wine	300	260
		Burgundy	300	240
		Sparkling Wine Flute	300	275
		Bowl, 22 cm	200	1980
		Bowl, 36 cm	200	1980
		Bowl, 42 cm	200	2880
		Candelabra, 20 cm	300	240
		Candelabra, 26 cm	300	280
		Candelabra, 32 cm	300	320
"	1981	Glass Collage Bowl	50	2990
"	1988	Year Object Glass Wings	Year	1485
Bugaev, Sergei	1994	Gropius Pot Derevolution	99	1480
Chia, Sandro	1986	Artist Plate no. 24	Year	145
"	1987	Porc. Obj. Dolore da cani	125	2800
"	1987	" Seated Man	40	12500
"	1989	" Palio white	125	2800
"	1989	" Palio black	125	2800
"	1989	" Pygmalion	50	3300
"	1991	" Seated Figure	50	5000
Cimiotti, Emil	1968	Vegetative Panel Relief	100	1135
Cocteau, Jean	1974	Artist Plate no. 2	5000	
Croissant, M.	1968	Relief	100	950
Dali, Salvador	1976	Suomi Objects:		
		No. 1 Bowl with Cover	500	2200
		No. 2 Bowl	500	1900
		No. 3 Coffeepot	500	1700
		No. 4 Teapot	500	1500
"	1976	Year Plate in Porcelain	3000	1780
"	1978	Artist Plate no. 12	5000	480
"	1979	Gilded Relief	97	13950
"	1979	Platinum Relief	91	13950
"	1979	Year Plate in Glass	3000	1250
"	1980	Angelic Messenger Ceramic	2000	1290
Dubuffet, Jean	1984	Ceramic Object Encrier	25	6500
Fetting, R.	1993	Pelican 15-piece Service	99	4900
"	1994	Gropius Pot Fatamorgana	99	1480
Fontana, Lucio	1968	Concetto spaziale ovale	75	1620
"	1968	Concetto spaziale taglio	75	2450
"	1968	Concetto spaziale crater	75	2450
Fruhtrunk, G.	1974	Year Plate in Porcelain	3000	450
Fuchs, Ernst	1979	Suomi Objects "Lohengrin":		
		No. 1 Bowl with Cover	500	530
		No. 2 Bowl	500	490
		No. 3 Coffeepot	500	420
		No. 4 Teapot	500	440
"	1979	Vase, Eagle with Snake	3000	256
"	1980	Tea Serv. Magic Sea white	500	1360
		" blue	500	2119
"	1980	Year Plate Pegasus glass	3000	980
"	1981	Artist Plate no. 17	5000	185
"	1982	Candelabra Griffin+Snake	100	2600
"	1982	Year Object Lohengrin	1000	1850
"	1983	Porcelain Object Phoenix	50	5860
"	1988	Porcelain Mask Incognito	500	1200
"	1988	Porcelain Object Pegasus	99	3700
Giovanopoulos, Paul	1994	Gropius Pot Hearts	99	1480
Gomringer, E.	1974	Artist Plate no. 3	5000	
Gräsel, Friedrich	1980	Ceramic Sclupture Torso	50	2790
Grass, Günther	1973	Artist Plate no. 1	5000	
Grieshaber, HAP	1968	Porcelain Relief Pan	75	1790
"	1976	Suomi Objects:		
		No. 1 Bowl with Cover	500	720
		No. 2 Bowl	500	750
		No. 3 Coffeepot	500	520
		No. 4 Teapot	500	470
"	1978	Suomi Vase Object no. 5	500	1320
"	1980	Suomi Obj. Carmina burana:		
		No. 1 Bowl with Cover	500	1817
		No. 2 Bowl	500	1313
		No. 3 Coffeepot	500	1248
		No. 4 Teapot	500	1122
"	1981	Year Object The Pair	3000	980
"	1982	Vase Knight with Angel	300	1190
Groen, Daniel	1991	Porcelain Raphael Motif	100	1350
"	1994	Artist Espresso Year Cup	3000	130
"	1994	Artist Place Plate	2000	250
Hadzi, Dimitri	1968	Sculpture studies white	1998	
"	1968	" yellow, 50 in all	2333	
"	1968	Porcelain Relief King	50	2440
Hadju, Etienne	1968	Porcelain Relief Tate	50	2773
Hajek, O.H.	1968	Porcelain Relief Farbwege	100	2060
"	1980	Year Plate Road Sign	3000	1300
"	1981	Porc. Vase Color Symbol	100	410
"	1981	" Color Labyrinth	300	313
"	1982	Artist Plate no. 18	5000	158
"	1984	Year Object Glas Sign	750	1450
"	1994	Gropius Pot Avalon	99	1480
Hartung, Karl	1968	Porcelain Relief I	75	1135
"	1968	" II	75	1135
Hauser, Erich	1980	Wall Relief Landscape	100	3750
Heiliger, B.	1968	Relief Block matte white	1375	
		" or gilded, 75 in all	2124	

Artist	Year	Title	Issue	Price-DM
Henze, Hans W.	1975	Artist Plate no. 6	5000	110
Hundertwasser, Fr.	1983	Ceramic Spiralental	2000	1595
“	1983	“ Flower House	500	2490
Immendorf, J.	1989	Lehmbruck Saga Object	99	6500
“	1991	Artist Plate no. 27 Time	195	
“	1994	Gropius Pot Vowels	99	1480
Kanyak, Zsafia	1979	Ceramic Lamp no. 0	1000	300
“	1979	“ no. 1	1000	300
“	1979	“ no. 2	1000	300
“	1979	“ no. 3	1000	300
“	1979	“ no. 4	1000	500
“	1979	“ no. 5	1000	500
“	1979	Amethyst Box no. 1	1000	317.50
“	1979	“ no. 2	1000	278.10
“	1979	“ no. 3	1000	257.20
“	1979	“ no. 4	1000	167.30
“	1979	“ Object 1	1000	430.70
“	1979	“ Object 2	1000	290
“	1979	Opal Box no. 1	1000	317.50
“	1979	“ no. 2	1000	278.10
“	1979	“ no. 3	1000	257.20
“	1979	“ no. 4	1000	167.30
“	1979	“ Object 1	1000	430.70
Kass, Janos	1987	Head on Wood Base black	100	1850
Knef, Hildegard	1976	Artist Plate no. 9	5000	
König, Fritz	1968	Porcelain Relief Window	100	2398
Kokoschka, Oskar	1979	Wall Relief The Potter	20	9000
Kolar, Jiri	1986	Porcelain Still Life	75	3600
“	1986	Year Object Ars poetica	1000	1875
“	1986	Ceramic Object Gold Fever	75	3900
“	1990	Porcelain Clock Ars tempi	50	1950
“	1990	Artist Plate no. 26 Time	165	
“	1994	Artist Place Plate	2000	239
Kopystiansky, Igor	1994	Gropius Pot	99	1480
Kriwet, F	1975	Artist Plate no. 8	5000	
Lang, Ernst M.	1979	Satirical Plate 26 cm:		
“		“ Heuss	5000	
“		“ Scheel	5000	
“		“ Schmidt	5000	
“		“ Brandt	5000	
“		“ Strauss	5000	
“		“ Kohl	5000	
“		“ Rühmann	5000	
“	1980	“ Kreisky	5000	55
“	1988	Marlene Dietrich Plate	5000	55
“	1988	Mao Tsetung Plate	5000	55
Leissler, A.	1979	Year Plate no. 9	3000	950
Lichtenstein, R.	1984	Porcelain Tea Service	100	15000
“	1990	Artist Plate	3000	295

Artist	Year	Title	Issue	Price-DM
Loth, Wilhelm	1968	Käthe Kollwitz Relief	100	1122
		in memoriam		
Matschinsky-	1980	Sculpture Blossoming Tree	50	13500
Denninghoff	1982	Porcelain Vase	300	853
		Autumn Wind		
Mavignier, A.	1968	Flat and Convex Relief:		
		matte white	50	2200
		gilded	50	3500
“	1979	Artist Plate no. 14	5000	148
Menuhin, Yehudi	1977	Artist Plate no. 10	5000	120
Moore, Henry	1971	Porcelain Relief Moonhead	6	19000
“	1973	“ Rings	6	44000
“	1979	“ in wood frame, white	50	14100
“	1979	“ black	25	18100
Morandini, M.	1980	Sculpture Onda construtta	100	6296
“	1981	Year Object Dimensioni	2500	1500
		(Tri onda)		
“	1982	Vase Movimento 30 cm	150	278.20
“	1982	“ Notturno 26 cm	150	278.20
“	1982	“ Crescendo 20 cm	150	278.20
“	1983	Porcelain Vase Arcus	200	660
“	1986	Year Obj. Foro geometrico	500	1850
“	1987	Service 15-piece Color	250	3500
“	1989	Artist Plate no. 25 Time	145	
“	1990	Service 15-p. Circolo nero	250	2950
“	1991	Porcelain Object		
		Rondo magico bianco	40	2870
		“ nero	40	3270
“	1992	Porcelain Object Empora	99	2200
“	1994	Gropius Pot Architee	99	1480
Nele. E.R.	1968	Porcelain Relief Anti War	100	1108
Paolozzi, Ed.	1977	Suomi Objects:		
		No. 1 Bowl with Cover	500	1660
		No. 2 Bowl	500	990
		No. 3 Coffeepot	500	880
		No. 4 Teapot	500	1100
“	1978	Porcelain Year Plate	3000	1380
“	1979	“ wood frame matte white	150	1780
“	1984	Porcelain Dog 2000	50	3850
“	1984	Artist Plate no. 20	3000	145
“	1985	Ceramic Year Object:		
		Tottenham Court Road	500	1250
“	1987	Portrait of an Actor	50	6800
“	1988	Porcelain Clock Belltower	99	5400
“	1993	Gold Relief on wood plate		
		with plexiglas cover	50	3500
“	1994	Gropius Pot Mekka-No	99	1480
Pasmore, Victor	1968	Porcelain Relief	50	3170
Peters, Herbert	1968	Porcelain Relief Ombroso	100	1035
Piene, Otto	1973	Porcelain Year Plate	3000	320

Artist	Year	Title	Issue	Price-DM
"	1974	Artist Plate no. 4	5000	160
"	1974	Rainbow Object 7-color	200	750
"	1974	" with platinum	30	1680
"	1975	Gold Bow Object	100	720
"	1975	Rainbow Service Object	200	1220
"	1977	Suomi Objects:		
		No. 1 Bowl with Cover	500	1050
		No. 2 Bowl	500	840
		No. 3 Coffeepot	500	1100
		No. 4 Teapot	500	990
Pomodoro, Gio	1968	Porcelain Relief Urania		
		" Center black		
		" platinum		
		" blue total:	75	1750
"	1968	Porcelain Relief Crowd	75	1199
Portanier, G.	1987	Artist Plate no. 23 Time	145	
"	1988	Ceramic Mask Pallas Athene	500	780
Portanier, Pasquale	1992	Artist Espresso Year Cup	3000	110
Pucci, Emilio	1977	Artist Plate no. 11	5000	110
Rabuzin, Ivan	1976	Suomi Objects:		
		No. 1 Bowl with Cover	500	755
		No. 2 Bowl	500	690
		No. 3 Coffeepot	500	650
		No. 4 Teapot	500	599
"	1978	Year Plate in glass	3000	520
"	1978	Artist Plate	5000	235
"	1979	Porcelain Vase 32 cm	300	585
"	1979	" 22 cm	300	485
"	1981	Year Object Four Seasons	3000	980
"	1983	Artist Espresso Year Cup	3000	110
Ris, G.E.	1968	Porcelain Relief	50	5100
"	1977	Year Object in glass	3000	550
"	1983	Year Object in porcelain	500	960
deSaint Phalle, Niki	1973	Porcelain Object Nana	200	550
Salomé	1985	Porcelain Sea-rose Pond	50	2900
"	1985	Year Object Mephisto	500	1875
"	1985	Ceramic Sumo Wrestler	50	2500
"	1986	Artist Plate no. 22	3000	145
"	1987	Porcelain Object Dancer	100	3950
"	1988	Ceramic Object Waterfall	299	2200
"	1989	Porcelain Obj. Berlin Mask	500	1200
"	1990	Porcelain Clock Timeless	99	4500
"	1992	Porz. Tigerman black/white	75	2900
"	1992	" black/yellow	75	2900
deSantillana, Laura	1991	Glass Object Mme. Wassily	75	2450
"	1991	" Monsieur Wassily	75	2650
Sapone, Natale	1972	Porcelain Object A 1	500	99
			300	170
			300	222
			300	150
Sapone cont'd			300	244
			300	222
"	1972	" B 1	200	166
			200	250
			200	380
			200	235
			200	340
			200	320
"	1972	" C 1	300	150
			200	222
			200	270
			200	266
			200	333
			200	270
"	1974	Object Vase 24 cm	400	110
			400	110
			400	110
"	1974	" 18 cm	400	66
			400	66
			400	66
"	1974	" 14 cm	400	48
			400	48
			400	48
"	1974	" 28 cm	400	155
			400	222
"	1974	" 32 cm	400	240
			400	322
"	1974	" 38 cm	400	290
			400	420
"	1974	Chop Dish	400	77
"	1974	Object Bowl 36 cm	400	110
"	1974	" 2/20 cm	400	55
"	1974	" 4/26 cm	400	59
"	1974	Object Vase 28 cm	500	340
"	1974	" 18 cm	750	177
"	1974	" 22 cm	750	150
"	1974	Year Plate in porcelain	3000	190
Seitz, Gustav	1968	Porc. Relief Loving Couple	75	1931
"	1968	" Torso	75	1670
"	1968	" Torso	75	761
Siesby, Alev	1982	Ceramic Bowl Object:		
		Taurus 13 cm	300	140
		" 16 cm	500	125
		" 20 cm	500	125
Uecker, Günther	1968	Porc. Relief White Rain	100	1088

Artist	Year	Title	Issue	Price-DM
"	1973	" Nail Object I round	50	2170
"	1973	" II oval	50	2450
"	1975	Year Plate in glass	3000	270
Valenti, Italo	1975	Porc. Relief The Sorceress		
		" white	25	1326
		" green	25	1860
		" gilded	25	2221
Vasarely, Victor	1968	Porcelain Relief NB 11		
		black/green		
		white		
		undecorationated total	50	3440
"	1968	" NB 22 Caope	50	16435
"	1971	"	100	990
			100	990
			100	990
			100	990
"	1971	"	75	1700
			75	1700
			75	1700
			75	1700
"	1971	"	50	2499
			50	2499
			50	2499
			50	2499
"	1971	"	100	3445
"	1976	Suomi Objects:		
		No. 1 Bowl with Cover	500	695
		No. 2 Bowl	500	560
		No. 3 Coffeepot	500	620
		No. 4 Teapot	500	950
"	1977	Year Plate in porcelain	3000	958
"	1978	Vase Object 24 cm	300	485
"	1978	" 44 cm	200	1200
"	1978	Artist Plate no. 13	5000	198
"	1979	Vase Object 28 cm	300	690
"	1979	" 32 cm	100	790
"	1979	" 24 cm	200	395
"	1982	Year Object Erebus glass	2000	1250
Weizsäcker,	1989	Conversation Landscape	50	1500
Andreas von	1990	" Evoluzione	50	2900
"	1991	Ceramic Mask Thinker	299	1250
"	1992	Porc. Clock Time Swings		
		I white	99	3750
		II black	99	3950
Wesselmann, T.	1982	Ceramic Still Life	25	10000
"	1984	Year Object Seascape	500	1250
"	1985	Artist Plate no. 21	3000	145
"	1986	Ceramic Bedroom	100	4750
		Blonde		
"	1988	Still Life on wood plate	299	3400
"	1993	Wall Landscape/	99	5900
		wood plate		

Artist	Year	Title	Issue	Price-DM
Whitaker, A.	1980	Object Series Tissu		
		Table Bowl 30 cm	300	892
		Bowl 14 cm	500	449
		Bowl 18 cm	500	589
		Vase 18 cm	500	195
		Vase 22 cm	500	248
Wiinblad, Björn	1975	Artist Plate no. 7	5000	480
"	1976	Year Plate in glass	3000	480
Wirkkala, Tapio	1971	Year Plate in glass	3000	480
"	1974	Vase Object Aphrodite	200	422
Wotruba, Fritz	1968	Porcelain Relief 3 Torsi	50	3199
Wunderlich, Paul	1979	Porcelain Object	150	2700
		Ellipsoid		
"	1980	Ceramic Sculpture	100	6400
		Anubis		
"	1983	Porcelain Object Vagant	50	1820
"	1983	Year Object Languste	1000	1250
"	1983	Artist Plate no. 19	5000	145
"	1984	Porcelain Mask I Terra	75	350
"	1984	" II Herba	75	350
"	1985	Year Object Horus I	1000	1450
"	1986	Tea Service	500	3200
		15-piece Leda		
"	1986	Porcelain Object	75	7800
		Horus II		
"	1987	Ceramic Strelizia I light	350	1490
"	1987	" dark	350	1490
"	1988	Porcelain Mask Wolf	500	1075
"	1989	Glass Object Massai	300	1650
"	1990	Glass Object Massai	300	1650
"	1993	Portrait of a Young Man	99	2900
"	1993	Artist Espresso Year Cup	3000	129
Zauli, Carlo	1980	Ceramic Sculpture	50	1330
		Quader		
"	1980	" Idol	100	1250

Limited Art Plates since 1973

1 G. Grass
2 J. Cocteau
3 E. Gomringer
4 O. Piene
5 M. Bill
6 H.W. Henze
7 B. Wiinblad
8 F. Kriwet
9 H. Knef
10 Y. Menuhin
11 E. Pucci
12 S. Dali
13 V. Vasarely
14 A. Mavignier
15 I. Rabuzin
16 O. Alt
17 E. Fuchs
18 O.H. Hajek
19 P. Wunderlich
20 E. Paolozzi
21 T. Weesselmann
22 Salomé
23 G. Portanier
24 S. Chia
25 M. Morandini
26 J. Kolar
27 J. Immendorf

Biographies of Designers, Modelers and Decorators

Data on well-known modern artists and designers who occasionally worked for Rosenthal since the sixties but not primarily in porcelain can be found in any modern art encyclopedia.

Aigner, Richard, ?, Munich sculptor, busts and statues, ca. 1911 free colleague of Rosenthal, Selb works; his models bear the misspelling Aichner.

Bachem, Bele, b. 1916 Düsseldorf, stage artist, painter, sketcher and author, 1951-1966 free colleague of Rosenthal, Selb works; for figures, decoration designs for utility and ornamental porcelain.

Backmund, Klaus, ?, sculptor, 1955 free colleague of Rosenthal, Selb works, for figures.

Baumann, Hans Theo, b. 1924 Basel, designer, free colleague of Arzberg, Daum, Gral, Schönwald, Berlin State Porcelain, Süssmuth, of Rosenthal 1954-1970, Selb and Thomas works; decorations for art and tableware departments, utensils.

Bendixen, Klaus, b. 1924 Hannover, painter, graphic artist, teacher, 1954-57 free colleague of Rosenthal, vase decorations.

Boess, Berthold, b. 1877 Karlsruhe-?, sculptor, 1913-34 free colleague of Rosenthal, Selb works, for figures.

Bontjes van Beek, Jan, 1899 Vejle, Jutland-1969 Berlin, ceramic artist who worked in Germany, teacher, 1952-53 free colleague of Rosenthal for vases.

Caasmann, A., ?, sculptor, 1912-13 free colleague of Rosenthal, Selb works, for figures.

Charol, Dorothea, 1889 Odessa-1963 London, sculptress, free colleague of the Schwarzburg Workshops, Volkstedt and Wedgwood, and Rosenthal, Bahnhof-Selb works, in the twenties, for figures.

Colnai, Luigi, * 1928 Berlin, designer, free colleague of Melitta, 1970-72 of Rosenthal for services and furniture.

Diller, Fritz, dates unknown, 1913-27 free colleague of Rosenthal for figures and animals.

Ebüzziya-Siesbye, Alev, * 1938 Istanbul, ceramic artist, free colleague of Füreya, Dümler and Breiden, Eczaciba, Royal Porcelain of Copenhagen, since 1975 of Rosenthal for decorative porcelain.

Falchi, Aldo, * 1935 Sabbionetta, sculptor and modeler, since 1959 free colleague of Rosenthal for animals and reliefs.

Fischer-Treyden, Elsa, * 1901 Moscow, ceramic artist and form designer, since 1953 free colleague of Rosenthal, Selb and Thomas works, for porcelain, ceramics and glass.

Fleischmann, Friedrich, 1887 Munich-1943 Munich, architect and commercial artist, 1926-31 free colleague of all Rosenthal works, services, writing implements, lamp bases, anniversary vases 1929.

Förster, Richard, 1873 St. Petersburg-(Berlin)?, sculptor and medalmaker, after 1919 free colleague of Rosenthal, Bahnhof-Selb works, for figures.

Freyer, Martin, 1909 Hannover-1974 Pfaffenhofen, painter and graphic artist, interior architect, designer, stage artist, 1964-1974 free colleague of Rosenthal, relief decorations for glass and porcelain.

Friedrich-Gronau, Lore, * Görlitz, sculptress and ceramic artist, 1939-61 free colleague of Rosenthal, Selb works, chiefly for dancer figures.

Friling, Hermann, 1867 Cologne-(Berlin)? painter and commercial artist, circa 1902 free colleague of Rosenthal, Selb works, for a service.

Fritz, Max D.H., 1873 Neuhaus, Thuringia-1948 Dresden, sculptor, medalmaker, plastic artist, colleague of L. Hutschenreuther, Meissen, at Rosenthal, Selb and Bahnhof-Selb works, circa 1930, for figures.

Geibel, Hermann, 1889 Freiburg in Breisgau-1972 Darmstadt, sculptor, graphic artist, teacher, free colleague of Rosenthal, Selb works, circa 1927, for an animal figure.

Grath, Anton, 1881 Vienna-(Vienna)?, sculptor and medalmaker, colleague of Frauenreuth, at Rosenthal, Selb works, 1918-1929, for figures.

Gross, W. ?, porcelain painter, circa 1925 colleague of Rosenthal, for decorations.

Gross, Karl, 1869 Fürstenfeldbrück-1934 Munich, sculptor, goldsmith, metal artist, teacher, circa 1900 free colleague of Rosenthal, for vases.

Guldbrandsen, Julius-Vilhelm, 1869 Stagelsee-1960 Humbleback, painter, at the Royal Porcelain Factory of Copenhagen, Hutschenreuther, 1909-24 at Rosenthal, directed the art department at the Selb works, influenced the painting (underglaze, limited "Rosari decorations").

Harth-Altmann, Thekla, 1887-1968, commercial artist, colleague of Rosenthal 1913-1923, for figures.

Heidenreich, Fritz, 1895 Mähring-1966 Selb, ceramic and plastic artist, employed by Rosenthal since 1919, since 1934 modeler of animal figures etc., first asymmetrical vase in 1950.

Hennig, Artur, 1880 Dresden-?, painter, graphic artist, teacher, colleague of F. Kaestner, Krister, at Rosenthal 1929, for decorations.

Hidding, Hermann, 1863 Nottnen, Westphalia-?, sculptor, circa 1900 free colleague of Rosenthal, Kronach works, for vases.

Hildebrand, Margret, b. 1917 Stuttgart, decorationator, teacher, free colleague of Rosenthal, Selb and DOMUS works, 1952-66, for service decorations.

Himmelstoss, Karl, 1878 Breslau-1967 Munich, free colleague of the Royal Porcelain Factory in Berlin, since 1912 also of Rosenthal, Selb works, for figures, at first the second busiest designer, after Liebermann.

Hoffmann-Lederer, Hans, 1899 Jena-1970 Achberg, sculptor, designer, teacher, free colleague of Rosenthal, Selb works, 1953-55, for vases and bowls.

Holzer-Defanti, Constantin, 1881 Vienna-1951 Linz, sculptor, 1918-27 free colleague of Rosenthal, Selb and Bahnhof-Selb works, mainly for dancer figures.

Kärner, Theodor, 1884 Hohenberg on the Eger-1966 Munich, animal plastic artist and painter, free colleague of Nymphenburg and Allach, since 1918 also of Rosenthal, Selb and Bahnhof-Selb works, mainly for animal figures.

Kaesbach, R., ?, sculptor?, free colleague of Rosenthal, Selb works, 1936-39, for acts.

Kittler, Philipp, 1861, Schwabach near Nürnberg?, sculptor, 1925-26 free colleague of Rosenthal, Selb works, for sporting figures.

Klimsch, Fritz, 1870 Frankfurt on the Main-1960 Saig, Black Forest, sculptor, teacher, since 1935 free colleague of Rosenthal, Selb works, for acts.

Koch, Otto, 1901 Bozen-1974 Selb, sketcher, sculptor, 1920-1966 at Rosenthal, as of 1920 director of the art department, Bahnhof-Selb works, 1960-63 director of porcelain painting in Munich, designer and decorator in all fields.

Kriesch, Laura, 1879 Budapest--ca. 1955 Gödöllö, Hungary, commercial and graphic artist, circa 1900 presumably free colleague of Rosenthal for painting and relief vases.

Kuhn, Beate, b. 1927, Düsseldorf, ceramic artist, modeler, 1953-62 free colleague of Rosenthal, Selb works, for vases and bowls.

Küspert, Georg, 1903 Selb, porcelain painter, modeler, 1916-68 employed by Rosenthal, Selb works, designer since 1927.

Küster, Hans, 1899 Selb-1963 Erlangen,

modeler, sculptor, 1913-1928 employed by Rosenthal, Selb works, for animal and grotesque figures, ornamental and utilitarian dishes, later at Krautheim & Adelberg.

Langenmantel-Reitzenstein, Erna von, 1890 Munich-?, sculptress, silhouette artist, free colleague of Rosenthal, Selb works, 1912, for three figures.

Latham, Richard S., 1920 Kansas City, Missouri, designer, since 1925 free colleague of Rosenthal, at first under contract to Loewy, for services, glass and utensils.

Liebermann, Ferdinand, 1883 Judenbach, Thuringia-1941 Munich, sculptor, teacher, free colleague of the Royal Porcelain Factory of Berlin, since 1901 also of Rosenthal, Selb works, had a major influence on its figure program.

Löffelbardt, Heinrich, 1901 Heilbronn-1979 Stuttgart, sculptor and designer, free colleague of Arzberg, Bauscher, Jena Glass Works, Schott, Schönwald, United Glassworks, Lusatian Glassworks, 1936 at Rosenthal, Bahnhof-Selb works, for a service.

Loewy, Raymond, 1893 Paris-?, designer, 1951-55 his firm collaborated with Rosenthal for services.

Loon, Johan van, b. 1934 Rotterdam, ceramic artist, designer, teacher, free colleague of the Royal Porcelain Factory of Copenhagen, since 1980 also of Rosenthal, for bowls and vases.

Lunghard, Rudolf, b. 1902 Höxter, ceramic artist, colleague of Bauscher, Hutschenreuther, etc., also of Rosenthal, Bahnhof-Selb works, circa 1950, for a service, and at the Bad Soden glass-works.

Marcuse, Rudolf, 1878 Berlin-?, sculptor, free colleague of the Schwarzburg Workshops, Royal Porcelain Factory of Berlin, 1913-? also of Rnsehthal, Selb works, for figurss.

Meisel, Hugo, 1887 Lichte, Thuringia-1966 Rudolstadt, Thuringia, sculptor, modeler, colleague of the Oldest Volkstedt Porcelain Factory, Schwarzburg Workshops for Porcelain Art, of Rosenthal, Bahnhof-Selb works, in the thirties, for figures.

Mondenhauer, Dorothea, 1879 Dreidorf-1968 Munich, animal sculptress, free colleague of Rosenthal 1924-26, for animal figures.

Mutze, Walter, 1893 Dresden-1963 Naila, Upper Franconia, porcelain painter, at Rosenthal 1913-1961, chief and pattern painter, art department, Selb works, patented painting process in granular technique in 1951.

Obermaier, Ottmar, 1883 Inzell, Upper Bavaria-(Munich?), sculptor, circa 1934 free colleague of Rosenthal, Selb works, for five figures.

Opel, Adolf, ?, modeler, 1900-20 free colleague of Rosenthal, Selb and Kronach works, for figures and vessels.

Oppel, Gustav, 1891 Volkstedt, Thuringia-1971 Berlin, modeler, free colleague of the Oldest Porcelain Factory, Volkstedt, 1924-36 of Rosenthal, Selb works, for figures and ornamental porcelain.

Otto, Edmund (a.k.a. Otto-Eichwald), 1888 Rixdorf-1959 Berlin, animal sculptor, free colleague of Berlin and Nymphenburg porcelain factories, circa 1926 also of Rosenthal, Selb works.

Paul, Bruno, 1874 Seifhennersdorf, Upper Lusatia-1968 Berlin, architect, painter, graphic artist, designer, teacher, free colleague of the Karlsruhe Majolica Factory, 1913 also of Rosenthal, Selb works, for a service.

Peynet, Raymond, b. 1908 Paris, illustrator, designer, 1955-65 free colleague of Rosenthal, figures, decorations for utilitarian and decorative porcelain.

Pozzi, Ambrogio, 1931 Varese, ceramic artist, designer, own ceramic firm since 1967, free colleague of Rosenthal.

Reinstein, Hans Günther, 1880 Plauen-(Berlin?), commercial artist, 1902-04 member of the Darmstadt Artist Colony, free colleague of L. Hutschenreuther, Rosenthal circa 1903-05, for two or three services and vignettes.

Röhrig, Karl, 1886 Eisfeld, Thuringia-1973 Munich, sculptor, ceramic artist, free colleague of Rosenthal, Selb works, circa 1927, for two figures.

Rosenthal, Philipp, 1855 Werl-1937 Bonn, company owner and designer of models.

Sarpaneva, Timo, b. 1926 Helsinki, painter, graphic artist, designer, free colleague of Iitala, Puuvila, AB Kinnasand, since 1958 also of Rosenthal, for services and vases.

Scharrer, Richard, b. 1914 Nürnberg, modeler, 1929-33, 1936-78 at Rosenthal, finally in design studio for utilitarian and ornamental porcelain and glass.

Scheibe, Richard, 1879 Chemnitz-1964 Berlin, sculptor, painter, teacher, free colleague of the State Porcelain Factory in Berlin, Velten-Vordamm Ceramic Factory, 1925 and 1950 also of Rosenthal, Selb works, for acts.

Schelenz, Erich, b. 1930 Munich, sculptor, free colleague of Rosenthal, Selb works, 1955-56, for figures.

Schiffner, Hans, 1876 Selb-1965 Selb, porcelain painter, trained at Rosenthal, as of 1918 director of hand painting ("Meissen Department"), 1927-34 director of the art department, Selb works, famous for relief etchings and gold, and since 1921 for matte coral red background decorations ("Rosenthal Red") with dragon drawings in gold.

Schliepstein, Gerhard, 1886 Braunschweig-1963 Berlin, sculptor, free colleague of the State Porcelain Factory of Berlin, 1925-27 also of Rosenthal, since 1929 exclusively for the Selb and Bahnhof-Selb worls, for figures, lamp bases, writing implements, clock casings.

Schott, Walter, 1861 Ilsenburg in the Harz-1938 Berlin, sculptor, painter, etc., 1912 free colleague of Rosenthal, Selb works, one figure.

Schwartzkopff, M., ?, also designed for the Schwarzburg Workshops for Porcelain Art.

Severin, Karl, 1896 Berlin-1970 Wolkersdorf near Nürnberg, graphic artist, porcelain painter, free colleague of Hutschreuther, at Rosenthal, Selb works, 1924-28, as pattern painter, famous for "Indian painting."

Stangl, Hans, 1888 Munich-1963 Munich, sculptor, free colleague of Rosenthal, Selb works, in the fifties, for hollow three-dimensional figures.

Steger, Milly, 1881 Rheinberg-1948 Berlin, sculptress, graphic artist, 1925 free colleague of Rosenthal, Selb works, for six acts. *Stockmayer, Fritz von*, 1877 Stuttgart-1940 Stuttgart?, porcelain painter and ceramic artist, free colleague of Arzberg, Fürstenwald, Schönberg, 1932-40 employed by Rosenthal, Thomas works, as of 1935 director of the art department, Selb works, vases, boxes, services, lively hand painting, set new decoration style and glazing technique.

Valentin, Max, 1875 Fürstenwalde on the Spree-?, sculptor, colleague of the Vienna Fayence Factory of F. Goldscheider, of Rosenthal, Selb works, circa 1929, two designs.

Vierthaler, Ludwig, 1875?-1967 Hannover, ceramic artist, teacher, free colleague of E. Teichert, Karlsruhe Majolica Factory, 1914 also of Rosenthal, Selb works, for two figures.

Vogeler, Heinrich, 1872 Bremen-1942 Kazakhstan, painter, graphic artist, illustrator, as of 1898 focal figure of the Worpswede Artist Colony, circa 1910 free colleague of Rosenthal, one Christmas plate.

Wagenfeld, Wilhelm, b. 1900 Bremen, industrial designer, teacher, colleague of Fürstenberg, United Lusatian Glass-works, WMF, etc., 1937 and 1952-55 free colleague of Rosenthal, Selb, Bahnhof-Selb and Thomas works, for services, etc.

Weber, Max, b. 1922 Oberkotzau, Upper Franconia, painter, designer, employed by Rosenthal, Thomas works, Marktredwitz, and Studio-Line, since 1954, for utilitarian and ornamental porcelain.

Weiss, Claire, b. 1906 Budapest, sculptress, free colleague of Bing & Gröndahl, Hutschenreuther, 1932-33 also of Rosenthal, Selb and Bahnhof-Selb works, for figures.

Wenck, Ernst, 1865 Reppen near Frankfurt on the Oder-1929 Berlin, sculptor, free colleague of the State Porcelain Factory of Berlin, 1925-29 also of Rosenthal, Selb and Bahnhof-Self works, for figures.

Wendler, Kurt, 1893 Wernigerode in the Harz-?, graphic artist, painter, 1920-30 free colleague of Rosenthal, Selb works, designs for "Indra decorations" (signed hand painting), lamps, writing implements.

Wersin, Wolfgang von, 1882 Prague-?, free colleagueof the German Workshops, Fürstenberg, Nymphenburg, 1936-38 also of Rosenthal, Selb and Thomas works, for services.

Whittaker, Alan, b. 1953 St. Helens, Lancashire, ceramic artist, free colleague of Rosenthal, Studio-Line, since 1979 for vases and bowls.

Wiinblad, Björn, b. 1918 Copenhagen, illustrator, stage artist, free colleague of Nymölle, since 1957 also of Rosenthal, for services, vases, glass, utensils, vases, pots, candelabras, ceramics.

Wirkkala, Tapio, b. 1915, Hanko, Finland, graphic artist, designer, interior architect, free colleague of Arabia, since 1956 also for Rosenthal for services, vases, bowls, utensils, glass, ceramics.

Wohlrab, Hans, b. 1913, modeler, since 1927 at Rosenthal, since 1949 in the art department, Selb works, since 1956 for services, since 1958 in the design studio, for bowls, vases, services.

Zoelch, Tono, 1897 Regensburg-1955 Rome, sculptor, painter, free colleague of Rosenthal, Selb and Bahnhof-Selb works, circa 1929 for busts and on-glaze painting.

Zschäbitz, Grete, b. 1904 Braunschweig, designer, 1924-33 free colleague of Rosenthal, Selb works, for figures.

Zügel, Willy, 1876 Munich-1950 near Murrhardt, animal artist, modeler, sketcher, free colleague of Meissen, Nymphenburg and Philipp-Dietrich Porcelain Factory, 1911-26 also of Rosenthal, Selb and Bahnhof-Selb works, for animals.

Bibliography

Particularly important titles are marked with a *.

Aries, Philippe, and Georges Duby (ed.), *Geschichte des privaten Lebens*, Vol. 4, von der Revolution zum Grossen Krieg, Michelle Perrot, Frankfurt 1992.

Arnold, Klaus-Peter, (ed.), Wolfgang Hennig, Annette Loesch et al., *Rosenthal Porzellan. Vom Jugendstil zur Studiolinie*, Exhibition Catalog, Staatliche Kunstsammlungen Dresden Dresden 1991.

Baumhauer, Joachim F., *Disneyana. Sammelbares aus der Welt der Micky Maus*, Battenberg Antiquitäten-Katalog, Augsburg 1993.

Europarat (ed.), *Tendenzen der Zwanziger Jahre*, Exhibition Catalog, Berlin 1977.

* Fritz, Bernd, *Die Porzellangeschirre des Rosenthal-Konzerns 1891-1979*, Stuttgart 1989.

Hantschmann, Katharina, *Du Paquier contra Meissen, Frühe Wiener Porzellanservice*, Exhibition Catalog, Munich 1994.

* Honisch, Dieter, and Philip Rosenthal, Hermann Schreiber, Ferdinand Simoneit, *Die Rosenthal-Story*, Düsseldorf-Vienna 1980.

Just, Johannes, and Jürgen Karpinsky, *Meissener Jugendstil-Porzellan*, Leipzig 1984.

* Kestner Museum Hannover (ed.), *Rosenthal. Hundert Jahre Porzellan*, Exhibition Catalog, Stuttgart 1982.

Livingstone, Marco (ed.), *Pop Art*, Exhibition Catalog, Munich 1992. Loewy, Raymond, *Hässlichkeit verkauft sich schlecht*, Düsseldorf 1953.

Maenz, Paul, *Art déco, Formen zwischen zwei Kriegen*, Cologne 1978.

Münchner Stadtmuseum (ed.), *Anziehungskräfte. Variétè de la Mode 1786-1986*, Exhibition Catalog, Munich 1987.

Nipperdey, Thomas, *Deutsche Geschichte 1866-1918*, Vol. I, Munich 1990.

Ohff, Heinz, *Anti-Kunst*, Düsseldorf 1973.

Pechmann, Günther von, *Franz Anton Bustelli. Die Italienische Komödie in Porzellan*. Der Kunstbrief No. 39, Berlin 1947.

Rosenthal, Philip, *Einmal Legionär*, Hamburg 1980.

Rosenthal, Philipp, *Exportsteigerung--ein brennendes Problem*, no place, 1928.

------*Sein Leben und sein Porzellan*, Leipzig 1929.

Rosenthal-Bibliothek, Vol. I-3, no place or date.

Rosenthal (ed.), *The Catalogue. Selections and New Lines*, Selb 1993.

------*Hommage à Gropius und die Klassiker von morgen*, Selb, no date.

Rötzler, Willy, *Objektkunst, Von Duchamp bis zur Gegenwart*, Cologne 1975.

* Siemen, Wilhelm (ed.), Beate und Karl Hilser, Maria Schweizer, Wilhelm Siemen, *So fing es an, so ging es weiter. Deutsches Porzellan und Deutsche Porzellanfabriken 1945-1960, Schriften und Kataloge des Museums der Deutschen Porzellanindustrie*, Vol. 11, Hohenberg/Eger 1989.

------(ed.), *175 Jahre Hutschenreuther. Ein Beitrag zum Firmenjubiläum 1814-1989, Ausstellung zur Form und Dekorgeschichte am Beispiel der Service-Entwicklung. Schriften und Kataloge des Museums der Deutschen Porzellanindustrie*, Vol. 17, Hohenberg/Eger 1989.

Staatliche Museen Preussischer Kulturbesitz (ed.),*Historismus, Kunsthandwerk und Industrie im Zeitalter der Weltausstellungen, Kataloge des Kunstgewerbmuseums Berlin*, Vol. VII, Berlin 1973.

Stadt Gelsenkirchen, Städtisches Museum (ed.), *Gelsenkirchner Barock*, Exhibition Catalog, Gelsenkirchen 1991.

Verkaufsförderung der Rosenthal-Porzellan AG (ed.), *WIR + SIE*, Vol. No. 1-6, Selb, 1963-65.

Walcha, Otto, *Meissner Porzellan*, Dresden 1973.

Wedewer, Rolf, (ed.), *Kunst--Form--Design, Porzellan von Rosenthal*, Stadt Leverkusen, Der Oberstadtdirektor, Museum Morsbroich, Leverkusen 1989.

Werner, Petra, (ed.), *Deutsches Porzellan zwischen Inflation und Depression--die Zeit des Art déco, Schriften und kataloge des Museums der Deutschen Porzellanindustrie*, Vol. 30, Hohenberg/Eger 1992.

Wichmann, Siegfried, *Jugendstil floral funktional in Deutschland und Österreich und den Einflussgebieten*, Herrsching 1984.

Württembergischer Kunstverein (ed.), *50 Jahre Bauhaus*, Exhibition Catalog, Stuttgart 1968.

Zischka, Ulrike, and Hans Ottomeyer, Susanne Bäumler, *Die Anständige Lust. Von Esskultur und Tafelsitten*. Exhibition Catalog, Munich 1993.

Plus a multitude of brochures and advertising material, as well as magazines of all kinds.